BROOKINGS FOCUS BOOKS

Brookings Focus Books feature concise, accessible, and timely
assessment of pressing policy issues of interest to a broad audience.
Each book includes recommendations for action on the issue discussed.

Also in this series:

Fast Forward: Ethics and Politics in the Age of Global Warming
by William Antholis and Strobe Talbott

Brain Gain: Rethinking U.S. Immigration Policy
by Darrell M. West

*The Next Wave: Using Digital Technology
to Further Social and Political Innovation*
by Darrell M. West

The Pursuit of Happiness: An Economy of Well-Being
by Carol Graham

Bending History: Barack Obama's Foreign Policy
by Martin S. Indyk, Kenneth G. Lieberthal, and Michael E. O'Hanlon

The Opportunity: Next Steps in Reducing Nuclear Arms
by Steven Pifer and Michael E. O'Hanlon

Mr. Putin: Operative in the Kremlin
by Fiona Hill and Clifford G. Gaddy

AVOIDING ARMAGEDDON

A BROOKINGS FOCUS BOOK

AVOIDING ARMAGEDDON

AMERICA, INDIA, AND PAKISTAN TO THE BRINK AND BACK

Bruce Riedel

BROOKINGS INSTITUTION PRESS
Washington, D.C.

Copyright © 2013
THE BROOKINGS INSTITUTION
1775 Massachusetts Avenue, N.W., Washington, D.C. 20036
www.brookings.edu

Library of Congress Cataloging-in-Publication data

Riedel, Bruce O.
  Avoiding Armageddon : America, India, and Pakistan to the brink and
back / Bruce Riedel.
    pages ; cm. — (Brookings focus books)
  Summary: "Traces the history of the United States, India, and Pakistan
as British colonies and their interaction in the twentieth and twenty-first
centuries, particularly in regard to relations between India and Pakistan,
nuclear proliferation, the global jihad movement, and U.S. diplomatic efforts
to stabilize conditions on the subcontinent"—Provided by publisher.
  Includes bibliographical references.
  ISBN 978-0-8157-2408-7 (hardcover : alkaline paper)
  1. United States—Foreign relations—South Asia. 2. South Asia—Foreign
relations—United States. 3. India—Foreign relations—Pakistan. 4. Pakistan—
Foreign relations—India. 5. Terrorism—South Asia—Prevention. 6. Nuclear
arms control—South Asia. I. Title. II. Series: Brookings focus books.
  DS341.3.U6R54 2013
  327.73054—dc23   2012046847

9 8 7 6 5 4 3 2 1

Printed on acid-free paper

Typeset in Sabon

Composition by Cynthia Stock
Silver Spring, Maryland

Printed by R. R. Donnelley
Harrisonburg, Virginia

This book is dedicated to my son,
Christopher.

CONTENTS

PREFACE

PRESIDENT-ELECT BARACK OBAMA made his first substantive call to a foreign leader on November 28, 2008, amid terrible tragedy. India, the world's largest democracy, was still in shock from an attack by ten Pakistani terrorists that had killed more than 160 people, six of them Americans, and wounded hundreds in the city of Mumbai, the country's financial capital. Obama began his conversation with Prime Minister Manmohan Singh, who had called Obama just two weeks earlier to congratulate him on his stunning election victory, with words of condolence: "I wish it was a happier time. America is with you in these days; all my hopes and prayers are with you today, and all the hopes and prayers of America." The prime minister responded by saying that the call meant a lot to him and to India. "Your call is a ray of sanity in this time," he said, adding that their two countries needed "to fight the curse of terrorism" together. Then he told the president-elect that "all indications point to Karachi as the launch site for this attack. I have told this to Pakistani President Asif ali Zardari." Obama noted that he was not yet sworn in as president but vowed that once in office, "I will work with you to ensure this tragedy is never allowed to happen again."

Now, four years after the Mumbai attack, a great deal more is known about its perpetrators and objectives than Obama and Singh knew in 2008. It was the result of a very complex plot involving an equally complex cast of deadly actors. It was also a turning point in the history of America's relations with India. For the first time, American and Indian citizens had been targeted together by the global jihad movement. For more than 200 years, America and India had been distant and often cold friends. The United States had watched with admiration India's fight for independence from Great Britain and more recently its rise as a global power, but there had also been many years of tension between Washington and New Delhi. Now, for the first time, the two had a common enemy. As the president-elect's adviser on South Asian issues during the campaign and the transition and as the note taker for this call, I felt that history was changing in front of me.

At the same time it was déjà vu. During their short history as independent nations, India and Pakistan have fought four wars against each other and have often edged to the brink of yet another one, and in 2008 there was widespread concern that the horror in Mumbai would lead to a fifth. Fortunately it did not, but the next mass casualty terrorism attack in India may well bring the two nuclear-armed states not just to war but to nuclear war. The risk of war in South Asia is all too real. The last war that India and Pakistan fought, over Kargil, threatened to expand to a nuclear conflict. Since the Kargil war the two countries have experienced several dangerous crises. In 2001 and 2002 they mobilized for war. In 2008 Mumbai exploded. But the two nations can also create a better future—Nirvana, if you like—in South Asia. By focusing on ending their differences and building bridges to each other, literally and figuratively, India and Pakistan could together become one of the most prosperous parts of the globe in the twenty-first century.

India was the richest country in the world in the fifteenth century, when Europeans found both the passage around Africa to India and the Atlantic path to the Western Hemisphere. At that time, India and China together produced about 40 percent of the globe's gross national product. However, the rise of the European empires that followed the great explorers like Vasco da Gama, who first reached India, and Christopher Columbus, who discovered North America, changed the locus of the world's economy, and by 1900 India and China accounted for only 20 percent of global product. Now at the dawn of the third millennium, the pendulum has shifted back. By 2030, the two Asian giants will again produce 40 percent of the world's GNP.

This book is in part about America's relationship with one of these giants: India, the world's largest democracy and soon to be the most populous country on the planet. The rise of India—or the return of India to global power status—is a good-news story. Hundreds of millions have escaped poverty in India in the last few decades and more will do so in the decade ahead. As a democracy, India holds the world's largest elections, and each time that it does it breaks the record for the largest organized human activity in history. India today is a great success.

America and India are often described as natural allies. To some extent that is true. Since they sit on opposite sides of the globe, they have no territorial disputes. They are both democracies that prize their citizens' civil liberties and freedoms. Both have created entrepreneurial geniuses who have built thriving middle classes. Yet the history of the relationship between the two countries has not been one of natural allies. Both were born of the British Empire, which ruled more of the world than any other nation in history, but independence came to America just as India was being conquered by the British. Once India achieved its freedom (with a little backstage help from Washington), the relationship between India and the United States was far from close or warm. Indeed, for most of its first fifty years, India was as much an adversary of America as anything else, and even the end of the cold war did not bring greater harmony. In 1998 relations dipped to a low when India tested nuclear weapons. Today there is much talk about the natural alliance, but in practice the partnership is still thin, arguably more hype than fact. Certainly, much of the potential of the U.S.-India relationship is still to be achieved.

A major reason for the disharmony in the U.S.-India relationship—perhaps the most important reason—is a third party, Pakistan. Pakistan, today the sixth-largest country in the world and soon to be the fifth, was born, as was India, in the partition of British India in 1947. From the start, the two great powers of South Asia have been deadly rivals. Pakistan is a rising power in its own right, a fact too often lost on those dazzled by India's rise next door. If Pakistan were situated anywhere but next to India, it would be recognized as a power at least as influential today as Turkey, Brazil, or Indonesia. In fact, with its nuclear arsenal, the fastest growing in the world, it is of great importance. That is not to say that the two countries are identical or equivalent powers; obviously India is much larger, and so far it has been much more successful on many accounts. Pakistan meanwhile has become a center of terrorism, a victim and patron of terror at the same time. But both are very important nations whose future will have a great impact on that of the United States.

So the real challenge for America in South Asia in the twenty-first century is coping with the rise of two powers, India and Pakistan. America has tried to maintain good relations with both and to deal with each on its own merits—a policy called, in the jargon of South Asia watchers in America, "dehyphenating the relationship." It is a laudable goal, but geography makes it a mirage. The two rivals cannot be separated in many important ways, and U.S. policy cannot undo geography. Tailored policies are needed for each, and bilateral relations must be separate and specific to each. Washington should not hyphenate when it does not need to, but it should not pretend that geography and history are irrelevant. The interplay between the two cannot be ignored.

India's rise to global power in both economic and strategic terms is one of the defining events of the twenty-first century. How

America interacts with India is among the most important foreign policy challenges that Washington faces, and it will be harder to meet than many assume. The history of the two is more troubled than is often realized, and Pakistan casts a complex and controversial shadow over the relationship. Simplistic suggestions such as the proposal that India and America "gang up" on Pakistan are recipes for disaster. Ignoring the issue is foolhardy.

This book describes how America and India have interacted since 1500, with the emphasis on recent times. It shows that their natural alliance is not natural at all, that it requires hard work and compromise. It also explains the tortured path of America's relationship with Pakistan, in particular the challenge that Pakistan presents to building a strong U.S.-India partnership and to managing U.S.-Afghanistan policy. Ultimately, it highlights the urgent need for Washington, New Delhi, and Islamabad to find new solutions to the problems in their traditional interactions before disaster strikes.

The book begins with a detailed analysis of what is now known about the Mumbai terror attack, the worst in the world since 9/11 and a very important case study in American diplomacy during an Indo-Pakistani crisis. Then, for some historical perspective, it looks back at how today's India, Pakistan, and America were born of a common parent, the British Empire. The book next focuses on the relationship among the three countries since 1947, examining how twelve American presidents have engaged with India and Pakistan. Although much could be said about the economic relations of the three, I am not an economist, so I leave that for others to do. The primary focus here is on diplomacy, counterterrorism, and nuclear affairs.

India and Pakistan attract and dazzle even as they sometimes confound and confuse. For me they are the most interesting and exciting countries in the world—very different from America in many ways and yet very similar in others, changing faster than ever and yet ancient and eternal. I have spent much of my life trying to understand India and trying to build the "natural" alliance between India and the United States, and I have spent an equal amount of time trying to find common ground with Pakistan so that an enduring partnership with America can emerge. I have had the honor of working for four presidents as they grappled with India and Pakistan in the White House. This book is the result.

Over the last several years I have also had the honor of teaching students at Georgetown University's School of Foreign Service and the Johns Hopkins School of Advanced International Studies about the politics and history of America's relations with the countries of South Asia. My students have made me smarter and more thoughtful about these issues, and I want to thank them for doing so. I am grateful to Dan Byman and Walter Andersen for asking me to teach at these great institutions.

I also want to thank my colleagues at the Brookings Institution for their insights and comments on my work. Stephen Cohen is the dean of South Asian scholarship in America, and he has been an immense source of inspiration and insight. Both Strobe Talbott and Martin Indyk, who were my partners in government and who brought me to Brookings in 2007, are mentors and friends. Michael O'Hanlon, research director in Foreign Policy at Brookings, provided excellent insights on the manuscript. Two fantastic research assistants, Aysha Chowdhry and Irena Sargsyan, have given me tremendous assistance with the project. Special thanks is also due to the Brookings Institution Press, especially its director Robert Faherty and my editor, Eileen Hughes, for their friendship and fine work.

Throughout the book I have tried to let the Americans directly involved in the diplomatic interactions among the United States, India, and Pakistan—from Admiral Nimitz and John Kenneth Galbraith to Strobe Talbott and Rick Inderfurth—speak for themselves through their own words and memories. I am, of course, solely responsible for any errors of fact or judgment. The Central Intelligence Agency has reviewed this book to ensure that there is no disclosure of classified information. Nothing in the following pages should be construed as asserting or implying that any branch of government has authenticated the information herein or endorsed my views. All the statements and opinions herein are solely mine. This book is dedicated to my son, Christopher, who has always made me very proud. Finally, my deepest thanks are to my wife, Elizabeth, for making the journey so joyful.

CHAPTER ONE

MUMBAI ON FIRE

THE VIEW FROM my room in the Oberoi Hotel was beautiful at dusk, with the sun setting over the blue Arabian Sea while down below the traffic flowed on Marine Drive, which curves along the beachfront in Mumbai. As the lights came alive in the late afternoon sky, the streets of the financial capital of India throbbed with activity. Mumbai, formerly Bombay, the most populous city in India and the sixth most populous in the world, has more than 20 million inhabitants, from some of the world's richest billionaires to some of the world's most destitute poor.

I was there in advance of the coming visit of my boss, William J. Clinton, the forty-second president of the United States. It was my job as special assistant to the president and senior director for Near East and South Asia issues on the National Security Council to oversee Clinton's March 2000 visit to India, Bangladesh, Pakistan, Oman, and Switzerland. It would be the first visit by an American president to South Asia in a quarter-century. The Oberoi and its great rival, the Taj Mahal Palace, were competing to host the president during his visit to the city. Both were trying to explain to me why the president should stay in their hotel.

Just over eight years later both the Oberoi and the Taj would be the targets of the deadliest terrorist attack since 9/11. The two hotels would be attacked by teams of terrorists from Pakistan-based

Lashkar-e-Tayyiba (LeT), along with the city's train station, a restaurant that catered to foreign visitors and the rich, a Chabad house for visiting Israeli and American Jews, and the city hospital. Between November 26 and 29, 164 people would die and more than 300 would be injured by the ten terrorists. In India the horror is known as 26/11 and the battle to kill the terrorists is known as Operation Black Tornado.

LeT had carefully chosen the targets and meticulously researched them over several years. It received considerable assistance in doing so from two sources, the Pakistani intelligence service, called the Directorate for Inter-Services Intelligence (ISI), and al Qaeda. Each had its own agenda for the operation. But the targets were the same—Indians, Americans, and Jews, the targets of the global jihad started by al Qaeda in the late 1990s. Although the attack was in India, America was among the targets, and al Qaeda was a common enemy. I pointed that out to President-elect Obama at the time in several briefings by e-mail and telephone.[1] The attack was intended to change the future of South Asia dramatically, perhaps even by provoking a war between India and Pakistan, the two nuclear powers rising in the subcontinent.

Understanding the Mumbai terrorist attack and its consequences is critical to understanding the challenges that America faces in dealing with the rise of India and Pakistan. Simply put, the United States cannot manage one without managing the other. Ensuring the political stability of both states and easing the rivalry between them is an American national security interest of the highest importance in the twenty-first century. The crisis in Mumbai, the first foreign policy crisis for President Obama, demonstrated dramatically how the rise of India and the rise of Pakistan will challenge America in the century ahead.

THE RISING TIGER AS TARGET

In a sense, India itself was the terrorists' target on 26/11, and Mumbai was chosen because it represents India's ascent over the last two decades. The simplest measure of India's importance is population. Its growth has been phenomenal. At the time of the Indian revolt against England in 1857, India had 200 million people; at independence in 1947, it had 325 million. But according to its latest census, today, only sixty-five years later, India has 1.15 billion people—one-sixth of humanity. It is now the second-largest country in the world, after China, but by 2030 it will be larger than China. And it is a young, amazingly diverse, country. Sixty percent of Indians today are under thirty years of age. There are 22 official languages, 216 ethnolinguistic groups, and an estimated 1,500 dialects in India. The population is 80 percent Hindu, 14 percent Muslim, 2.5 percent Christian, and 2 percent Sikh. India's 140 million Muslims make it the third-largest Muslim country in the world, after Indonesia and Pakistan. India is also the second-largest Shia Muslim state in the world, after Iran.

The pace of change in India today is staggering. While in 1985 there were only 2 million phones in the country, by 2011 there were 600 million cell phones and 15 million more were being added every month. Poverty remains a huge problem, but that also is changing rapidly. According to a 2011 Brookings Institution study, the poverty level in India is dropping very quickly. In 2005 about 41 percent of Indians were living below the poverty level—defined as living on less than a $1.25 per day—but by 2015 only 7 percent will be living below the $1.25-per-day line (amounts adjusted for inflation). From 2005 to 2010, 230 million Indians escaped poverty; by 2015 another 137 million will have done so. The graduation of 360 million Indians from abject poverty in ten years is more than the rest of the world's progress in poverty alleviation combined; not even China has reduced poverty levels as fast as India has today. While India has had the dubious honor of hosting the most poor people on Earth since 1999, when it overtook China, by 2015 it will have relinquished that distinction to Nigeria.[2]

The change has not been easy. In August 2012, when an estimated 640 million people lost power at the height of summer, India had the largest electrical blackout in history. Next door in Pakistan, the blackouts were just as severe and they lasted longer. To produce power, between 2002 and 2012 India doubled its consumption of coal and increased oil consumption by 52 percent and natural gas consumption by 131 percent, but even that was too little to provide enough energy. India's urban population will have increased from 340 million people in 2008 to almost 600 million by 2030, when it will have 68 cities with more than 1 million inhabitants and 6 cities with more than 10 million. In 2030 two of the world's five largest cities will be in India—Mumbai and New Delhi.[3]

Pakistan also is a large country, with almost 190 million people, of whom 97 percent are Muslim—77 percent Sunni and 20 percent Shia. When it became independent in 1947, it had only 33 million (counting only what was then called West Pakistan, not what is now Bangladesh). Like India, Pakistan is growing fast. If fertility rates remain constant (3.2 percent today), there will be 460 million Pakistanis by 2050; with a modest decline in fertility rates, the number will be around 335 million. The most conservative population estimate puts Pakistan at 310 million people in 2050. Today Pakistan is the sixth-largest country in the world and the second-largest Muslim state. By 2030 it will be the fourth- or fifth-largest country and the most populous state in the Islamic world.[4]

If India itself and its rise were a target of the terrorists on 26/11, Mumbai, as India's largest city and home to its financial center and many of its new millionaires, was the logical place to strike. It is also a media center, home to India's huge film industry, Bollywood, and it is filled with journalists and television cameras. Mumbai symbolized the rise of the new India, which, with its international connections, challenged the anti-India ideology of the terrorist group Lashkar-e-Tayyiba and its sponsors.

THE PLOT AND ITS MECHANICS

The Mumbai attack was planned after extensive intelligence had been collected and the terrorists were well-trained and -equipped.

In July 2009 the lone survivor of the terrorist team, Mohammad Ajmal Amir Qasab, surprised prosecutors during his Mumbai trial by confessing in open court that he and his nine comrades had been recruited by Lashkar-e-Tayyiba; trained in commando tactics at LeT camps in Pakistan; equipped by LeT with AK-56 automatic assault rifles (the Chinese version of the Russian AK-47, which is standard equipment for the Pakistani army), hand grenades, GPS sets, cell phones, and other equipment; and dispatched by senior members of LeT from Karachi, Pakistan, in a small boat. As ordered, they hijacked an Indian boat at sea to take them into Mumbai. In Mumbai the group split into four teams, which attacked their prearranged targets—the city's central train station, a hospital, two famous five-star hotels known for hosting Western visitors as well as the cream of Indian society, a Jewish residential complex known to host visiting Israelis, and a famous restaurant also known for attracting a foreign clientele. The terrorists also set small bombs to add to the confusion and terror after they had fired indiscriminately into the crowds at the various target sites.[5]

It was an extraordinary attack in many ways. Throughout the siege of the city, the terrorists stayed in touch by cell phone with their LeT masters back in Pakistan. The handlers provided the terror teams with updated intelligence on the tactical situation around them, gleaned from watching Indian television reports. The Indian authorities have released the chilling transcripts of their calls, showing that the masterminds provided guidance and encouragement to the killers, even ordering them to kill specific hostages. In his confession Qasab identified the leader of the operation as an LeT senior official, Zaki Rehman Lakhvi, who oversaw his training and was actually present when the team left Karachi. His training included three months of intense small-arms exercises with a group of LeT members; afterward Qasab was selected to receive more specialized training in how to launch the attack itself. The team then waited another three months while the LeT leadership determined the best timing for the attack.

The masterminds of the plot were very careful not to reveal their plans through electronic media. They used multiple Internet websites to communicate, jumping from one to another to avoid detection. LeT had set up a special section to ensure the security of its communications, led by Lieutenant Colonel Saadat Ullah, a retired officer from the special communications division of the Pakistani army.[6] As a foot soldier Qasab did not know everything about the plot, but he was briefed along with his comrades on the plans and targets. For the most part the goal was just to create carnage, to kill as many people as possible. The team that was headed to the Chabad house, however, had a more elaborate mission: they were to take hostages to use them to demand the release of Palestinian prisoners in Israeli jails. To work, this part of the plot required the terrorist team at the Chabad house to communicate with the masterminds back in Pakistan. According to Qasab's account of their briefings, the terrorists were shown videos and photos of all of the targets and maps to find them on laptop computers.[7] The Chabad house in particular, which is on a back street in Mumbai, is not easy to find (it took me considerable effort in 2011).

The videos, photographs, and maps had been carefully collected for Lashkar-e-Tayyiba by David Coleman Headley, an American citizen of Pakistani descent. In fact, for Americans the most shocking element of the Mumbai attack was the role that he played in the collection of intelligence that preceded the attack. Headley was born Daood Sayed Gilani in 1960 in Washington, D.C., where his Pakistani father worked for Voice of America. He got into trouble with the law as a youth and was arrested on drug charges. Headley pleaded guilty in March 2010 to a charge of conspiracy to commit murder based on his role in the Mumbai attack. According to his guilty plea, he joined LeT in 2002 on a visit to Pakistan. Over the next three years he traveled to Pakistan five times for training in weapons handling, intelligence collection, surveillance, clandestine operations, and other terrorist skills.[8]

Headley, whose confession of guilt is available on the website of the U.S. Department of Justice, has been an extraordinary source of information on the plot, Lashkar-e-Tayyiba, al Qaeda, and the Directorate for Inter-Services Intelligence. In 2011 he was the key witness for the prosecution of his partners in the plot, and the Department of Justice (DOJ) provided considerable additional evidence from e-mails and intercepted phone calls to back up his claims. As part of the plea agreement that Headley signed to avoid execution, he consented to be interviewed by Indian security officials. Their report on their interview with him has been provided to me by friends in India, and much of the key material is available in the Indian media.[9] In short, the United States has unique and voluminous insight into the Mumbai plot from a key participant.

Beginning in 2005, Headley was given the task of traveling to India from the United States to conduct surveillance for the Mumbai attacks. As a first step, Lashkar-e-Tayyiba told him to change his name to David Coleman Headley in Philadelphia to hide his Pakistani identity when traveling abroad. He then made five trips to India between 2005 and 2008, visiting all of the targets, recording their locations with a GPS device, and carefully studying the security around each. On the way back, he stopped in Pakistan each time to get new instructions from LeT and the ISI and to present his surveillance reports. He thus became one of the masterminds of the plot. During his interrogation by the Indians and in his confession, Headley said that the raid was planned with active ISI involvement at every stage and that at each of his meetings in Pakistan he met with ISI officers as well as LeT leaders. Sometimes the ISI gave him tasks separate from those assigned by LeT; for example, the ISI asked him to take photos of an Indian nuclear facility near Mumbai. ISI provided money to help him set up his cover in Mumbai, including an initial $25,000 in cash. Headley also said that the ISI provided some of the training for the attackers, including training by elite Pakistani naval commandoes.

7

According to Headley, the ISI was especially pleased with the choice of the Chabad house as a target.[10]

Headley could not answer the question of at what level in the Pakistani intelligence service his activities had been approved; as an intelligence asset, he did not have access to that information. He has allegedly said that ISI leaders did not know.[11] But it is hard to believe that an asset like Headley, an American citizen operating for years in India, would not get the constant attention of officials at the highest levels of the ISI. No intelligence service would "run" an agent like Headley, an American citizen plotting mayhem, without the direct supervision of the top leadership. Headley had a co-conspirator in Chicago, Tahawwur Hussain Rana, a Canadian citizen, who helped devise a cover story for Headley: he was working for a travel agency, which Rana had set up in Chicago. Rana also traveled to Mumbai and stayed in the Taj Hotel to assist in the reconnaissance mission. Rana has been convicted of his role in the attack; at his trial he said that he believed that he was working for the ISI all the time.

The arrest of Sayeed Zabiuddin Ansari, alias Abu Jindal, at New Delhi airport in June 2012 was another major breakthrough in the investigation of the deadliest terror attack in the world since 9/11. Abu Jindal, an Indian citizen traveling with a Pakistani passport, was in the control room in Karachi in 2008 talking on the phone to the ten terrorists. He gave them advice on where to look for more victims in the Taj Hotel, for example, and instructed them when to murder their hostages. His voice was recorded by the Indian authorities listening in on the phone calls and has been replayed in chilling detail by the Indian police since then for all to hear. Abu Jindal has also been linked to other attacks in India, including the bombing of the Mumbai metro and train system in July 2006, which killed more than 180 people. According to press reports from India, Jindal was arrested after being deported from Saudi Arabia to India. The arrest was a joint counterterrorism effort by India, Saudi Arabia, and the United States. Abu Jindal was in Saudi Arabia recruiting and training new LeT volunteers from the enormous Pakistani diaspora in the Persian Gulf states and was allegedly in the final stages of plotting a "massive" new terrorist operation. He told the Indian authorities that two members of the ISI were also in the control room, both allegedly majors in the Pakistani army. That confirmed the long-standing accusation that the 2008 plot was orchestrated and conducted with the assistance of the ISI, but because Abu Jindal was actually in the control room in Karachi, his accusation is more powerful.[12]

Lashkar-e-Tayyiba used a criminal network—the infamous Dawood Ibrahim gang, which was responsible for an earlier terrorist attack on Mumbai on March 12, 1993—to try to cover up its involvement in the 26/11 attacks. Dawood Ibrahim Kaskar, one of the world's most wanted criminals and drug dealers, operates from Dubai and Karachi. LeT contracted with the gang to send a professional assassin to Mumbai to kill Qasab to eliminate the human evidence of their involvement in the crime. The Indian security services reportedly disrupted the hit man's plans before he could carry out his mission.[13]

LeT continued to use Headley to collect intelligence after the Mumbai attacks. First, LeT sent him back to India to look at more targets, including Israeli targets like the offices of El Al airlines. But it also outsourced him to al Qaeda for another intelligence collecting mission in Europe. LeT and al Qaeda sent him to Denmark, where his task was to do surveillance of the offices of a Danish newspaper that had published cartoons mocking the prophet Mohammad. The cartoons had aroused a storm of anger in the Islamic world, where depictions of the prophet in any form are rare but ones making fun of him are considered heresy. Al Qaeda had promised to make Denmark pay and had already attacked the Danish embassy in Pakistan. Headley made at least two trips to Denmark to survey the newspaper's offices in Copenhagen; he even got inside the offices by using his cover as a travel agent.

This time he reported directly to al Qaeda in Pakistan, meeting with Muhammad Ilyas Kashmiri, a senior al Qaeda operative who had once worked for the ISI. Kashmiri told him that the "elders" of al Qaeda were very interested in this project and that an al Qaeda cell already in Europe was ready to conduct the operation once Headley collected all the necessary intelligence. They would mount a mini-Mumbai operation, seizing the newspaper's offices, beheading all the employees captured with maximum media coverage, and finally fighting to the death with the police and Danish security forces. According to his guilty plea, Headley had a meeting with the al Qaeda team in England to prepare for the attack.[14]

Headley was arrested at Chicago's O'Hare airport in October 2009 before he could get on a flight back to Pakistan for a final planning session with Kashmiri. There is speculation among Danish authorities that the plan was set to take place in December 2009, when Copenhagen would host the Climate Change Summit and dozens of world leaders including Obama and Singh would be in the city along with major media outlets from around the world. Kashmiri was killed in a drone attack in Pakistan in June 2011.

THE IMMEDIATE GOAL: WAR IN SOUTH ASIA

Lashkar-e-Tayyiba, which is formally banned in Pakistan but nonetheless operates relatively freely, has denied any role in the attack, and senior officials of the movement claim no knowledge of the attackers. Therefore the motives of LeT in attacking Mumbai must be gleaned from the circumstances surrounding the attack rather than from the masterminds directly. Exactly who in LeT beyond Lakhvi ordered the attack is unknown, but it is clear that whoever did so had powerful political leverage in Pakistan and powerful protectors. What is also clear is that the specific targets of this attack—India's major financial capital, Westerners visiting Mumbai and its luxury hotels, Israelis, and Jews—are the targets of the global Islamic jihadist movement led, symbolically at least, by Osama bin Laden before his death. Bin Laden and his deputy Ayman al-Zawahiri have long urged the Islamic community to wage jihad against the so-called Crusader-Zionist-Hindu alliance, which, in their narrative, seeks to oppress the Muslim world.

The timing of the attack also was significant. In the fall of 2008 India and Pakistan were slowly and haltingly moving toward improving their long-tense bilateral relationship. As noted, since the partition of the subcontinent, the two have fought four wars and several smaller skirmishes. A peace process was begun in 1999—after the two had tested nuclear weapons a year earlier—by India's prime minister, Atal Behari Vajpayee, and his Pakistani counter-part, Nawaz Sharif. Vajpayee came to Lahore in February 1999 to begin talks on the peace process, and he and Sharif agreed to look for ways to defuse tensions. They set up a back channel for quiet negotiations on the most difficult issues dividing the two, especially Kashmir. As Sharif has described it, the goal was to end the arms race between the two and resolve their underlying differences.[15]

The process began in Lahore and moved forward bit by bit, with some major setbacks along the way. The Kargil war in the summer of 1999, initiated by Pakistani army leader and future dictator Pervez Musharraf, halted it altogether for some time. Musharraf had opposed the Lahore process and actually snubbed the Indian prime minister by not showing up for some of the events scheduled for his unprecedented trip. Instead, the next spring he ordered the Pakistani army to take positions inside Indian-controlled territory across the line of control (LOC) in Kashmir, near the town of Kargil—a move that sparked a limited war between India and Pakistan in mid-1999. (Lashkar-e-Tayyiba was an enthusiastic supporter of the Kargil adventure and was highly critical of Sharif when he ordered the army to withdraw behind the LOC.) The peace process was further damaged by the terrorist attack on the Indian parliament on December 13, 2001, which led to the mobilization of more than 1 million soldiers along the border. The threat of war again loomed large. This attack, which is examined in more detail in chapter 6, came after Musharraf had taken power in a coup.

It is deeply ironic that in time Musharraf would become the principal agent of the peace process. After trying limited war, nuclear blackmail, and terrorism, Musharraf finally settled on the back channel, and by 2008 it had achieved significant progress under the new Indian prime minister, Manmohan Singh. It even survived other major acts of terror, such as the attack on Mumbai's subway and train system in 2006. The details of the back channel talks, discussed below, have been well reported,[16] and Musharraf himself has confirmed the story.[17]

The back channel did not reach a final settlement of all the issues dividing the two, but it did produce an understanding that any deal would include two key points. First, the LOC would become an international border, with only minor adjustments mutually agreed to; second, the border would be a soft one—that is, it would permit maximum movement of Kashmiris between the two states. Local issues like tourism and the environment would be handled by the local governments of Pakistani Azad Kashmir and Indian Jammu and Kashmir. India could claim that it had achieved victory because the LOC was recognized as the official border; Pakistan could argue that because the border was porous, it was no longer relevant.

The back channel stalled when Musharraf's political position in Pakistan collapsed in late 2007 and early 2008. The Indian government became leery about whether Musharraf could deliver, rightly noting that he had done very little to prepare the Pakistani people and army for a deal. Musharraf's successor, Benazir Bhutto's widowed husband, Asif Ali Zardari, began to pick up the pieces of the peace process after he was elected and came to power. Most important, he publicly began to change Pakistan's posture on terrorism, nuclear strategy, and India in a dramatic way. In a number of press interviews, Zardari said, in effect, that for years the Pakistani army and the ISI had been breeding terrorist groups like LeT—that they had been playing a double game, appearing to fight terror while actually sponsoring it—and that terrorism might destroy Pakistan.[18]

In the summer of 2008 Zardari declared that India was not Pakistan's inevitable enemy, and, in a striking reversal of Islamabad's strategy, he proposed in a video linkup to an Indian think tank that Pakistan should adopt a no-first-use policy regarding nuclear weapons.[19] In addition, for the first time in decades, small but important steps were taken to open trade across the line of control in Kashmir and to expand transportation links between India and Pakistan. Many in Pakistan, including in the army and the jihadist camp, were appalled at Zardari's statements and at the confidence-building steps that were being taken.

Zardari was threatening to fundamentally change South Asia. It is reasonable, therefore, to assume that one of the key targets, if not the key target, of Lashkar-e-Tayyiba in Mumbai was the peace process itself, which they succeeded in stopping at least for a time. Singh was forced by the horror of Mumbai to suspend the dialogue. Almost certainly those dark forces in Pakistan who sent the LeT team to Mumbai had intended that outcome, if not even more: war with India.

An important book by a Pakistani expert on al Qaeda has argued that the ultimate objective of the Mumbai operation was in fact to provoke a full-scale war. Syed Saleem Shahzad based his conclusions on exclusive interviews with Kashmiri, who told him that al Qaeda manipulated the planning of the operation to make it bigger than the ISI expected or even the LeT senior leadership wanted.[20] Headley's interrogation and confession make clear that al Qaeda was involved in the planning of the plot, operating independently of the ISI and keeping its profile low. According to Kashmiri, al Qaeda wanted a nuclear war between India and Pakistan in order to disrupt the global counterterrorism efforts against al Qaeda, to complicate NATO's war in Afghanistan, and to polarize the world between Islam and the "Crusader-Zionist-Hindu conspiracy." For al Qaeda, a war between India and Pakistan would be a global game changer, disrupting the U.S. campaign to defeat al Qaeda, weakening global unity in the battle against terrorism, and creating a whole new environment for al Qaeda to operate in.

There is no doubt that Kashmiri was very important to al Qaeda. After the SEAL raid in which Osama bin Laden was killed on May 2, 2011, in Abbottabad, Pakistan, the Central Intelligence Agency (CIA) carefully studied the material found in his hideout. One forty-eight-page document showed that bin Laden had ordered Kashmiri to develop a plan to assassinate President Obama. According to the message, killing Obama "will lead the U.S. into a crisis as Vice President Biden is totally unprepared for the post." He urged "brother Ilyas" to find a way to attack the president's jet, Air Force One, the next time that the president came to South Asia.[21]

It is hard to prove or disprove Shahzad's claim. Shahzad was murdered shortly after his book came out. According to Admiral Mike Mullen, the chairman of the Joint Chiefs of Staff, the ISI was responsible for Shahzad's death. Kashmiri himself was killed by a drone a few weeks after Osama bin Laden was killed. While there is no way to check Shahzad's interview and story, a careful study of LeT itself tends to confirm the outline of his analysis.

HOW LASHKAR-E-TAYYIBA FITS IN INDIA AND PAKISTAN

Lashkar-e-Tayyiba, or the Army of the Pure, was created in 1987 by three Islamic scholars, Hafiz Saeed and Zafar Iqbal, who were then teaching at the Engineering University in Lahore, and Abdullah Azzam, then at the International Islamic University in Islamabad.[22] Saeed, who took the lead role, is rightly considered the founder and leader of LeT; however, he has publicly distanced himself from the organization in recent years after taking on the leadership of Jamaat-ud-Dawa (JuD), a humanitarian organization that is also a cover for LeT's activities. Saeed is a Punjabi whose family lost many of its members in the bitter communal fighting in the Punjab that followed the partition of British India in 1947. In the 1980s Saeed traveled to Saudi Arabia to further his Islamic education, where he was heavily influenced by its extreme Wahhabi brand of Islam. He became a charismatic speaker known for his fiery rhetoric.

Abdullah Azzam, a Palestinian born in the West Bank, was educated in Islamic law and philosophy in Syria and Jordan and at Egypt's prestigious Al Azhar University. He is rightly regarded by many experts as the father of the modern Islamic global jihadist ideology. Azzam also taught in Saudi Arabia, where he proposed that jihad should focus first on the "far enemy"—the United States and the Soviet Union, which sought to control the Islamic world—and defeat them before turning to the "near enemy," Israel. Azzam had tremendous influence on the young Osama bin Laden during his formative years fighting alongside the mujahedin in Afghanistan and Pakistan. Azzam and bin Laden created an office to assist Muslims from around the world who sought to fight in Afghanistan, known as the Services Bureau, which had close connections to Pakistan's Directorate for Inter-Services Intelligence. Bin Laden, who then had access to his family's massive wealth, was an early source of funding for Lashkar-e-Tayyiba. Azzam was assassinated in 1989. The ISI believes that the Israeli secret intelligence service Mossad was responsible; others believe that the Russians killed him.[23] Al Qaeda, on the other hand, accused the Jordanian intelligence service of killing Azzam; it says a Jordanian intelligence officer told an al Qaeda triple agent of the Jordanians' responsibility in 2009.

The Directorate for Inter-Services Intelligence also played a key role in the creation and development of LeT. In the late 1980s the ISI was eager to take control of the Kashmiri Muslim separatist movement in Indian-controlled Kashmir. Pakistan had demanded the annexation of Kashmir since 1947, and the issue is at the core of the tension between Pakistan and India. However, a home-grown Kashmiri movement—the Jammu Kashmir Liberation Front (JKLF)—emerged during the 1980s that sought independence for Kashmir, not unity with Pakistan.[24] The army and ISI wanted to encourage anti-Indian resistance and violence but not independence, so alternatives to the home-grown movement were encouraged. LeT was one of several such groups.

LeT's ideology as laid out by its founder Saeed goes far beyond Kashmir, however; it seeks the creation of a Muslim caliphate over the entire subcontinent. The role model is the old Mughal Empire of the seventeenth and eighteenth centuries, under which a Muslim minority ruled the Hindu majority and dominated most of the subcontinent. The vision of Saeed and his fellow LeT leaders requires the destruction of India as a state. Saeed declared that goal in a speech in 1999 after the Kargil war with India: "Today I announce the breakup of India, Inshallah [God willing]. We will not rest until the whole of India is dissolved into Pakistan."[25] One LeT newspaper captured the spirit of LeT's ideology with this passage: "Kashmir can be liberated in six months. Within a couple of years, the rest of the territories of India could be conquered as well, and we can regain our lost glory. We can bring back the era of Mughal rule. We can once again subjugate the Hindus, like our forefathers."[26]

In seeking to revive a lost Islamic empire, LeT's ideology is by definition violently anti-Western, since the British Raj is blamed for the downfall of the Mughals. LeT therefore opposes any manifestation of British or Western influence in Pakistan and South Asia. For example, it routinely denounces cricket, the country's national sport, as a colonial implant; Pakistanis should instead wage jihad. Or, as another LeT paper has written: "The British gave the Muslims the bat and snatched the sword and said to them: 'You take this bat and play cricket.' We should throw the bat and seize the sword and instead of hitting 'six' or 'four,' cut the throats of the Hindus and Jews."[27]

Since its founding, LeT has trained thousands of volunteers from around the world in its camps in Pakistan, which are scattered from Kashmir to the tribal areas along the border with Afghanistan and particularly around Lahore, in the Punjab. According to one Pakistani estimate, more than 200,000 jihadis have been trained in LeT's camps over the last twenty years.[28] In 2009, according to a

Pakistani intelligence source quoted in the *New York Times,* LeT had an active membership of 150,000 in Pakistan.[29] Its main head-quarters in Muridke, near Lahore, has a campus of several hundred acres with schools and dormitories for thousands of students, a garment factory, an iron foundry, and a huge mosque.[30]

The organization has wide popularity in Pakistan, especially in the Punjab. Its strong roots in the Punjab set it apart from many other jihadist groups in Pakistan, which have their strength in the tribal areas or Kashmir. LeT recruits from the same areas where the Pakistani army recruits, indeed from the same families. Because of LeT's Punjab connection, it is far less vulnerable than any other Pakistan-based network to a crackdown by the army and the government. It even attracts major speakers to its events. The self-described father of Pakistan's nuclear bomb, the famous nuclear technology proliferator A. Q. Khan, was the keynote speaker at LeT's annual public conference in 2001 and is reported to be a member of the organization.[31]

LeT has taken credit for dozens of attacks on Indian targets in Kashmir since the late 1980s. By its own account, it has killed thousands of Indian soldiers. At the same time, it has been respon-sible for the deaths of hundreds of innocent Kashmiris, Hindus, Sikhs, and Muslims in the Kashmiri insurgency. It was proba-bly behind the slaughter of a Sikh village in 2000 on the eve of President Clinton's visit to the subcontinent. It has also taken the conflict into India proper on numerous occasions. LeT was a co-conspirator in the attack on the Indian parliament in 2001 and was principally responsible for the multiple attacks on the Mumbai metro system in 2006 and the bombing at the famous Gateway Arch in Mumbai in 2003.

LeT's public name has changed frequently over the years as it has evolved and come under pressure for its acts of terrorism. When it was created in 1987 as an allegedly humanitarian agency, Saeed and Azzam called it the Markaz-ud-Dawa-wal-Irshad, or the Cen-ter for Preaching and Guidance. The leadership officially named the militant wing Lashkar-e-Tayyiba in the early 1990s in a meeting in Afghanistan. After the December 2001 attack on the Indian parliament by another Pakistan-based terrorist group, Jaish-e-Mohammad (in which LeT probably played a supporting role), LeT was officially banned in Pakistan. The group then reappeared under the title Jamaat-ud-Dawa, which claimed to be a purely humanitarian organization that provides aid to those in need in Pakistan, such as the victims of the earthquake in Kashmir in 2005.[32]

In fact, JuD is an elaborate cover for Lashkar-e-Tayyiba. It has an extensive humanitarian infrastructure that provides both real assistance to the needy and a useful cover for terrorism. After the Mumbai attacks in 2008 and subsequent international pressure, JuD renamed itself again; it currently operates under several cover names. Saeed now leads a group of Pakistani jihadist organizations calling themselves the Defense of Pakistan movement. In April 2012 President Obama offered $10 million for information leading to Saeed's arrest for his role in Mumbai, making him one of the most wanted men in the world. Despite the reward, he is not in hiding. Indeed, he regularly appears on Pakistani television and at large rallies organized with the help of the ISI, whose protection makes him immune to arrest.

In addition to its infrastructure of terror camps and humanitarian agencies inside Pakistan, Lashkar-e-Tayyiba also operates an extensive network outside the country, often among Pakistani diaspora communities around the world. LeT cells have been identified in the United Kingdom and other European countries, in the Persian Gulf states, and in the United States. LeT also operates in Nepal and Bangladesh, where it uses cells in those countries to support its operations inside India. The links to cells outside Pakistan are also important for fundraising, in the Gulf states in particular. Saudi Arabia is an especially attractive place for LeT fundraising, both among Pakistanis living in the kingdom and Saudis who are attracted to LeT's jihadist ideology and actions.[33]

LASHKAR-E-TAYYIBA AND AL QAEDA

Lashkar-e-Tayyiba has extensive links to al Qaeda that go beyond sharing a similar list of enemies and a common link through the connection to Azzam. Bin Laden was an early funder of LeT. After the U.S.-led NATO International Security Assistance Force (ISAF) attack on Afghanistan following the 9/11 attacks drove al Qaeda out of Afghanistan, LeT provided refuge for many al Qaeda operatives seeking to hide out in Pakistan. LeT camps and safe houses became critical to the survival of al Qaeda.

The first major terrorist figure linked to 9/11—a Palestinian named Zayn Muhammad Husayn, better known as Abu Zubaydah—was captured in an LeT safehouse in Faisalabad, Pakistan. According to the account of the CIA officer who captured him, it was clear that LeT was serving as a knowing host for Zubaydah.[34] In fact, LeT was providing its network of safe houses and friendly mosques to help hide al Qaeda fugitives all over Pakistan. As al Qaeda recovered from the shock of its defeat in Afghanistan, it also used LeT training camps to train its operatives.[35] LeT itself has sent fighters to Afghanistan and Iraq to participate in the jihad against Western armies in both countries. LeT has a long-standing interest in supporting the Taliban in Afghanistan and has been especially active in Konar Province. The dispatch of fighters to Iraq was a response to the Anglo-American invasion and occupation, which LeT publicly characterized as a threat to the Islamic community.

There is also evidence of LeT support for al Qaeda terrorist operations in the West. Shahzad Tanweer, the leader of the al Qaeda cell that carried out multiple suicide bombings on the London underground on July 7, 2005, had been to an LeT camp in Pakistan before the attacks. A second bomber in that attack, Mohammad Sidique Khan, may also have trained in an LeT camp. Both appeared in martyrdom videos aired by al Qaeda after the attack. LeT also provided some of the funding for the al Qaeda cell that planned to blow up ten jumbo jets over the Atlantic en route from the United Kingdom to Canada and the United States in the summer of 2006.[36]

Immediately after American commandoes killed bin Laden in 2011, Hafiz Saeed proclaimed the fallen al Qaeda leader a hero of Islam. At Friday prayers that week, Saeed acknowledged LeT's debt to bin Laden and promised that LeT would avenge his death. Documents found in bin Laden's hideout show that the two were in close contact right up to bin Laden's death. Given the two groups' close connections and shared ideological viewpoints, it is odd indeed that al Qaeda's leadership said very little about the Mumbai operation in the months following the attack. Bin Laden and Ayman al-Zawahiri each issued several statements afterward on numerous issues, including developments in Pakistan, but none made any mention of the Mumbai attacks.[37] Why?

Al Qaeda's unusual silence about the Mumbai attack may be an attempt to protect its ally Lashkar-e-Tayyiba from more international scrutiny. Once an organization is openly affiliated with al Qaeda, it gets more attention from the security services of the world, including the CIA, Britain's Secret Intelligence Service (MI6), and others. It joins, in effect, the A team of international terrorists and therefore gets more attention in counterterrorism operations. Al Qaeda probably also wanted to cover its own hand in the Mumbai operation to avoid bringing more pressure on Pakistan to break the ISI's ties to LeT and to make a more serious effort to combat al Qaeda itself. Bin Laden was not hiding from the ISI in 2008; he was hiding in its midst.

REACTIONS TO THE MUMBAI MASSACRE AND THEIR IMPLICATIONS

Pakistan initially denied any involvement in the 2008 Mumbai attack, even trying to suggest that the bombers were not Pakistanis and the attack was not staged from Karachi. There was considerable confusion in the early Pakistani response. President Zardari said at first that he would send the head of ISI to India to help with the investigation. The army and ISI quickly made it clear that they did not think that that was a good idea, and Zardari dropped it. Only in January 2009 did Sherry Rehman, then the Pakistani information minister, acknowledge publicly that the terrorists were Pakistanis. Under enormous international pressure, Islamabad banned Jamaat-ud-Dawa and put Saeed under house arrest. He was released in June 2009. Several other LeT officials have been arrested and are awaiting trial. Pakistan rejected India's request that Saeed and others be extradited to India to stand trial. The Pakistani government has consistently denied that it or the ISI had any connection to the bombers and the attack. While some Pakistani officials quietly have admitted that the ISI had links to LeT in the past, they deny that it had any foreknowledge of or role in the Mumbai operation itself.

There has been no systematic crackdown on LeT's infrastructure and apparatus in Pakistan. Many Pakistanis are in denial about their country's relationship to the tragedy in Mumbai. Despite India providing Pakistan with dossiers of evidence linking the attack to Pakistan, many Pakistanis believe that it was plotted and conducted by someone else. Some blame the Indian intelligence service, claiming that the Indians wanted to divert attention from Hindu extremists involved in anti-Muslim pogroms in India. Others have argued that Israel was the real perpetrator, hoping to provoke a war between India and Pakistan in order to destroy Pakistan's nuclear arsenal. One Pakistani think tank has argued India and Israel did it together.[38] India, of course, blamed Pakistan for the attack from the start, and it suspended all diplomatic engagement with Pakistan immediately after the massacre. India has presented detailed dossiers that lay out the evidence of a Pakistani hand in the attacks, including transcripts of the chilling calls from the terrorists to their handlers in Pakistan, the weapons and other material found in Mumbai at the crime scenes, and the results of the interrogations of Qasab and Headley.

21

It is important to note what India did not do after 26/11 as well as what it did. Although the alert levels in the Indian and Pakistani air forces increased during and immediately after the attacks, there was no general mobilization of the Indian army as occurred after the December 2001 attack on the parliament or any military strikes on LeT targets in Pakistan. Pakistan, apparently fearing an Indian air strike or some other military attack, put its air force and advance ground units on alert. However, as the Indian air force commander later said, "We exercised restraint and did not give Pakistan any excuse for a misadventure."[39] India's restraint is especially significant in light of an intense effort by the Indian military after the attack on Parliament in 2001 to develop the capability to strike Pakistan quickly after any new terrorist incident, avoiding a lengthy national military mobilization. Announced in 2004, the new doctrine for rapid response to a provocation is called the Cold Start approach. Indian forces have trained and conducted exercises to carry out a limited military attack on Pakistan since 2004.[40] The Cold Start doctrine and plans were designed specifically to give New Delhi a military option for retaliation against attacks like the Mumbai massacre.

Instead Singh, Congress Party leader Sonia Gandhi, and the rest of the ruling Congress Party leadership chose a political response, despite intense pressure for a stronger response from the opposition Bharatiya Janata Party (BJP), or Indian People's Party, amid the run-up to the national elections in May 2009. During the campaign BJP leaders repeatedly suggested that Singh's response had been too pacific and would only encourage further terrorism. The argument did not resonate with Indian voters, who returned the Congress Party to office with a larger mandate that it had won previously. Nonetheless, it is clear that another mass casualty attack on the level of the Mumbai attack would lead to intense political pressure on New Delhi for a more forceful response, possibly including military action. In a brave and prudent political move, Singh agreed to restart diplomatic engagement with Pakistan despite the failure of Islamabad to take on LeT or to extradite its leadership. In July 2009 at the Summit of the Non-Aligned Movement in Egypt, Singh agreed to reopen the diplomatic process with Pakistan. The BJP again attacked him as naïve and weak for doing so, but Singh understood the dangers of escalation for India.

Led by the United States, France, and the United Kingdom, the international community was quick to condemn the attacks in a statement by the UN Security Council in the days just after the attack. In June 2009, the United Nations added four officials from LeT to the consolidated list of individuals associated with bin Laden and al Qaeda created under UN Security Council Resolution 1267 (passed in May 2005), which obligates all UN members to freeze their funds and assets. The U.S. Department of the Treasury followed suit, freezing the assets of the four in July 2009.

In the immediate aftermath of the massacre, the United States, the United Kingdom, and other states appealed to India to show restraint and to Pakistan to cooperate with the investigation into the attacks. President George W. Bush and Secretary of State Condoleezza Rice spoke directly with both Zardari and Singh to try to caution them to avoid letting the situation get out of hand. As noted in the introduction to this volume, President-elect Barack Obama also called Singh to express his condolences and urge restraint. Such calls to India's leaders for restraint and a cool response have now become an all-too-familiar reaction to acts of terrorism in India. In 1999 President Clinton urged restraint during the Kargil war; President Bush did the same after the attack on the parliament in 2001, after the Mumbai metro attacks in 2006, and after the Mumbai massacre in 2008.

The 2008 attack on Mumbai came only days after Obama was elected president of the United States. His new team was confronted with an enormous international crisis as they were still celebrating their victory and starting to prepare to run the country. Obama was careful throughout the crisis to make clear that Bush was still president and that he was not yet in charge, but the events in

Mumbai shaped his thinking about the world and the rise of India and Pakistan. Mumbai showed graphically that America's deadliest enemy, al Qaeda, was deeply entrenched in a larger terrorism syndicate in Pakistan that threatens America, India, and even Pakistan itself. Six Americans were directly murdered by the terrorists in Mumbai, symbolizing the stakes for America. Others, like my friend and occasional coauthor Gary Samore, the president-elect's soon-to-be arms control czar, were staying at the Taj and could have been killed.

The complex web of ties between al Qaeda, Lashkar-e-Tayyiba, and the Pakistani army are a direct threat to American strategic interests beyond Mumbai itself. Pakistan has become a hothouse of terrorism, creating a global menace. The crisis would have been much worse, of course, if al Qaeda and its friends had gotten all that they wanted. If Singh and Gandhi had responded with force, not restraint as both Bush and Obama urged, this gang of terrorists could have created the war that they hoped for. A war between India and Pakistan, even if conducted on a limited basis with conventional weapons, would have been devastating to U.S. interests. Obama and his aides understood that completely. We knew that his call to Singh was immensely important, and we waited anxiously to hear how Singh had portrayed his options for action. Thankfully, he chose well. A war would have been devastating in many ways to many more countries than India and Pakistan. In the fall of 2008 the world economy was in free fall. Banks were failing, jobs were fading, and a deep recession loomed ahead. War in South Asia would have accelerated all the downward trends in the global economy. Not only would India's rising economy be threatened, the global economy itself would be threatened.

The longest war in American history, the battle to free Afghanistan of al Qaeda and terrorism, would have been vastly complicated. In 2008 more than 80 percent of NATO supplies for the war came through Pakistan, the bulk through Karachi, the port that the terrorists departed from on their journey to Mumbai. If

India and Pakistan had gone to war, that supply line would have been instantly put in jeopardy. Al Qaeda and LeT understood that completely. If the war had escalated to a nuclear exchange, the implications would have been even more disastrous for America and the world. India and Pakistan have the capability to destroy each other's cities. The destruction of just Mumbai and Karachi would mean the deaths of millions. The economic, political, and climate implications are self-evident.

The Mumbai crisis highlighted the vital interests that the United States has in the rise of India and Pakistan, and determining how to cope with their emergence as major world powers is among its most urgent priorities. The next chapter turns to understanding America's relationship with them and how it has evolved.

CHAPTER TWO

AMERICA, THE RAJ, AND PARTITION

India is the richest and most splendid country in the world.
—Marco Polo

THE CABINET DINING room at Number 10 Downing Street is a historic, impressive place to meet. I was a guest of Prime Minister David Cameron, who had invited me to participate as an outside expert in a meeting of the United Kingdom's National Security Council in December 2011 to take stock of British policy toward Pakistan and Afghanistan. More British soldiers are deployed to Afghanistan than to any other conflict zone in the world, and many have paid the ultimate price in service to their country. The key decision-makers of the United Kingdom—the prime minister, deputy prime minister, chancellor of the exchequer, foreign secretary, minister of defense, chief of staff, and the head of the Secret Intelligence Service (SIS, also known as MI6)—were seated around the table to review the state of war in South Asia. John Sawers, or M, the head of SIS, was an old friend. As an American, I considered it a singular honor to be asked to address this group.[1]

For centuries, that particular room had seen generations of British leaders discuss and review policy toward India, the jewel in the crown of the British Empire. No analysis of the rise of India and

Pakistan can begin without a proper understanding of their modern origins in the British Raj. In many ways, the British were the godfather of Pakistan; it was on the banks of the River Cam, not far from London, that the idea of Pakistan developed in the 1930s. At the end of the Raj, the idea of partition became reality and India and Pakistan became the states that they are now.

To understand America and the rise of India and Pakistan today, then, one must begin with the British Empire. America, India, and Pakistan are all products of that empire, and their political systems are derived from their common British heritage, to which they also owe a common language. But their experiences with the United Kingdom also differed in important ways. In addition to the Native Americans already living in the New World, who were soon outnumbered, America was populated primarily by immigrants from Europe and by African slaves. Most of the European immigrants, at least, came willingly. India is populated by the descendants of its original inhabitants, not those of colonial settlers. There were never more than 100,000 Europeans in the Indian Empire. While for Americans the memory of the British Empire is fairly benign, the memory of the Raj is bittersweet for Indians and Pakistanis. Many appreciate the benefits that it provided and still enjoy some of its legacy, but it also led to partition, pain, and the enduring conflict over Kashmir. The legacy of the Raj also deeply affected the future foreign policy strategies of India and Pakistan. It left India with an abiding distaste for great power politics and a fierce determination to maintain full independence in making decisions on national security. India does not want to be a partner, especially not a junior partner, in constraining alliances against communism, China, or anything else. The legacy of the Raj left Pakistan the weaker and more vulnerable state, always at war with its bigger neighbor. It needs a partner—or better, multiple partners—to stand up to India. These legacies are as alive today as they were in 1947.

America and British South Asia also have had very different timelines. The United States fought for and gained its independence from Great Britain at the end of the eighteenth century, just as India was losing its independence to the British East India Company at the end of the eighteenth and the beginning of the nineteenth century. America would fight a terrible civil war in the middle of the nineteenth century; at about the same time, India would fight a terrible war to gain independence, lose the war, and formally become a part of the British Empire. By the end of World War I, in 1918, America would be a global power; India would be just beginning its successful battle to achieve independence.

ORIGINS

Europeans "found" America and India at the same time, when Portuguese and Spanish explorers were looking for a new way to access the wealth of India and Asia. Their direct path through the Middle East had been blocked by the growing power of the Ottoman Empire, so they sought new paths. One was around the African continent, the other across the Atlantic and Pacific. The lure was spices, especially the spices and peppers of India. Vasco da Gama won the race on May 20, 1498, when he and his fleet arrived in India after sailing around Africa. Christopher Columbus, of course, had found America six years earlier, although he was in denial for a time, still believing that he was dealing with the Indians of the subcontinent.

Da Gama made three voyages to India before dying in Kochi in 1524. The Portuguese king made him admiral of the Indian seas and viceroy of Portuguese India. For a time, Portugal dominated the ocean highway to India, building trading stations and forts and fighting naval battles with the Ottomans to protect its access. Portugal grew fabulously wealthy from its monopoly of trade with India. Portugal's key base in India was at Goa, which the Portuguese occupied in 1510 and kept until 1961, but they also had possessions on both the east and west coasts of India. In 1535 Portugal acquired part of what would become Bombay, where it built the city's first church.

The India that Portugal discovered was richer than any state in Europe and probably better governed and administered. The Mughal Empire was in its ascendency in the sixteenth century. The empire was founded in 1525 by Babur, a descendant of Genghis Khan and Tamerlane, when his army invaded the subcontinent from Afghanistan equipped with Turkish cannon and matchlock muskets that gave him a technological advantage over the Indian armies that he encountered and defeated. His son Humayun expanded the empire, and Humayun's son, Akbar the Great, took it to its apogee. From 1556 to 1605, Akbar ruled over an empire that stretched for more than 1,200 miles, from Kabul and Kandahar in the northwest to the Bay of Bengal in the southeast. Most of today's Afghanistan, Pakistan, India, and Bangladesh were under Akbar's reign; only the far south of the Indian peninsula was beyond his reach.

Akbar's Islamic empire, which was administered by officials of his Persian-speaking royal court, had some 100 million subjects in 1600. The majority were Hindus, but Akbar was careful not to antagonize them with an overzealous approach to Islam. He celebrated Hindu festivals, took Hindu wives, and tolerated diversity. His son, Jahangir—or "conqueror of the world"—would rule from 1605 to 1627, succeeded by Jahangir's son, the famous Shah Jahan, who would build the Taj Mahal during his thirty years on the throne.

The Portuguese never tried to conquer the Mughal Empire; they knew that it was vastly more powerful than any army and fleet that they could possibly muster. Instead, they traded with it. Other European states fought Portugal for part of the action, and the Dutch, Danes, and French also took possession of forts and trading stations around the Indian Ocean. The British arrived on the stage in 1600, when Queen Elizabeth I granted a charter to 218 merchants who formed The Governor and Company of Merchants of London Trading into the East Indies, which would later become the East India Company. Its first trading station was set up in

1608 in Surat. By the middle of the seventeenth century, Portugal was fading as a great power and needed English help to defend its realm. On May 11, 1661, King Charles II married Catherine of Braganza, daughter of King John IV of Portugal, and acquired Bombay as her dowry. The king leased the Bombay settlement to the East India Company, firmly establishing England's presence in India. The settlement grew quickly from a population of 10,000 people in 1661 to some 60,000 fifteen years later.[2]

From the beginning, the British Empire in India was dominated by the quest for profit; it was built not to acquire territory for the greater glory of the monarchy but to make money. The East India Company represented the royal family and the state, of course, but its principal objective was to engage in and profit from trade. As it gradually expanded its influence and control over parts of India, it raised its own armies and fleets and called on the government in London for assistance when threatened by enemies, Indian or European. At its height it controlled an army of 200,000 men, but it was run from a tiny headquarters in London, staffed by only 159 employees in 1785 and 241 in 1853.[3] At the same time, Britain was building its colonies in North America. The first settlement came in 1607 in Jamestown, Virginia, quickly followed by others in Massachusetts and Maryland. Through conquest and settlement, the English would establish thirteen colonies in America by the end of the seventeenth century. While in 1750 the Mughal Empire encompassed 180 million people, in 1755 the thirteen colonies had only 1.2 million inhabitants of European descent.

The people living in the growing British possessions in both North America and South Asia would become participants in the series of conflicts that established Great Britain as the world's preeminent global power in the seventeenth and eighteenth centuries. In America those conflicts are referred to collectively as the French and Indian wars, and in India they are seen as wars to conquer the subcontinent, but they were in fact global conflicts—usually pitting England against France—and British politicians, soldiers, and merchants saw them as such. British soldiers could expect to fight in both North America and South Asia. For example, in America Lord Cornwallis is famous for losing the battle of Yorktown in 1781 to a combined French and American army, setting the stage for the Treaty of Paris, which resulted in American independence. However, Cornwallis went on to have a more victorious career in India as a general and governor. He helped to expand the domain of the East India Company, not only on the subcontinent but also throughout the Indian Ocean littoral; Fort Cornwallis in Penang, Malaysia, is named for him. And Sir Charles James Napier, of the Royal Navy, who ravaged the Chesapeake Bay area in the War of 1812, conquered the Sindh in the 1830s.

The epic British-French rivalry for North America and South Asia began in earnest with the War of Austrian Succession in the 1740s, and battles raged around the world between the forces of the two great colonial empires. When the war ended in 1748 with the Treaty of Aix-la-Chapelle, the two powers exchanged the conquests that each had made in America and India. France was given back the fortress of Louisburg on Cape Breton Island in return for giving back Madras to the English. America and India were now pawns in European rivalries.

The first major milestone in the British East India Company's conquest of the subcontinent came on June 23, 1757, when a small English and Indian army led by Robert Clive defeated a much larger Bengali army at the battle of Plassey near Calcutta. The Bengali army was supported by French advisers, and the war in India was part of the next major global struggle, known in Europe as the Seven Years' War. By then the British East India Company had three main bases in India, at Fort St. George in Madras (today's Chennai), Fort William in Calcutta (Kolkata), and Bombay (Mumbai). Louis XIV, France's Sun King, had created the French East India Company, which had bases in Chandernagar in Bengal and Pondicherry on the coast of the Bay of Bengal. Although Clive commanded only 700 or so European troops at Plassey and his total force of around 3,200 was dwarfed by the opposing Bengali army, which was almost 70,000 strong, his victory was decisive. The East India Company acquired effective control of Bengal as a result. A decade later, the company controlled Bengal completely, putting 30 million Indians under the British crown. England's dominance in South Asia would never be seriously challenged by another European power.

The British emerged from the Seven Years' War as the dominant power in North America as well as South Asia. The war began with a military disaster near Pittsburgh, Pennsylvania, when the largest British army that had yet been sent to America was ambushed and annihilated by a French and Indian (Native American) force in 1755. General Edward Braddock's defeat (his aide-de-camp was the young George Washington) was followed by a series of campaigns that culminated in the taking of Quebec in 1759 by General James Wolfe. Wolfe's decisive victory would lead to the British conquest of all of North America east of the Mississippi.

After the Seven Years' War, American and Indian fortunes in the British Empire diverged dramatically. The thirteen colonies fought for their independence from England in another global struggle, the American Revolution, which ended with the American victory at Yorktown, in which France's support had been crucial. French arms triumphed not only in North America but also in South Asia. The French navy scored impressive victories in both arenas, and by the end of the American Revolution, France had more troops in India than in America. With the signing of the Treaty of Paris in 1783, the United States of America became free and independent. America would fight a second war with Britain in 1812, in which it sought and failed to acquire Canada, but its independence was never in doubt after Yorktown. With the end of direct American involvement in the affairs of the British Empire, the formal bond between America and India came to an end as well. Trade continued, of course, but Americans no longer saw themselves as part of the larger British Empire. India, however, was moving in the opposite direction.

In India, the Mughal Empire was dissolving. The emperor in Delhi was becoming a figurehead, with no control over most of his empire. The East India Company still regarded him as the legal ruler of most of the nation and theoretically accepted his writ because the Mughal emperor had granted them their original trading rights. Even as the company chipped away at the emperor's real authority, they maintained the façade of his sovereignty for several more decades.

The British and the East India Company fought a series of wars with local Indian rulers to further consolidate British control over the subcontinent. The French tried to hold the British tide back, but in the end the British defeated all of India's various warlords and kings. In the battle of Assaye, on September 23, 1803, Arthur Wellesley, the future Duke of Wellington, won a decisive victory that brought most of southern India into the empire. With the defeat of Napoleon by Wellington at Waterloo in 1815, British domination of the subcontinent was complete. At the Congress of Vienna (1814-15), held to resolve a number of issues of concern to European states, Britain also gained control of Holland's last colony in South Asia, the island of Ceylon, which became part of the British Empire. British armies would go on to fight the Burmese twice, finally annexing Burma to the empire in 1852, and they also defeated the Sikhs twice, annexing the Punjab and Kashmir by 1849. Nepal too was defeated and its territory reduced; ultimately it became a satellite of the British Empire in India. The Sindh was annexed and Baluchistan made a puppet princely state.

By the middle of the nineteenth century, Britain and the East India Company dominated South Asia from Afghanistan to Thailand and from Nepal to Sri Lanka. All of today's India and Pakistan were under British control. Meanwhile, with the acquisition of the Louisiana Territory from France in 1803, the acquisition of

Oregon from Britain in 1846, and the acquisition of Texas follow-ing the defeat of Mexico in 1848, America had expanded from the Atlantic to the Pacific Ocean.

India and America then encountered their own most severe cri-ses of the nineteenth century. Two wars were fought, one in South Asia and one in North America, that would be defining events in the development of India, Pakistan, and the United States. The so-called Indian Mutiny, also described as the First Indian War of Independence (1857–58), and the so-called War between the States, better known as the Civil War, would radically change each coun-try's fate, leaving India deeply entrenched in its colonial status and launching America as an emerging world power. Conventional his-tories have generally agreed that 100,000 Indians and 11,000 Brit-ish soldiers perished in the 1857 war. New historians in India claim that the Indian death toll following the campaign and its aftermath was actually much higher, perhaps 1 million or more. In the Civil War, some 600,000 to 750,000 Americans died on both sides.

The war in India began after the British introduced a new rifle for its Indian troops, or sepoys. Rumors spread that the Enfield rifle would use cartridges greased with fat from pigs or cattle, thus alienating both Muslim and Hindu soldiers. Muslims do not eat pork, and Hindus revere cows. But the roots of the rebellion were much deeper. The British had become contemptuous of their Indian subjects. While the British had begun in India as humble traders seeking favor from the emperor and his court, now they were rulers who considered the Indian population, Hindu and Muslim alike, as second-class human beings. Indians were treated as inferior to Englishmen in their own country.

Racism was to be found in all of the East India Company's deal-ings with Indians, but worse was the British effort to try to convert Indians to Christianity. The company had been very careful for two centuries to leave India's religions alone, prohibiting mission-ary activity in South Asia; it understood that the combination of Islam and Hinduism was already an explosive one. If the British added Christianity to the mix, using their secular power to promote theological power, they would be riding a very angry tiger. But hubris and arrogance overtook caution. The company began to allow missionary activity, and in the great revival that swept nineteenth-century England, eager Anglican missionaries were sent to the subcontinent.

The mutiny began in April 1857 in a garrison at Meerut just north of Delhi. Soldiers who refused to use the new cartridges were sentenced by court martial to ten years' hard labor, and the entire garrison rose up against the British. The revolt quickly spread throughout the Bengali army of the East India Company. Thousands deserted and took up arms against the company and the British. British civilians, including women and children, were massacred across the country. The rebels took Delhi and pressed the reigning Mughal emperor, Bahadur Shah Zafar II, to lead them. Zafar, a gentle man who preferred poetry to politics, was not interested in becoming a revolutionary, but he had no choice. Soon almost all of north India was in rebel hands. The uprising rapidly gained the support of extremists in both the Hindu and Muslim communities, who saw it as a chance to oust the hated British from India and return the subcontinent to native rule. Some Muslim clerics called for a jihad against the British.

The mutiny, the most serious challenge to the British Empire in the nineteenth century, was by far the most serious challenge to British rule in India until the twentieth century. London mobilized troops from Indian garrisons that remained loyal, especially Sikhs and Gurkhas, and from bases in the Middle East and Malaya. Some troops came from England. Fed on stories of atrocities committed by the rebels, the British counterrevolution was brutal and remorseless. Captured Muslims were forced to eat pork and Hindus forced to eat beef and then executed. Often captives were tied to the mouth of cannon and blasted apart.

Not all of the Indian troops in the British army had defected, and there was never any real threat to the capital in Calcutta or to Madras and Bombay. After a siege, a relief force regained control of Delhi, killed all of Zahar's family, and captured Zahar, who was hiding in the tomb of his ancestor Humayan. After putting him on display and trying him by court martial, the British sent him into exile in Burma, where he died. The Mughal Empire was formally dissolved. The British almost destroyed the Red Fort, where the throne was located, and the massive Jama Masjid mosque before cooler heads prevailed and it was decided that their destruction would only further inflame passions. Delhi was a ghost town for a time as the British purged it of any and all who had backed the mutiny.

The English public had been horrified by the news of massacres of English civilians and terrified by the thought that Britain could lose the "jewel in the crown" of its empire, as the young Queen Victoria had labeled India. On August 2, 1858, the government dissolved the East India Company, transferred all its rights to the British monarchy, and took formal control of India for the British monarchy and nation. No longer would profit be the overriding mission of the British in India; now imperial objectives would come above all others.

India would indeed be the jewel in the crown of the empire, and the British viceroy in Calcutta would rule as a sovereign power not only over the subcontinent but over the entire Indian Ocean basin. British possessions in the Persian Gulf and at Aden in Yemen as well as Singapore and Malaya were under the control of the British Indian Empire. India became the base for British military expeditions throughout the region. For example, in a short Anglo-Persian war in 1856, 4,000 British and Indian troops dispatched from Bombay to the Persian Gulf captured the Iranian city of Bushire to compel the Qajar Shah to make peace.[4] Of course, ultimate decisionmaking authority resided in London, but the viceroy was, in effect, master of the largest part of the British Empire. The government would now spend resources developing its new jewel. In 1876 Victoria took the title of Empress of India, after Prime Minister Benjamin Disraeli pushed approval of the title through Parliament.

Americans watched the spectacle of the mutiny largely through the eyes of English newspapers. Not surprisingly, their sympathies lay with their fellow white Christians, especially in the American South, where the mutiny fed fear of slave uprisings. Americans were not generally friends of the British Empire; after all, they had fought it twice. However, they had no affection for Indians. Racism ran deep in America, and most Indians, whether Muslim or Hindu, were dark-skinned people. The *New York Times,* for example, called the mutiny "a Mohammedan conspiracy" to restore the Mughal Empire.[5]

But in the late 1850s American attention was increasingly riveted on the crisis brewing at home between the slave-holding South and the industrializing North. The four-year civil war that erupted after President Abraham Lincoln's election in 1860 was the bloodiest conflict in American history. Traditional estimates put the number of war dead at more than 620,000 (360,000 for the North and 260,000 for the South), although more recent research puts the total at around 750,000.[6] The Federal government was transformed by the struggle. More than 2 million soldiers were under arms for the Union, and in 1865 General Ulysses S. Grant commanded the largest army in the world; for a brief period, the United States also had the largest and most advanced navy in the world. The American economy too was transformed by the war effort.

Above all, the war propelled America onto the global stage. In its aftermath the Grant administration built what would come to be called the Old Executive Office Building next to the White House to provide quarters for the departments of state, war, and the navy and the nation's nascent national security bureaucracy. Upon completion it was the largest office building in the world. It was a concrete manifestation of a new reality: America was a global player as never before. Having defeated Mexico, its only rival for dominance in North America, before the Civil War, America was the preeminent power in the Western Hemisphere, with a navy that rivaled the British Royal Navy in size and quality.

Grant also became the first American president to visit India. After leaving the White House in 1876, he embarked on a world tour, during which he visited British India. He traveled from Egypt to Bombay, New Delhi, Jaipur, Agra, Benares, and Calcutta. He and his wife Julia visited the Taj Mahal and were entranced by its beauty. They stayed at Government House in Bombay on Malabar Point, where they and the viceroy discussed the Second Anglo-Afghan war, which was then under way; as a result of the war, a British protectorate was established in Afghanistan. From India they went on to Rangoon, Burma, and then China and Japan. Plans to visit Lahore, Madras, and Ceylon were scrapped due to lack of time, but Grant saw more of India than any American president since.[7]

Washington's relationship with London changed as a result of the Civil War. In its early months, there was a real danger that the British Empire would recognize the Confederate States of America and even intervene on their behalf. Once Lincoln issued the Emancipation Proclamation, that danger receded. Although some of his cabinet, especially Secretary of State William Seward, longed to seize Canada, war was avoided. After the war the two English-speaking North Atlantic powers would increasingly engage in peaceful cooperation and trade. The long border between America and the new Canadian federation that emerged right after the Civil War would become increasingly open.

In short, while India was becoming an integral part of the British Empire after the middle of the nineteenth century, America was becoming Britain's equal. The paths of the two countries were diverging dramatically. In 1911 George V became the first monarch to visit the subcontinent, and he announced the decision to move the capital from Calcutta to New Delhi. A grand new city was designed by Edwin Lutyens to impress the world with the power of the Raj and to symbolize the enduring strength of British rule in India. But the Indian economy was stunted by colonialism. India did not undergo an industrial revolution like that in America and Europe, and many Indians blame the Raj.[8] Nonetheless, India would be a vital part of the British war effort during World War I. More than 1 million Indian soldiers fought for the empire, some 140,000 in France alone, in the trenches on the Western Front. Indian forces conquered Iraq and Tanganyika. For the most part, Indians saw service as a patriotic duty. Mahatma Gandhi, the rising star of Indian politics, organized an ambulance corps to assist the war effort (he had done the same thing a decade before, during the Boer War in South Africa).

America was a very reluctant warrior in the Great War. President Woodrow Wilson won reelection in 1916 in part on the basis of the slogan "He kept us out of war," and he was not eager to join a battle between rival European colonial empires. When war finally came in 1917, he promised a "war to end all wars," which would usher in a new era of open diplomacy, ending the world domination of the European great powers, and of self-determination for all peoples—or at least for Europeans and Americans. His Fourteen Points promised freedom, not more imperialism. The British government was appalled. It was determined to use the war to annex more colonies, not to give up the ones already in hand and certainly not the jewel in the crown.

Indians expected some governance reforms as their right for sending so many troops to fight for the empire, of whom 90,000 had died. But Winston Churchill, the colonial secretary after the war, was determined to give nothing. As a young man Churchill had fought in India on the frontier with Afghanistan. He had deeply held views about India, and he hated Hindu politicians like Gandhi who were pressing for reform, considering them a threat to the survival of the Raj. He dismissed Gandhi as a "fakir" and charlatan. India was not to be given to the Indians; it was to remain the centerpiece of the empire.[9] When in 1919 in Amritsar, the Sikh holy city, British troops massacred hundreds of Indians pressing for political change in a peaceful demonstration, London rewarded the commander of the troops responsible. The massacre would prove to be a turning point. Thereafter, Indians understood that reform was a chimera. Independence was essential.

ROOSEVELT AND PARTITION

Gandhi would lead the Indian nationalist movement from the end of World War I until his murder in 1948. His nonviolent approach would gain worldwide renown and favor, especially in the United States, where his marches, speeches, and fasts would be followed with rapt attention. Gandhi and his struggle later inspired the American civil rights movement of the 1960s. But Gandhi had little impact on the British before World War II. They imprisoned him for a total of 2,089 days of his life in British jails in either Africa or India. Churchill was determined not to free India, and as a member of both the government and the opposition, he made sure that India remained a colony in the interwar years. He became prime minister in 1940, absolutely determined never to cede India.

The Japanese attacks on Pearl Harbor and Singapore in 1941 would transform Asia's history and put the future of India on America's agenda with England. In the early months of 1942, Japanese armies overran Burma and threatened Calcutta while a Japanese aircraft carrier group raided the Bay of Bengal, sank a Royal Navy carrier, and forced the Royal Navy to retreat to East Africa, leaving India vulnerable to invasion. One of Gandhi's closest lieutenants, Subhas Chandra Bose, broke with Gandhi and was supported by the Nazi regime. Bose had gone to Berlin, where, in broadcasts over German radio, he urged Indians to join the Axis powers to free India. He denounced the United States as a pawn of the British Empire and declared the United States as well as the United Kingdom as enemies of Indian freedom.[10] Then Bose sailed by U-boat to Japan, where he organized an army of Indian prisoners captured by Japan in Singapore to liberate India. The situation was alarming. His charge that America was the enemy of Indian freedom was taken very seriously in Washington, where Bose was seen as a real menace to the stability of India and the Allied war effort there. President Franklin

D. Roosevelt felt that the war had to be a war for freedom and that London and Churchill must do something to accommodate India's legitimate demand for self-determination. India would become the most acrimonious issue between Churchill and FDR during the war. The war also transformed average American perceptions of India. For the first time, large numbers of Americans arrived in India, as part of the war effort. A quarter of a million had come to support the air bridge to China over the Himalayas ("the Hump") or to support the British army in India in fighting Japan; most served in eastern India around Calcutta.[11] A young Julia Child served in Ceylon and India with the Office of Strategic Services, the predecessor of the Central Intelligence Agency. She and her colleagues would bring home new American impressions of life in the subcontinent.[12]

Two and a half million Indian soldiers served with the British army during the war, of whom forty received the Victoria Cross, the highest military honor that the British Empire awarded. Indian military forces were critical to British and Allied operations in Burma, the Middle East, and Italy, and India was the most crucial base in supporting Chinese armies fighting the Japanese.[13] India's people, however, would pay a horrendous price for the war. Famine broke out in Bengal in 1943. Sufficient food was available elsewhere in the empire to avert starvation, but the war effort required all the available ocean-going vessels, or so Churchill argued. More famine followed in 1944, and again the ships were said to be needed elsewhere. Estimates of the cost in lives range from half a million to more than 4 million. Some Indian authors have argued that in allowing so many to starve, Churchill was more than negligent; they assert that he wished to punish India.[14] His chief of the imperial general staff, Field Marshal Viscount Alan Brooke, blamed the United States for not providing enough ships.[15] It was to be the last famine in India. The democratic government that replaced the Raj never allowed its people to die as Britain had.

Roosevelt pressed Churchill after Pearl Harbor to respond to Indian nationalist demands for greater self-determination. He sent

Churchill private letters imploring him to be more open to the Indian nationalist movement and sent an envoy to India to represent American interests. For the British, especially the viceroy in Delhi and Churchill, that constituted interference in the internal affairs of the empire and showed a flagrant disregard for an ally's independence. Churchill was so angered by Roosevelt's moves that he even considered resigning as prime minister in protest, the only time during the war that he considered such a step.

Gandhi saved Churchill. In August 1942, under pressure from Bose and his radio broadcasts in exile, Gandhi began the "Quit India" movement, demanding immediate independence for a united India and urging peaceful nonviolent resistance to the war effort. For example, Indians were to block convoys or rail trains supplying the British army in India. The British responded with a major crackdown on Gandhi and the Congress Party, and thousands of party activists were arrested and imprisoned for the rest of the war. For a time, India was on the verge of revolt. The viceroy warned Churchill that he faced "the most serious rebellion since that of 1857."[16] In the end the British managed to curb Indian anger and repress the Congress Party.

But Quit India had a major impact on American thinking about Indian nationalism. The United States was engaged in a "great crusade" to defeat Nazi Germany and Imperial Japan, one in which "anyone not with us was against us." After August 1942, it became increasingly difficult for Roosevelt to lobby for Gandhi and India with Churchill and the United Kingdom. Still, in January 1943 FDR sent another envoy to India to press his case one more time for giving India the promise of freedom after the war. William Phillips was a Boston aristocrat, Harvard graduate, and career diplomat who had been ambassador to Mussolini's Italy. In 1943 he was the chief of station in London for the Office of Strategic Services. Churchill assumed that with his background, Phillips would favor the Raj.

Instead, Phillips pressed the viceroy for a meeting with the imprisoned Gandhi and urged FDR to convene a conference of

Indian politicians to establish an all-party, Muslim and Hindu, administrative body to prepare to take over governance of India after the war. Even Roosevelt thought the proposal "amazingly radical." Phillips was refused access to Gandhi, who was fasting to protest British policy. He did meet with the leader of the Muslim cause, Muhammad Ali Jinnah. After the meeting, Phillips wrote the president that "the more I studied Jinnah's Pakistan, the less it appealed to me as the answer to India's communal problems. To break India into two separate nations would weaken both."[17] The British were not amused, and FDR did not push Churchill again.

Churchill was determined not to relinquish the Raj, but in 1945 he lost his reelection bid. The British Empire had been devastated by the war, Britain was deeply in debt to America, and times were very hard in London. British policymakers began to look for a new way to preserve British influence in South Asia, and they chose partition. Behind the scenes, in correspondence with Jinnah, the leader of the Pakistan movement, Churchill encouraged the drive for a Muslim state in the subcontinent. Jinnah's private correspondence with Churchill has never been made public.

Jinnah was British educated. He dressed like a well-to-do English gentleman and savored English style. Earlier in life, he had been a supporter of the Congress Party and a united India, but in the 1930s he embraced the new idea of a state for Muslims in South Asia. That idea was given a name by a group of Muslim students from the subcontinent at Cambridge University, who proposed *Pakistan,* to stand for Punjab, Afghania, Kashmir, Sindh, and Baluchistan. The word also means "land of the pure" in Persian and Urdu.

Jinnah was the driving force behind Pakistan's creation. He refused any compromise that would fall short of independence. He understood that Gandhi's Quit India movement had damaged the ties between the nationalist Hindus and America and England. He also understood that the British wanted to maintain their strategic position in South Asia somehow and that promises of a close alliance with Pakistan after independence would appeal to British policymakers. He gauged correctly that London would back partition, despite the wish of the majority of the people of the subcontinent for a unified state. Jinnah remains a divisive figure in South Asia today. His portrait can be found in every office in Pakistan, his expression usually one of stern defiance. In India he is the symbol of partition. When Jaswant Singh, a prominent member of the Bharatiya Janata Party and former foreign minister, published a massive biography of Jinnah that was a fair portrait of his strengths and weaknesses, Singh was expelled from the party and vilified as soft on Pakistan.

On August 14, 1947, Pakistan became the first country to become independent of the British Empire after World War II and the first country created as a homeland for Muslims. India followed the next day. Two future world powers were born. The Raj, however, left a tremendous legacy to both India and Pakistan. India emerged from centuries of British rule determined to maintain its independence at all costs; it was never again going to be told what to do by a foreign power. It would make any decision to go to war, not London or Washington. It would pursue a third way during the cold war and beyond. It would be friends with all powers, the ally of none. The closing years of the Raj had been especially bitter for India, with the threat of Japanese invasion, massive famines, and draconian political crackdowns. Indians admired much about the British, but they were happy to see them go. Pakistanis were equally determined to keep their newfound independence, but they were convinced that they needed an ally against their bigger rival next door. They wanted to be part of a global alliance with a major power to protect them from the perceived Indian threat. America would be that ally. When America disappointed Pakistan, Pakistan would turn to China.

It is, of course, deeply ironic that today the largest manufacturer in the United Kingdom is an Indian firm, Tata, which began as a small company in Bombay under the Raj and now owns the largest steel mill in England and the country's premier automobile company, Jaguar.[18]

CHAPTER THREE

IN THE SHADOW OF THE COLD WAR:
THE FIRST FORTY YEARS

HAWAII WAS AN unlikely place to meet with the Pakistani minister of defense and the fiftieth anniversary of Japan's surrender in World War II was an unlikely occasion for the meeting. But in 1995 Secretary of Defense William J. Perry and I were in a conference room of a five-star hotel there to honor Pakistan's role in Japan's defeat and to discuss the future of U.S. relations with Pakistan after the cold war. It was all a bit absurd. Pakistan had not existed in World War II, but it was invited to the commemoration ceremony to represent the Indian soldiers who fought for the Raj. India was invited too, but New Delhi declined since it did not have warm memories of Churchill's war or of being an instrument of the Raj's other wars.

The conversation with the Pakistanis went nowhere. By 1995 America and Pakistan were caught in their deadly embrace, prisoners of their history of seduction and betrayal throughout the cold war. The Pakistani team was headed by the minister of defense, a civilian who had only the most nominal influence and no control over the military. The Pakistani military does not let civilians interfere in its affairs and certainly not on important issues like nuclear weapons. The Pakistani team in Hawaii was there only to complain. They spent forty-five minutes railing against America's betrayal of Pakistan in 1990, when, under the Pressler amendment,

America had cut off Pakistan's supply of military equipment. The amendment was named after the South Dakota senator who sponsored the bill in 1985, whose name is better known in Pakistan than it is in any town in the Dakotas today. Not only had the United States refused to deliver the F-16s that Pakistan bought in the 1980s, it refused to return Pakistan's money and was charging them for the maintenance of their aircraft! It was unfair and arrogant, the Pakistanis charged; America was the global bully. Perry was ready for the tirade; he had heard it all many times before. His goal was to try to get beyond that issue, on which his hands were tied, to see whether better military-to-military relations were possible despite the Pressler amendment. It was a worthy effort, but a futile one.

Honolulu is home to the Pacific Command (PACOM), the regional military command that includes India (but not Pakistan) in its area of operations (AOR). Since World War II the American military has seen India largely from the perspective of the Pacific and East Asia. In PACOM's plans, India, which sits at the remote far end of the AOR, is often seen more as a potential counterbalance to China than anything else. But just as India did not want to attend the 1995 ceremony, it generally does not want to be seen as a counterbalance to China or as a player in Washington's grand geopolitical strategies. It has serious concerns about China—it was, after all, attacked by China in 1962—but it does not want to be stuck in American-made alliances. It is determined to keep the independence that it fought so long to gain from the British.

The United States played little part in the historic transformation of South Asia that followed the end of the Raj; Washington left partition to the British to execute and watched from the sidelines. The last viceroy of India, Lord Mountbatten, would become a household name in America for his role in presiding over the mass violence and huge refugee flows that followed partition, but American diplomacy stayed on the margins as this catastrophic human tragedy played out. For the next fifty years, American strategic thinking about the subcontinent was always a function of a larger conflict, the cold war with the Soviet Union and Communist China. The cold war dynamic drew the United States into an alliance with Pakistan and into an adversarial relationship with India. The alliance with Pakistan, however, was deeply troubled by the divergent goals of the two parties. America wanted an alliance to contain Russia; Pakistan wanted an alliance to confront India. The resulting tension would bedevil the allies for decades. The United States also was uncomfortable with being an adversary of India, which it considered too big and too democratic to divorce. So several presidents tried to have it both ways—maintaining an alliance with Islamabad as well as pursuing good relations with New Delhi. Their efforts consistently failed, a fact that should serve as a lesson for today's policymakers.

India and Pakistan went to war almost at their birth as independent states, in a conflict centered in Kashmir, at the northern tip of the subcontinent. The first war ended in the division of Kashmir, a division that endures to this day. The two states also evolved differently internally. Pakistan was a divided state from the start, with 42 million people in East Pakistan and 33 million in West Pakistan, 1,000 miles away.[1] The military officer corps came from the west. Pakistan's democratic government was overthrown in a military coup in 1958; four army dictators would follow, with brief periods of weak civilian government. India would remain a vibrant democracy with not one coup attempt by the army and only a brief period of undemocratic government imposed by a prime minister. Pakistan would become an increasingly dysfunctional state, unable to address its poverty and illiteracy; India would make slow progress on eliminating both, setting the stage for more rapid progress after the cold war.

The unresolved Kashmir conflict is central to the fate of both countries. India and Pakistan were born with a wound, and the wound has not healed in the decades since; instead it has become more infected, giving rise to terror and violence. Kashmir is not the only reason for Indo-Pakistani enmity, but it is the most obvious and the most subject to resolution. It is a concrete dispute at heart, even if it has taken on many symbolic and ideological aspects. American policymakers from Truman to Kennedy recognized this reality and tried hard to advance a solution to bring peace to South Asia. They failed for a variety of reasons, and their failures led their successors to give up trying. That was the wrong answer.

TRUMAN AND EISENHOWER

India and Pakistan were born in great violence and misery. More than 1 million died and another 10 million became refugees as the two new states were torn out of the Raj.[2] Partition, Britain's solution to the end of its empire, left a legacy of hatred and violence that endures to this day and may someday lead to even greater disaster. Harry Truman would be the first American president to deal with this situation. Washington recognized both countries upon independence and dispatched ambassadors to their respective capitals. But for Truman, South Asia was still a British preserve and a backwater for America. The president's focus was on the emerging cold war with Russia, the takeover of Eastern Europe by the Soviets, and the civil war in China, which ended in communist victory. Truman responded with the Marshall Plan to rebuild Europe, created NATO to defend it, and initiated U.S. alliances with Japan, Australia, and New Zealand in the Pacific.

Like his successors, Truman wanted to build good relations with both India and Pakistan. But Truman, again like his successors, would find that harder to do than most assumed. Almost from the beginning, India and Pakistan were at war over the future of Kashmir, a princely state ruled by a Hindu maharajah but populated by a Muslim majority. Both Pakistan and India wanted Kashmir to join their respective nations, but the maharajah hesitated, hoping for independence. Pakistan sent in a Pashtun army to annex the province in October 1947, and India responded with an airlift of troops to the capital, Srinagar, to prevent annexation. The war in

Kashmir continued until December 31, 1948, costing the lives of about 1,500 soldiers on each side.

The United Nations, which had brokered the cease-fire, adopted a resolution to bring in observers to help maintain the truce. The UN Military Observers Group in India and Pakistan (UNMO-GIP) monitored the 400-mile-long cease-fire line with troops from around the world, although in the early years Americans made up the largest contingent. Pakistan was to withdraw all of its forces—irregular as well as regular—from the province. India was allowed to keep minimum-strength forces to preserve law and order. A plebiscite was to decide the fate of the province. Although both India and Pakistan accepted the UN resolution, neither carried it out. Instead, each held onto the territory that it had acquired in the war, leaving India in possession of two-fifths of the province, including the Valley of Kashmir, the most populated area. Pakistan acquired three-fifths of the province and a border with China. It would later cede territory in Kashmir to China, and today the original province is divided in three parts: 43 percent is held by India, 37 percent by Pakistan, and 20 percent by China.

The UN then sought to send a delegation to New Delhi and Karachi, Pakistan's capital until 1958, to arrange a plebiscite and a settlement. Admiral Chester Nimitz, the World War II American naval hero, was to lead the talks, but his mission never materialized.[3] The Texas-born Nimitz moved to New York in March 1949 to work with the UN and to set up a staff to arrange the voting procedures. He enthusiastically wrote that India and Pakistan both had an "ardent desire to secure a peaceful solution."[4] He expected to leave for South Asia in April. However, Pakistan soon refused to withdraw its troops, and India refused to hold the plebiscite, which it knew it would lose. UN Secretary General Trygve Lie suggested that Nimitz arbitrate the dispute. Nimitz agreed and again waited for India and Pakistan to set dates for him to visit. Truman and the British prime minister both wrote to the leaders of both countries, urging support for the Nimitz mission.

It was India's prime minister, Jawaharlal Nehru, who turned Truman down. Nehru, who felt an emotional and family bond to the province, had made the decision to send troops to Kashmir in 1947, and he was determined not to give it up. After meeting with Nehru when he came to Washington in October 1949, Truman left it to others to push the Kashmir issue with him, and Secretary of State Dean Acheson and Nimitz met with Nehru to try to change his mind. Nehru insisted that all Pakistani troops had to leave Kashmir first while Indian troops stayed to maintain law and order, implicitly indicating that his troops would ensure the right outcome of the plebiscite. Acheson wrote later that Nehru was "one of the most difficult men with whom I have ever had to deal." Nimitz tried to budge him in two more meetings but got nowhere.[5]

In February 1950 the UN Security Council voted to send a representative to South Asia to try to break the deadlock. Pakistan insisted on Nimitz; India rejected him. The admiral never made it to South Asia, and he went home to California for good. He officially resigned his position only in 1953, but the effort was over long before then. Nehru told the American ambassador that "he was tired of receiving moralistic advice from the United States. So far as Kashmir was concerned, he would not give an inch."[6] Kashmir became a frozen conflict for more than a decade, preventing any real rapprochement between India and Pakistan. Occasional half-hearted efforts to resume a serious dialogue went nowhere.

Nehru, a hero of the independence struggle, was India's first prime minister, and he was determined to not take sides in the cold war. He wanted India to become a leader of a new third force, the Non-Aligned Movement. During his visit to Washington in October 1949, he had the first summit-level Indo-American talk with Truman. Kashmir was not the only problem. The personal chemistry between Nehru and Truman was poor, and they did not get along well. When, at the formal state dinner, Truman discussed the virtues of Kentucky bourbons, Nehru was not impressed. Nehru pushed Truman to accept the results of the Chinese civil war and to recognize the new communist government. He also pushed for bringing the communist government into the United Nations and for allowing it to take the Chinese seat on the UN Security Council. Under intense Republican criticism for "losing" China to the communists, Truman resisted.

Two years later Nehru tried to warn Truman that moving American and UN forces deep into North Korea to the Yalu River dividing Korea and China would spark a Chinese reaction. The Indian ambassador in Beijing, who was the only noncommunist envoy who had access to the leadership and to Mao, was told to warn the Americans not to get close to the Yalu. Truman refused to listen to Nehru, and Nehru was proven right. Thousands of American GIs and marines were killed or wounded as a consequence, and the war dragged on for two more years. Relations between India and the United States were cordial but not close. China was one stumbling block, and another, U.S. ties with Pakistan, quickly arose.

Pakistani-American relations were an altogether different matter. Muhammad Ali Jinnah died within a year of Pakistan's independence, and his successors were eager to find an ally to offset India's natural advantages of size and population. With the United Kingdom in decline, America was the obvious choice. Prime Minister Liaquat Ali Khan came to Washington in May 1950, on the eve of the Korean War, to seek military aid. Once the war began, Pakistan supported the Americans; although it did not send troops, it did send 5,000 tons of rice. Unlike with Nehru, Truman hit it off with the Pakistanis, and he was open to developing a close relationship with them. But the Truman team did not agree to provide arms to Pakistan, and repeated Pakistani requests were softly rebuffed. Liaquat was assassinated on October 16, 1951, the first in a very long series of violent deaths of senior Pakistani leaders. His assassination has never been fully resolved; like many of those that followed, it is still a mystery today, surrounded by elaborate conspiracy theories. At the time, the British were widely blamed for his assassination because he allegedly wanted Pakistan to leave the Commonwealth, but that was a canard.[7]

Washington paid little attention to Pakistan at first. Since America was stretched thin in Europe and East Asia, Truman was not really interested in helping the former British colony and spreading American assistance even further into the subcontinent. While Jinnah had sent a top aide to be ambassador in Washington in 1947, the first American ambassador to Pakistan arrived in April 1948. However, he left almost immediately because of poor health, and his successor did not arrive until February 1950.[8]

The Korean War dominated the last years of Truman's presidency. As the conflict bogged down in a stalemate with China, South Asia got little attention in Washington. By 1952 the American people were tired of the war and eager for a change. The Republicans took the White House in the November presidential elections, and Dwight David Eisenhower became president. Like Truman, Eisenhower would try to be friends to both states, but in the end he would build an alliance with Pakistan alone. Eisenhower brought to the job a very impressive resume as the wartime Allied commander in Western Europe and the first military commander of NATO. He had a solid understanding of geopolitics and was much less ideological than most of his cabinet. His vice president, Richard Nixon; his secretary of state, John Foster Dulles; and his CIA director, Allen Dulles, were more extreme in their cold war views and thus less likely to try to court India. Nixon developed an extreme dislike of India over the course of his career. The two Dulles brothers were influenced in their thinking by the writings of their grandfather, who had been a missionary in India under the Raj and was an enthusiastic supporter of British imperialism and an opponent of Indian independence. John Welsh Dulles's *Life in India* was not a book that Nehru would have recommended to the secretary if he wished to understand the country.

Nehru wanted to preserve Indian neutrality in the cold war. He wanted India to lead a third way, nonalignment, which would create from the newly decolonized countries of the world a powerful bloc between Moscow and Washington that would focus on further decolonization and economic growth. For Nixon and Dulles that was heresy. They wanted to build an alliance of states to contain communism and roll back its gains. In their view, democracies like India should recognize that the cold war was a conflict between good and evil and honor their moral obligation to choose good. In May 1953, Dulles became the first American secretary of state to visit South Asia. He was disappointed by Nehru's neutral stance and entranced by Pakistan's eager embrace of anticommunism. Nixon followed Dulles in December 1953, and an initial arms package agreement followed Nixon in early 1954. It was much less than Pakistan wanted, but it marked the beginning of a military relationship. Nehru was not pleased. He told the UN that the American observers in UNMOGIP had to leave, and in December 1954 they were replaced with military officers from other countries.

Eisenhower was more subtle in his thinking, but he let Nixon and Dulles pursue their alliance policy. At the same time, he sought to keep the lines open to Nehru and New Delhi. In 1956 Nehru was invited to stay at Ike's farm outside Gettysburg, Pennsylvania, where Nehru's photo can still be seen today. But just before the visit, two crises rocked the world. Israel, France, and Great Britain attacked Egypt to stop it from taking control of the Suez Canal, and Russia invaded Hungary to suppress an anticommunist uprising. While the United States condemned both actions, India was harder on the Suez aggression than the invasion of Hungary. The U.S.-India relationship remained cool and distant despite Ike's personal connection to Nehru. Indian suspicion of American intentions toward India was rife. Washington was often blamed for anything that went wrong in India or elsewhere in the world. In 1959 Nehru's private secretary, M. O. Mathai, who had worked for him since 1946, was hounded out of his position as private secretary for allegedly spying for the Central Intelligence Agency.[9] Eisenhower, in his second term, briefly flirted with the idea of mediating the Kashmir issue but gave it up when Nehru made it clear that he was not open to the idea. Ike instead supported a World Bank effort to broker a water-sharing agreement between the two countries, which worked out successfully.

In contrast, ties with Pakistan flourished on Eisenhower's beat. The key figure in the relationship would be Field Marshal Ayub Khan, who was born in 1907 near Abbottabad, the city where Osama bin Laden hid out for more than five years before he was killed in 2011. Khan was a graduate of the elite Royal Military Academy in Sandhurst, England, and he served as a battalion commander with the British 14th Army in Burma in World War II. He opted to join Pakistan in 1947 and in 1948 became commander of Pakistani forces in East Pakistan, today's Bangladesh, helping to consolidate Pakistani control over the Bengali half of the country. In 1951 he became the first native commander in chief of the army, replacing a British holdover from the Raj. He was a tall, physically imposing figure, the epitome of an officer in the British, now Pakistani, army. Shortly after Eisenhower took office, Khan sent a top secret memo to the State Department, making the case for sending aid to Pakistan to stop the Soviets from invading the subcontinent to grab a "ripe but undamaged plum into the Soviet paw." Ayub argued that Nehru did not understand the Russian menace.[10] In 1954, as chief of army staff, Ayub visited Washington, where he made a very good impression on the Eisenhower team, and while there he pressed for military assistance. With the Korean War over, the question of sending Pakistani troops to Korea was moot. Military assistance began to flow in ever-larger quantities to Pakistan. Vice President Richard Nixon, who became Pakistan's strongest advocate in the administration, would say that Pakistan "is a country I would do anything for. They have less complexes than the Indians."[11] It was the start of a long Nixon romance with Pakistan.

Pakistan, unlike India, wanted to form cold war alliances, and it soon became America's "most allied ally." First it signed a defense agreement with Turkey, a NATO ally. Then it joined both the South East Asia Treaty Organization (SEATO), in 1954, and the Central Treaty Organization (CENTO), in 1955, becoming the critical South Asia link in a global chain of alliances stretching from Norway to Japan and encircling the Soviet Union. In joining SEATO, Pakistan argued that East Pakistan was a Southeast Asian nation; in joining CENTO, it argued that West Pakistan was a Middle Eastern nation. Since Dulles was concerned that both regions were at grave risk after the French defeat in Indochina and the British collapse in the Middle East, Pakistan won key points with the secretary. Dulles was so proud of the alliances that he told a journalist that he had brought "the only Asians who can really fight, the Pakistanis, in the alliance. We could never get along without the Gurkhas." When Walter Lippman, the journalist, reminded Dulles that the Gurkhas are not Pakistanis, Dulles said that he was "nit picking."[12]

While Pakistan was seeking an external ally, Pakistani domestic politics was consumed by the struggle between West and East Pakistan. West Pakistan was controlled by the Punjabi majority there, which dominated the officer corps; East Pakistan felt like a second-class colony and resented West Pakistan's control of politics. Since more people lived in Bengal, East Pakistan would win in any truly free election. Consequently, Pakistani political leaders in West Pakistan dragged their feet on conducting truly free elections.

On October 7, 1958, Ayub Khan seized power in a coup, becoming chief marital law administrator. Two weeks later he dismissed the remnants of the civilian government and sent the president off to exile in London. Within two years Field Marshal Khan held a rigged referendum and was confirmed in office with a resounding 95.6 percent of the vote. Pakistan's democracy had died, and its first military dictatorship had begun. (In another fixed election in 1965, Jinnah's sister, Fatima, ran against Ayub and lost, although she won in Karachi and almost won in East Pakistan.) To cement his control of the country, Ayub decided to move the capital from Karachi, in the Sindh, to a new city, Islamabad, in the Punjab. He wanted to escape the influence of the "mob"; therefore "the capital must be moved out of Karachi."[13] Although there is no solid evidence that the CIA or any part of the U.S. government pushed Khan to stage the coup, there is also no evidence that Washington tried very hard to discourage him. The U.S. ambassador urged Khan, if possible, to make any military interregnum short. In July 1958 the pro-American government in Iraq had been toppled in a very bloody coup, ushering in a more radical pro-Soviet government and undermining CENTO. The Eisenhower team did not want a repeat in Pakistan, so it went along with Khan's coup and embraced the new strongman.

Pakistan now became a base for American secret operations on a grand scale. The CIA director, Allen Dulles, had been working with Khan behind the scenes for several years to cement a strong intelligence relationship with Pakistan. Construction of a secret base for the 6937 Communications Group began in mid-1958. Top secret U-2 aircraft began regularly overflying the Soviet Union from an airbase near Peshawar. A small town grew up around the base to provide the comforts of home to the American pilots and maintenance crews. In addition, the National Security Agency set up a listening post at Badaber, near Peshawar, to spy on Soviet and Chinese communications, gathering intelligence that was essential to the United States in the era before satellites. Pakistan became a vital ally and Ayub Khan a vital friend. Even after the Russians shot down a U-2 aircraft in 1960, exposing the entire secret project, Pakistan remained essential to American intelligence operations during the cold war.[14] Allen Dulles was the father of the CIA's critical alliance with Pakistan and its intelligence service, the Inter-Services Intelligence Directorate.

In December 1959 Eisenhower became the first sitting American president to visit South Asia. The trip was also the maiden voyage for his jet, the first Air Force One. He flew to Italy and then to Turkey, Pakistan, Afghanistan, India, Iran, Greece, Tunisia, France, Spain, and Morocco, visiting eleven countries in nineteen days. Ike was warmly greeted during all three South Asia stops, and his reception in Karachi on December 7 was especially warm. But he went as a lame duck president, and the U-2 crisis, which followed in March 1960, quickly overshadowed the goodwill that emerged from his trip. Moreover, the Russians had beaten him to India. Nikita Khrushchev had visited India in 1955, staying almost a month—much longer than any American president except Grant, who had left office in 1876.

As a parting gift to Ayub, in March 1960 the Eisenhower administration agreed to sell to Pakistan what was at the time one of America's most sophisticated combat jet aircraft, the F-104 Starfighter. It had just entered service with the U.S. air force in 1958, and its sale signified that Pakistan had indeed become America's "most allied ally" and Ayub Khan America's man in South Asia.

JFK AND INDIA

Nixon lost the 1960 election to John F. Kennedy, who promised a more vigorous, anti-colonial, and enlightened foreign policy than his Republican predecessor had adopted. Kennedy was a cold warrior, but he also recognized the winds of change in the world. He believed that the era of colonial empires was over—he had been an early critic of the French colonial war in Algeria—and he felt that America needed to understand that the new postcolonial countries did not always want to join one cold war bloc or another. So Kennedy, who as a senator had sponsored legislation to increase food aid to India, embarked on trying to woo India and Nehru into a closer relationship with Washington, without any formal anticommunist alliance. He sent a trusted close adviser, John Kenneth Galbraith, to be his ambassador in New Delhi. Galbraith frequently wrote JFK long letters from India in which he commented not only on India and South Asia but on global developments, domestic issues, economics, and especially the growing conflict in South Vietnam, where he was an early and prescient critic of the war. His letters and diary have been published, providing unique insight into this period.

Yet Kennedy was also eager to maintain a tight alliance with Pakistan. He invited Ayub Khan to visit the United States twice during his 1,000 days in office. In July 1961, Khan was feted in New York with a ticker-tape parade on Fifth Avenue, and in Washington he embarked on a full state visit, including a state dinner at Mount Vernon, the only time in the history of the first president's mansion that it had hosted a state dinner. His photo, taken with President Kennedy and Mrs. Kennedy, still hangs in the visitor center there. When Khan visited again a year later, in September 1962, JFK hosted him at the family home in Newport, Rhode Island, and at Kennedy's farm in Middleburg, Virginia. The Kennedy team hailed Pakistan as a reliable ally against communism and a model for development in the third world. But it was India that most preoccupied JFK in his relations with South Asia. His appointment of Galbraith put a Kennedy man, an advocate of the New Frontier, at the center stage of U.S.-Indian relations. No president since has sent such a close friend and high-powered representative to New Delhi.

President Kennedy never made a trip to India in his all-too-short presidency, but his wife, Jacqueline Bouvier Kennedy, did travel to India and Pakistan in March 1962. The charismatic and photogenic first lady was a very big hit with all, and she was met with an outpouring of affection that was unique in the travels of first ladies at the time. Massive crowds met her everywhere. Ayub Khan and the first lady discovered a mutual fondness for horses, and her Secret Service agent said that it was "love at first sight" when Ayub gave her a horse in Lahore.[15] Nehru was so entranced that he kept a photo of Mrs. Kennedy in his private study for the rest of his life.[16] Galbraith rightly saw the visit as a triumph for the Kennedy administration.

The United States and India drew closer with the sending of Peace Corps volunteers to India, an increase in American economic assistance, and genuine dialogue between the top leaders. Nehru visited the White House in November 1961, accompanied by his daughter Indira. However, the visit, conceived as an opportunity for the leaders to get acquainted, did not go well; Nehru, at the age of seventy-one, was old and tired and seemed disengaged. No personal bond developed between JFK and Nehru.

By far the most important development in the U.S.-India relationship was a result of the Chinese Communist invasion of India in October 1962. Like much of India's border, the boundary between China and India had been drawn by the British to their advantage, and it was revised various times from the late 1800s into the 1920s. In the west, the boundary, initially known as the Johnson line, divided Kashmir from China; in the east, the McMahon line—agreed on by British India and Tibet but not by China in the Simla Accord in 1914—divided eastern India, including Assam, from China. When China invaded Tibet in October 1950, it therefore inherited a border that it did not regard as legitimate or fair. Negotiations between Beijing and New Delhi in the 1950s did not reconcile the two claims. China did open negotiations with Pakistan on their new common border in Kashmir, which ended with Pakistan ceding a large part of northern Kashmir to China and Islamabad and Beijing drawing an agreed border between the two countries. The Chinese encountered significant resistance from the Tibetan people to China's occupation of their country, resistance that they blamed on India and the CIA. Both were in fact independently assisting the Tibetans.[17]

Nehru had been sharply critical of the American policy of not recognizing the Chinese Communist government, and he championed its right to take China's permanent seat on the UN Security Council, which was still held by the Nationalist Chinese government, based in Taiwan. He argued that China and India were very much kindred spirits—two great Asian countries that were finally free of the Western imperialist powers that had long exploited them. So it was a crushing blow to Nehru and India when China launched a surprise invasion on October 20, 1962, to seize control of the territories that it claimed along its 3,225-kilometer border with India. The Indians were caught unprepared; their intelligence had grossly underestimated the strength of the Chinese, who had 125,000 well-trained mountain troops poised on the border. The Indian forces had no mountain training and were armed with World War I–vintage rifles.[18] The much better led and equipped Chinese forces routed the Indian army, which retreated in some confusion from the Himalayas. The Chinese threat was most significant in the far eastern section of India, which is linked to the main land mass by only a narrow band of land north of what was then East Pakistan. After refusing to align itself for fifteen years with either the West or the communists in the cold war, India found itself the victim of a Chinese invasion that it could not halt with its own forces. Nehru was devastated by China's betrayal. He reluctantly turned to the United States and United Kingdom, asking for immediate shipment of supplies for the Indian army and, in panic, for the deployment of American bombers to stop the Chinese advance. America quickly found itself arming both Pakistan and India, with no assurance that they would not use the arms against each other.

It is clear from Galbraith's diary that the Americans also were surprised by the Chinese invasion. With no embassy in China, the United States was blind. This crisis coincided with the most dangerous crisis in the entire cold war, the Cuban missile crisis, which occurred when the Soviets built bases in Cuba where nuclear ballistic missiles capable of reaching most of the United States were housed. At the time, the two superpowers were on the brink of nuclear war. Since the entire bureaucracy in Washington was consumed by the life-or-death duel over Cuba, Galbraith was given almost no instructions from the White House or the State Department during the key period in the Indo-Chinese crisis. As a result, he was very much the main decisionmaker on the American side, a role that he relished. He wrote: "Washington continues to be totally occupied with Cuba. For a week, I have had a considerable war on my hands without a single telegram, letter, telephone call, or other communications or guidance."[19] To add one more level of drama, the crisis also coincided with the move of the ambassador and his family into a new residence, Roosevelt House, where the staff could not find any dishes and Galbraith could not find a room suitable for small intimate discussions.[20] Working closely with his British counterpart—a recurring approach to U.S. crisis management in South Asia over the decades—Galbraith fashioned a response that backed India and delivered much-needed military assistance to the Indians. Once a request for aid was formally transmitted, the first American shipments of arms and matériel arrived by air four days later. British support came as well.

The intentions of the Chinese were impossible to decipher. After their initial victories, they paused for several weeks and then attacked again, with devastating results, driving the Indians back in the east of India. If they had pressed on in the most vulnerable sector, they could have cut off Assam and eastern India and linked up with East Pakistan. Even Calcutta was at risk. Nehru asked for more aid—a dozen squadrons of American fighters and two squadrons of bombers—to shift the balance. He was so desperate that he was asking for direct American military intervention, at least in the air. That would have meant a major war with China. There were some very anxious moments in New Delhi, Washington, and London until, with no warning, the Chinese announced a unilateral cease-fire on November 21, 1962. JFK never had to answer the request for air power. The war was over. India was humiliated, Nehru was devastated, but U.S.-Indian relations were at an all-time high. Approval ratings among Indians for America soared from 7 percent at the start of the war to 62 percent at the end.[21]

Galbraith's memoirs also make it clear that even as he faced the Chinese threat, he had to devote as much of his energy and skill to managing Indo-Pakistani relations. Pakistan saw an opportunity in

India's distress and sought to exploit it. Ayub Khan's government suggested to the U.S. embassy in Karachi that Pakistani neutrality in the war could be ensured by Indian concessions in Kashmir, threatening, by implication, the opposite scenario if those concessions were not forthcoming. China tried to encourage Pakistan to attack India on its own by offering a nonaggression pact with Pakistan. Galbraith wrote that "my concern was about equally divided between helping the Indians against the Chinese and keeping peace between the Indians and Pakistanis. The nightmare of a combined attack by Pakistan and China, with the possibility of defeat, collapse, and even anarchy in India was much on my mind."[22]

In short, at a defining early moment in U.S.-Indian relations, when China and India were military adversaries, the United States found itself trying to manage the Indo-Pakistani rivalry in order to avoid a second front in the war. Pakistan was threatening to stab India in the back while it was fighting Communist China. Pakistan, outraged that America was arming its rival, wanted Indian concessions on Kashmir in exchange for staying out of the conflict. Working with the British, Galbraith and his counterpart in Karachi secured support for India and Pakistan to renew their dialogue on Kashmir. Nehru reluctantly agreed, understanding the need for a quiet Pakistani front. As Galbraith describes it, Nehru was a much diminished prime minister. He had fought his whole life for Indian independence, and now he had been forced to rely on Washington and London for assistance. American C-130s were delivering vital military aid, and an American aircraft carrier, USS *Enterprise,* was sailing in the Bay of Bengal and visiting Madras to show tangible support.

Galbraith suggested to Kennedy in one of his private letters that the United States and the United Kingdom seize the opportunity to quietly move toward a Kashmir settlement. Galbraith opposed a territorial settlement; he envisioned a much more subtle deal that would transform the entire nature of South Asian politics, a fundamental rapprochement based on regional cooperation that made Kashmir largely irrelevant. In a letter to the president dated December 6, 1962, the ambassador wrote:

> It would be fatal to show hesitancy at this moment when the Indians are relying on us and when the fear of the Chinese is so great. Now that we have got the Kashmir issue out in the open—a significant achievement in itself—we must press it, but in such a manner as not to involve ourselves in the inbuilt antagonisms between the two countries. We must continue to make it clear to the Indians that it is their task, not ours and not Pakistan's. In my view, incidentally, Kashmir is not soluble in territorial terms. But by holding up the example of the way in which France and Germany have moved to soften their antagonism by the Common Market and common instruments of administration, including such territorial disputes as that over the Saar, there is a chance of getting the Indo-Pakistani dialogue into constructive channels.[23]

Galbraith had reached the right conclusion about the proper American role in South Asia in the midst of a terrible crisis. But instead of taking Galbraith's sophisticated approach, the Kennedy team, working closely with the British, tried a more conventional approach. After Kennedy sent letters to Ayub and Nehru, the two reluctantly agreed to resume bilateral discussions on Kashmir, with American and British diplomats pushing each side to make compromise offers. On the eve of the first round, Pakistan's new foreign minister, Zulfikar Bhutto, announced that China and Pakistan had reached an agreement to demarcate their border in Kashmir, an agreement in which China had been given a considerable part of the territory of historic Kashmir. The Indians were furious. They had been attacked and invaded by China, and Pakistan had now given away part of the territory still in dispute and on which bilateral negotiations were just about to commence. Bhutto claimed that the Chinese had tricked him into prematurely announcing the deal. The United States and the United Kingdom accepted this farce; Nehru did not. Talks began, but they were bound to fail. After six desultory rounds, they collapsed.

Kennedy began his 1,000 days in office eager to build the ties with India that had languished under Eisenhower and Truman. By the end of that time, the United States was helping to build a new Indian army, including six mountain divisions to face China. India wanted more, including at least two squadrons of F-104 jets. But Kennedy and his successor, Lyndon Johnson, did not agree to send India high-performance jet aircraft like the F-104s that Pakistan was getting. Both Kennedy and Johnson considered the F-104 deal with Pakistan a foolish excess of the Eisenhower and Nixon days that should not be repeated.

JFK was equally determined to maintain a strong alliance with Pakistan, but Islamabad did not want an ally that armed both sides. It had not joined SEATO and CENTO to see American arms flowing into India; it wanted an exclusive alliance against its rival. The U.S.-Pakistan connection was coming apart, and Pakistan turned to China for a new ally. After the border agreement on Kashmir, Pakistan signed an aviation agreement with China, which broke an American-inspired campaign to isolate China both politically and physically. Pakistan International Airlines began regular flights between Dacca and Shanghai. The Kennedy team responded by canceling a deal to upgrade Dacca airport, the first of what would become a long list of sanctions against Pakistan. Pakistan in turn upgraded relations with China to full embassy status.[24]

In what would be his last days, Kennedy became more and more irritated with the Pakistanis and with Ayub. In one of his final meetings with his national security team, he asked, "What do we get from Pakistan? In return for the protection of our alliance and our assistance, what do they do for us?"[25] JFK's question was purely rhetorical. The answer was still the secret intelligence base that the CIA and National Security Agency used to eavesdrop on China and Russia—America's desire for which Ayub had skillfully exploited. The base was expanded considerably in a new secret protocol in

September 1963.[26] Less than two months later, Kennedy was dead. Sardar, the horse that Ayub had given Mrs. Kennedy in Lahore, followed his casket down Pennsylvania Avenue riderless.

The Indo-Chinese war had one more major consequence: India moved closer to a decision to develop a nuclear deterrent. India had begun a nuclear power program early after gaining independence and had acquired reactors from the United States and Canada. But Nehru had insisted that India would use them only for peaceful purposes. In his world view, the use of nuclear weapons was unthinkable, so they were not to be acquired. However, in the wake of the Chinese invasion the opposition party called for development of a nuclear weapons program to deter further Chinese aggression. Nehru still demurred, but India was on the path to conducting its first test of a nuclear bomb.

The Americans also had come to realize that America and India needed the bomb if they were going to be able to stop another major Chinese invasion. In 1963, shortly before his death, Kennedy met with his military advisers to review the options in the event of another Chinese attack. Secretly recorded tapes of the meetings reveal that Secretary of Defense Robert McNamara told JFK that "we should recognize that in order to carry out any commitment to defend India against any substantial Chinese attack, we would have to use nuclear weapons." Kennedy responded that "we should defend India, and therefore we will defend India if she were attacked."[27]

JOHNSON AND THE SECOND INDO-PAKISTAN WAR

Lyndon Baines Johnson, a senator from Texas, had been chosen by Kennedy as his running mate to capture Southern white votes for a Catholic liberal Democrat from Massachusetts. LBJ brought with him years of experience in domestic affairs but not a wealth of foreign policy experience. However, as vice president he had bonded with Ayub, and he had little of Kennedy's fondness for India. But the Pakistani leader made an early mistake in dealing with Johnson. Instead of coming to Kennedy's funeral himself, he sent his foreign minister, Zulfikar Ali Bhutto, who had already spoiled his copy book with Washington because of the Kashmir deal with China and his outspoken leftist rhetoric. Moreover, Bhutto insisted on a private session after the funeral to deliver an important message from Ayub; when an irritated Johnson reluctantly agreed, Bhutto only antagonized Johnson more by having literally nothing important to say.

The Vietnam War was Johnson's overwhelming priority in world affairs, and it came to consume his presidency. LBJ expected Pakistan to live up to its obligations as a SEATO member by sending troops to defend South Vietnam from communism, and he asked Pakistan at least "to show the flag" with a token deployment.[28] He argued that if the dominoes fell in Southeast Asia, then East Pakistan would find itself sharing a border with communist Burma. Nonetheless, Ayub refused repeated requests for a Pakistani troop deployment, including during a face-to-face encounter with Johnson in December 1967 when Johnson briefly stopped in Karachi on a flight home from Saigon. He was the second sitting American president to visit South Asia, although it was only for a few hours.

Pakistan had not joined SEATO to fight communism, of course, and it certainly did not want to antagonize its new ally China by fighting in Vietnam. It had become the "most allied ally" of the United States to enhance its ability to fight India. Now American arms were rapidly building a stronger India, thus tilting the balance of power even more against Pakistan. Bhutto turned to his foreign minister and the Directorate for Inter-Services Intelligence (ISI) to develop a plan to seize the initiative before American arms decisively gave India the upper hand.

In 1965 Bhutto and the ISI came up with Operation Gibraltar, a foolish and dangerous plan conceived as a clever scheme to create an insurgency in Kashmir that would provide an excuse for a massive Pakistani armored thrust across the border to separate the valley from India. The ISI, working with elite Pakistani commandoes, would send teams into Kashmir to start an uprising; once the turmoil began, an armored attack, code-named Operation Grand Slam, would follow. Gibraltar was named after the famous port in Europe where Muslim invaders first entered Spain; Grand Slam was apparently named after a fictional plot to rob Fort Knox in the hit 1964 movie *Goldfinger*. Both were poorly thought out and incompetently executed; even so, the plan was slavishly followed. Some 7,000 Pakistani commandoes and militants infiltrated the valley, but the insurgency was a bust. The ISI had done little or nothing to prepare the Kashmiris to revolt, and in any case the Indians arrested many of the infiltrators before they could do any damage. Nonetheless, Pakistani armor attacked, leading to some of the largest tank battles since World War II. The battle turned against Pakistan, and soon Indian armor was threatening to take Lahore. The war was a fiasco, and it would doom Ayub's government.

China briefly threatened to assist Pakistan. Beijing warned New Delhi that if India attacked East Pakistan, China would resume military operations along the McMahon line and possibly seize the tiny kingdom of Sikkim. It was a bluff. When China's ultimatum to India to stop the war expired, China just extended it a few more days. In the end, China let down Pakistan. American intelligence suspected that Pakistan, China, and perhaps Indonesia had plotted together against India, but in the end Pakistan was left alone.[29]

Remarkably, the plan's author, Zulfikar Bhutto, escaped blame for the disaster. He went to New York to present Pakistan's case for Kashmir to the United Nations, and he was seen on the world stage and at home as a passionate defender of Pakistan's position. He blamed America, because it had armed India, for what went wrong. He also blamed Ayub for not implementing the plan effectively, and he left the cabinet. Zulfi, as he was familiarly called, was a scion of one of Pakistan's richest families, large landowners in Sindh province, and he was a master at portraying himself and his country as victim. A rich man who had never worked the soil, he painted himself as a revolutionary socialist like Che Guevara or Yasir Arafat and his new political party, the Pakistan People's Party (PPP), as the party of the aggrieved and the underclasses. He made friends with revolutionaries like Mao Zedong and Muammar Qadhafi as well as royalists like King Faysal of Saudi Arabia and his old friend Richard Nixon and Nixon's national security aide, Henry Kissinger. Zulfi was educated in California and styled himself a modern Napoleon. He collected Bonaparte memorabilia and had a library with 10,000 books about the French military genius.[30]

Zulfi did not impress LBJ. The Johnson administration, distracted by Vietnam, decided to avoid significant involvement in the diplomacy surrounding the war, leaving it to the UN instead. However, it cut off military assistance to both parties. Although Pakistan was hurt much more because it was much more dependent on U.S. aid (U.S. aid to Pakistan in the period from 1954 to 1965 was twenty times the amount of aid to India), India was outraged because it was the victim of aggression and Kennedy had just promised a new era in American-Indian relations. As a consequence of the war, the United States, which went from arming both sides in the India-Pakistan rivalry to arming neither, lost the trust of both.

It got worse. The Soviets hosted a peace conference in Tashkent after the cease-fire to allow the belligerents to formally end the war, exchange prisoners, and return captured territory to restore the status quo ante. Moscow, not Washington, was the peacemaker in South Asia. Johnson was just too consumed with Vietnam. After signing the Tashkent communiqué, India's prime minister, Lal Bahadur Shastri, who had succeeded Nehru, suffered a massive heart attack at the close of the peace summit and died the next day, January 11, 1966.

Indira Gandhi, Nehru's daughter, took his place. She had traveled the world with Nehru when he was prime minister and had been his keenest student of global and domestic politics. She had served as minister of information in the 1962 war with China and in the 1965 war with Pakistan, giving her tremendous public visibility. The power brokers who ran the Congress Party in 1966 assumed that she would be a weak prime minister whom they could dominate and manipulate. They underestimated her badly.

Initially, Mrs. Gandhi and Johnson hit if off well. She came to Washington looking for the resumption of military aid and stepped-up economic assistance, which India needed to make its agriculture sector more efficient. LBJ was smitten with her at first, and a brief honeymoon ensued. It was not destined to last. As Vietnam's shadow grew ever darker, she denounced the war as an imperialist relic bordering on genocide, and she openly sympathized with North Vietnam and the Viet Cong. Johnson had no more use for her or India. His administration had begun with strong ties to India and Pakistan, but those ties were mutually antithetical. It ended with the United States being relegated to bystander status in South Asia.

For both Indians and Pakistanis, the Johnson era was a bitter disappointment. India thought that America would be its new ally against China and that the two democracies would finally escape the estrangement of the Nehru era. Although India had been receiving U.S. military aid, it was abruptly terminated, and Washington had sold the F-104s to Pakistan but not to India. India saw itself as the victim of unprovoked aggression from Pakistan and could not understand why LBJ did not see it that way too. The legacy of the Johnson arms cut-off remains alive today. Indians simply do not believe that America will be there when India needs military help. New Delhi turned elsewhere for arms, signing a major deal to build the MiG-21, the F-104's competitor, in India with Russian assistance.

Pakistanis were shocked that they, the "most allied ally," also were cut off from their main source of arms. SEATO and CENTO seemed to mean nothing when Pakistan really needed American help, nor did the secret U-2 and National Security Agency bases. Pakistan did not feel that it was an aggressor; it was simply trying to redress a wrong in Kashmir that the world was ignoring. It now would turn to other sources of arms, especially China, to replace the United States. The legacy of the U.S. "betrayal" still haunts U.S.-Pakistan relations today, but it would be only the first in a long line of American "betrayals" that Pakistani generals and politicians would nurture. The disastrous Operation Gibraltar fiasco had long-term consequences for South Asia. Until the second India-Pakistan war, it had been fairly easy for people to move between one country and the other, but India and Pakistan decided after 1965 to require visitors from the other nation to get a visa before entry. Consequently, travel, trade, and understanding between the two states began to dry up. As each developed trade partners outside the subcontinent, economic interaction would largely cease.

NIXON, INDIRA, AND THE 1971 WAR

Richard Nixon came to the Oval Office with more South Asia experience than any president before or since. He knew the players and had traveled in the region. In many ways, he was the founding father of the American-Pakistani alliance in the 1950s. When he traveled to South Asia in December 1953, he told the *New York Times* on background that "the time has come to put an end to Washington's patience with Nehru, who has often embarrassed the U.S."; in contrast, he praised Pakistan. So in 1969 Indians were understandably apprehensive about his election and Pakistanis hopeful that they would have a champion in the White House.

Nixon fulfilled the expectations of both. A new American rapprochement with Pakistan, based on Pakistan's channel to China, became the centerpiece of his South Asia policy, reversing two decades of American animosity to Pakistan's China connection and Nixon's own vehement China bashing. Another Indo-Pakistani war would take America and India to the brink of conflict in 1971 and move India to test a nuclear bomb.

Henry Kissinger was the guiding hand of Nixon's foreign policy, especially in South Asia. Kissinger's account of his experiences, published later in his memoirs, is unusually rich and detailed, but it raised considerable dissent among others in the administration, especially South Asia hands at the Department of State and other departments. Kissinger needed to explain his views in detail for several reasons, but the most urgent was that immediately after the 1971 crisis a journalist, Jack Anderson, obtained access to the detailed notes taken for the Pentagon leadership during the National Security Council crisis meetings and published them. They portrayed a Nixon White House at war with its own bureaucracy and very much isolated from outside opinion. Nixon saw the crisis as a global test of wills with Moscow while almost everyone else saw it as a regional battle over the future of East Pakistan, soon to be Bangladesh.

East Pakistan had always been the second-class citizen in the Pakistani state. While a majority of the country's population lived in the east, West Pakistan's Punjabi establishment dominated the state, especially the army. A disproportionate amount of development was sent to West Pakistan and virtually all officers in the military came from the west, mostly from the Punjab. In 1970 there were only 300 Bengalis among the 6,000-strong Pakistani officer corps. Moreover, although more Pakistanis spoke Bengali than any other language, it was not a recognized national language. Jinnah had insisted on that. For Bengalis, West Pakistan was another colonial master; it had simply replaced the British.

Ayub Khan had stepped down in 1969, exhausted and under fire for the 1965 war fiasco. East Pakistanis were especially angry, recognizing that Ayub had taken on India in a war that left them defenseless against New Delhi. Almost all of Pakistan's armor and airpower were in West Pakistan; had India chosen in 1965 to occupy East Pakistan, which it surrounds on three sides, it could have done so easily. In short, the Pakistani army was ready to lose Bengal to gain Kashmir. The Bengalis got the message.

Yahya Khan was Ayub's successor. A veteran of the British Eighth Army in World War II, he had fought in Libya and Italy. Yahya, who was a Shia but also a Punjabi, had a bad drinking problem and poor judgment. He reluctantly agreed to hold relatively free elections in December 1970. The separatist Awami League, led by Sheikh Mujibur Rahman, swept East Pakistan, winning all 167 seats. Zulfi's PPP did the best in West Pakistan, taking a majority of seats (81 of 138) there. The election results meant that power would shift from West to East Pakistan; the downtrodden Bengalis would run the country simply by virtue of being a majority of the population and having all voted for one party.

The Punjabis would not stand for that. Yahya and Zulfi both went to Dacca to talk to the Bengalis. After some ineffectual negotiations, Yahya flew home, drinking Scotch all the way, and ordered the Pakistani commander in Dacca, Lieutenant General Tikka Khan, to conduct a sharp crackdown on the Awami League and Bengali separatists.[31] Code-named Operation Searchlight, it became a massacre. American-made armored personnel carriers invaded the university in Dacca and killed thousands of students. Political leaders, poets, novelists, and the best of Bengal were rounded up or shot. Sheik Mujib, as he was called, was arrested, but not before he announced the independence of Bangladesh on March 26, 1971.[32] The Bangladesh government subsequently charged that the Pakistani army had engaged in genocide against its own people, killing 3 million people during the repression. Millions of Bengalis fled across the border into India, rapidly creating a major refugee problem for the Gandhi government. By May some 10 million Bengalis had escaped to India and the Awami League had set up a guerrilla front to wage an insurrection against Tikka Khan's army. India began to arm the insurgents.

To make matters worse, the Pakistani government had provoked India directly in the lead-up to the crisis. On January 30, 1971, an Indian airliner was hijacked by two Kashmiris after it left Srinagar and was forced to land in Lahore, Pakistan, where it was blown up after its passengers had deboarded. India, blaming Pakistani intelligence, closed Indian air space to Pakistani aircraft flying from the two halves of Pakistan, thus vastly complicating Pakistani logistics.

Pakistan proclaimed its innocence, charging that the two hijackers were Indian spies. After the 1971 war, the hijackers were freed in Pakistan and remained there, clearly indicating that they were in fact Pakistani agents. The hijacking and the massacres drove Indira Gandhi to take action. But first she looked to America to act.[33]

However, Nixon and Kissinger refused to take any serious action to halt the massacre. Acting under the president's guidance, Kissinger ordered the American government to "tilt" toward Pakistan and Yahya. Many in the bureaucracy resisted. At one National Security Council meeting, Kissinger, exasperated by the pushback from the regional specialists, exclaimed, "The President always says to tilt toward Pakistan, but every proposal I get is in the opposite direction. Sometimes I think I am in a nut house."[34] The American diplomats on the scene were appalled at their country's policy. In April 1971, virtually the entire country team in Dacca signed a dissent cable, which is worth quoting here in some detail.

Our government has failed to denounce the suppression of democracy. Our government has failed to denounce atrocities. Our government has failed to take forceful measures to protect its citizens [dual nationals of the United States and (East) Pakistan] while at the same time bending over backwards to placate the West Pakistan dominated government and to lessen likely and deservedly negative international public relations impact against [it]. Our government has evidenced what many will consider moral bankruptcy, ironically at a time when the USSR sent President Yahya a message defending democracy, condemning arrests of leaders of a democratically elected majority party (incidentally pro-West). But we have chosen not to intervene even morally on the grounds that the Awami conflict, in which the overworked term genocide is applicable, is purely an internal matter.[35]

The consul general, Archer Blood, sent the cable—the so-called Blood telegram—to Washington, and several officers in the department signed a letter to Secretary of State William Rogers supporting it. The consul general had classified the cable "confidential," but Nixon had it reclassified "secret/NODIS," the highest classification possible for a State Department cable, to restrict its dissemination. Nixon's tilt was only in part a reflection of his animus toward India and his fondness for Pakistan. Behind the scenes the president and his national security adviser were reversing over two decades of American policy toward China, and they needed Yahya and Pakistan to do it. It was a very closely held secret; not even Rogers, the secretary of state, knew what they were doing.

Nixon had visited South Asia three times as a private citizen between his years as vice president and his election to the presidency, and on each visit he was snubbed in India and hailed in Pakistan. In August 1969, Nixon again visited India and Pakistan, this time as president. His meeting with Mrs. Gandhi in New Delhi was strained and uncomfortable. Because he was now president, she could not snub him again (she had famously asked an aide in Hindi during an earlier visit, "How much longer must I talk to this man?"), but their contempt for each other was self-evident.

In Islamabad, Pakistan's new capital, the reception was much warmer. Nixon was greeted as a close friend by Yahya, for whom the president had a surprise request. He asked Yahya to use Pakistan's close ties to China, forged after the invasion of India in 1962, to pass a very important message to Chairman Mao: Nixon was interested in a dialogue at the highest level with the communist government, ending decades of isolation. Nixon told Yahya to communicate via very secure means and not to discuss the American opening with anyone in the U.S. embassy or State Department. The Pakistani ambassador in Washington was to communicate only with Kissinger regarding the message and China's response.

Beijing did not respond immediately. It was not until February 1970 that Yahya's ambassador reported a positive response from the Chinese to Kissinger. In October, as the crisis in East Pakistan was getting worse, Yahya came to the White House to meet Nixon personally once again. To greet his guest Nixon had arms sales to Pakistan, banned since 1965, lifted for selected equipment, including 300 armored personnel carriers.

On October 25, 1970, Nixon gave Yahya another message for Mao. He wanted to send a secret high-level emissary, Kissinger, to Beijing to start a direct dialogue with Mao and his comrades. Two months later, on December 8, 1970, the day after the Pakistani elections brought the Awami League to power, the Pakistani ambassador had a top secret positive response, in principle, to the request for a Kissinger visit. But the Chinese remained in no hurry, and the timing of a trip was still under consideration in Beijing.

After Operation Searchlight began, Nixon and Kisssinger felt that they could not afford to tilt away from Yahya and Pakistan without endangering their China connection, which remained a closely held secret. Rogers and the rest of the State Department and government bureaucracy were still out of the loop, and they could not understand why Nixon was so unwilling to criticize Pakistan.

On April 27, 1971, with Dacca under Tikka's boot, the Chinese gave their approval for a Kissinger secret mission. Kissinger told the Chinese in early June that he was coming, and he arranged a visit to Islamabad. The CIA and the ambassador were brought in on the secret, and they were told to work with Yahya's staff on a plan to disguise Kissinger's upcoming visit to China. After Kissinger had dinner with Yahya, Kissinger's staff told reporters that he was ill. Instead of flying to his next destination the following morning, Kissinger would spend a couple of days in the mountains north of Islamabad to recover. He would not see any journalists while he rested.

On July 10, 1971, Kissinger flew to Beijing on a Pakistani aircraft to see Mao and the Chinese leadership. He flew back to Islamabad the next day and resumed his schedule. The great secret was intact. A few days later, Nixon announced the breakthrough and told the American people that he intended to visit China himself. In a private letter to Yahya thanking him for helping to bring about the breakthrough, Nixon wrote: "Those who want a more peaceful world in the generation to come will forever be in your debt."[36]

Indira Gandhi saw her worst nightmare developing. A massive crisis in East Pakistan was destabilizing Calcutta and Assam, the Americans were backing Pakistan, and a new Islamabad-Beijing-Washington axis was developing. She went to Moscow to build a counteralliance. In August, India and Russia signed the Indo-Soviet Friendship Treaty, which bound the two countries more closely together than ever before. It was not a formal military alliance like NATO, but it symbolized India's growing reliance on Soviet military equipment and served to counterbalance any Chinese consideration of intervening on Pakistan's behalf in a future war. In short, Indira was telling China to stay out of the upcoming war or it might have a war in Siberia and Manchuria on its hands.

The war was now at hand. Mrs. Gandhi visited New York and Washington in November to gain United Nations and American support for the Bengali people and India. She met a brick wall in the Oval Office. Nixon saw her as a Soviet partner, if not client, and was deaf to her concerns. It was an ugly meeting by all accounts. Nixon called the Indian prime minister a "bitch" and much worse behind her back; she thought that he was a cold war fanatic who cared nothing about innocent lives. India mobilized, and Mrs. Gandhi told the army commander, Field Marshal Sam Manekshaw, to prepare for war. He told her that the army was ready.

Instead, Pakistan struck first. Operation Genghis Khan was a preemptive blow designed to get the upper hand by attacking Indian airbases on December 3, 1971, in an approach similar to that used by the Israelis against the Egyptians in 1967. It failed. India took the offensive, and Manekshaw had Pakistan on the run immediately. The 90,000-strong Pakistani garrisons in East Pakistan were in a hopeless situation: surrounded on three sides, with reinforcements a thousand miles away.

America sided with Pakistan. The U.S. ambassador to the UN, George H. W. Bush, called India "the major aggressor." Privately

Bush thought Kissinger an "arrogant paranoid," but in public he backed the White House line.[37] Kissinger and Bush met with the Chinese ambassador to the UN, and Kissinger gave China tacit approval to help Pakistan. Kissinger told the Chinese that although the arms ban was still in force, he was pressing American allies like Iran and Jordan to transfer U.S.-supplied jets to Pakistan—an illegal maneuver. The CIA was told to push the king and the shah to ignore démarches from the American ambassador in each country against the transfer of American F-104 jets to Islamabad. Jordan delivered several to the Pakistanis. China did nothing.

At just that point, the CIA delivered a secret intelligence report to Nixon suggesting that Mrs. Gandhi had designs beyond East Pakistan and was determined to destroy Pakistan entirely in the war. The report was judged alarming and probably incorrect by the CIA's own analysts.[38] Nonetheless, Richard Helms, the director of central intelligence, told the White House that "Gandhi intends to attempt to eliminate Pakistan's armor and air force" and "straighten out" Kashmir. Nixon called it "one of the few really timely pieces of intelligence the CIA had ever given me."[39] Helms later told me in a private conversation shortly before he died that the report was inaccurate but too important to be ignored. He felt that he had not handled it well by highlighting it to Nixon.

Nixon dispatched a carrier battle group led by the USS *Enterprise* into the Bay of Bengal from the Strait of Malacca to try to save Pakistan's fortunes by an intimidating show of support. He may have hoped that the Chinese would be emboldened by the move to attack India. It did not work. Indira, who probably had no designs on West Pakistan, was not easily intimidated. It was also too late for the Pakistanis. They asked the American consul in Dacca on December 14, 1971, to tell the Indians that they were ready to surrender. The darkest day in Pakistan's history followed. Ninety-three thousand Pakistani soldiers became prisoners of war, and the nation of Bangladesh, led by the Awami League, was born. Zulfikar Bhutto led the Pakistani delegation to the UN to make

Pakistan's case that it had again been victimized, and on December 18 he saw Nixon and Kissinger. Kissinger thought him "brilliant and charming," and they all but endorsed him as the next Pakistani leader. Two days later Yahya turned power over to Bhutto and stepped down in disgrace and humiliation.[40] In February 1972 Nixon went to Beijing.

The war ended in disaster for Pakistan and triumph for India, but both again felt let down by the United States. India had expected America to support a campaign to stop genocide; Pakistan had expected America and China to do something to stop India. Despite his sense that Pakistan had been betrayed again, Bhutto needed American support. He would spend the next five years trying to get Pakistan back on its feet, roaming the world looking for help from China to Saudi Arabia. In September 1973 he saw Nixon in the Oval Office one last time. He asked for arms sales and aid to be resumed and offered the United States a naval base at a new port in Baluchistan, Gwadar, as a sweetener. Nixon never seriously considered the offer. Behind the scenes Zulfi ordered Pakistan's scientists to develop a nuclear weapon at any and all costs. An unknown Pakistani engineer in Belgium, A. Q. Khan, offered his services, and the ISI began to assist him in stealing nuclear centrifuge technology from the Dutch company where he worked.

Indira Gandhi did not need America. She was convinced that Nixon was her enemy, and she harbored suspicions that the CIA was determined to assassinate her. Her suspicions intensified after the hero of Bangladesh's independence struggle, Sheikh Mujibur Rahman, was murdered in a bloody coup in the summer of 1975 that she believed was orchestrated to punish her for the 1971 war.[41] She won an overwhelming majority in the next elections. The prime minister had faced two nuclear powers backing Pakistan in 1971, America and China, but she had been too strong to let them intimidate her, even when the United States tried gunboat diplomacy to do so. She was seen around the world as a winner who had stood up to Nixon and prevailed. She did conclude that

India needed the bomb, and on May 18, 1974, India exploded a nuclear device and thereby joined the nuclear club.

THE BOMB AND FORD

The postmortem on India's nuclear test conducted by the U.S. intelligence community noted that "the intelligence community failed to warn U.S. decision makers that such a test was being planned. This failure denied the U.S. government the option of considering diplomatic or other initiatives to prevent this significant step in nuclear proliferation."[42] The postmortem concluded that the CIA and other agencies had long expected an Indian test—some since 1965 and the second Indo-Pakistani war—but that in 1974 there were simply too few intelligence collection assets (spies, satellites, and intercepted communications) against "an admittedly difficult target" to provide timely warning. Just two years earlier, a special national intelligence estimate (SNIE) had argued that "Mrs. Gandhi knows that a test would be popular at home, stimulate a rising sense of national pride and independence, and—in the eyes of many—reinforce India's claim that it should be taken seriously as a major power." Once a decision to test was made, the SNIE said, a test could come within a few days, and India could build a stock of ten to twelve low-yield weapons in a year. Within a few years it could build fifty to seventy devices a year.[43]

For the first but not the last time the CIA had rightly predicted India's ability to test a nuclear device but had been unable to provide timely warning of the preparations for an actual test. Over the course of the next four decades, the challenge of detecting test preparations in advance would be a key priority for the CIA. It would have successes and one more failure, in 1998. The 1974 test was one more negative factor in the already deeply strained U.S.-India relationship at the end of the Nixon administration. Washington protested the test, but Nixon was riveted on the collapse of his administration in the Watergate scandal. In August 1974, he resigned in disgrace. Gerald Ford became president and kept Kissinger as his secretary of state. Kissinger visited India in October for a three-day mission to try to repair the damage done by the 1971 crisis. He spoke publicly about the need for America to recognize India's rise to world power status and acknowledged past errors. In a very public snub, Mrs. Gandhi had lunch with the secretary on his first day in New Delhi and then left town for Kashmir. In February 1975 the embargo on sales of weapons to Pakistan and India was finally lifted by Ford, ten years after President Johnson had imposed it. Since that greatly benefited Pakistan, Mrs. Gandhi was not pleased. She got her revenge just two months later, when the American-backed regime in Saigon fell to the communists. India announced that it was a "gratifying vindication" of decades of Indian policy in Vietnam.

For forty years America had sought to build strong ties to both India and Pakistan. The attempt had failed. Two powerful Indian prime ministers, Nehru and his daughter Indira, had been difficult interlocutors for four American presidents; only Kennedy had succeeded in building a real partnership with India. In Pakistan, America had twice deeply disappointed the generals who ran the country by not treating Pakistan as an exclusive ally. It was not a promising start to the American involvement in the rise of India and Pakistan. It would get worse.

For forty years American presidents had also tried, to varying degrees, to resolve the Kashmir problem. The efforts of Truman and Kennedy were the most serious, but both failed. Nehru proved to be a very difficult interlocutor on Kashmir, but the Pakistanis made impossible demands; they would not accept anything less than possession of the valley. The lesson that American diplomats drew from years of failure was that Kashmir was too difficult to deal with and therefore best ignored—an understandable conclusion but the wrong one.

CHAPTER FOUR

THE CARTER AND REAGAN YEARS

TAMPA, FLORIDA, IS a long way from South Asia, but in mid-2011 I was there to attend a conference at the headquarters of the U.S. Central Command on Pakistan as a guest of General David Petraeus, the U.S. commander in Afghanistan. CENTCOM is the regional command of that part of the U.S. military whose area of responsibility includes Pakistan, but not India. I have been to CENTCOM many times over the past three decades to discuss American war plans and military missions. This time I was to review Pakistan's role in supporting the Taliban movement in Afghanistan. My message was simple: the United States was fighting a proxy war with Pakistan in Afghanistan.

The audience was not thrilled with the message. They knew that I was right, but the hard truth of it was not eagerly welcomed by American commanders. After all, only twenty-five years ago the United States had fought a war against the Soviets in Afghanistan with Pakistan's help. I was a junior player in that war effort, but even I could see that it would be much easier for the United States to win if Pakistan provided it and its allies with safe havens along the border and a sanctuary in which to train and prepare to fight. In the 1980s, President Ronald Reagan enjoyed Pakistan's support and won the war. Now, in the twenty-first century, America and

Pakistan are on opposite sides in the Afghan civil war. It's a lot harder to envision success.

CENTCOM planners look at Pakistan from the west. It sits at the edge of their area of responsibility (AOR), on the far end of the Middle East and the Persian Gulf; consequently, CENTCOM sees Pakistan primarily in terms of how its actions and policies affect Afghanistan and the Gulf. Pakistan's military leaders, of course, look primarily the other way, east toward India. They are obsessed with India and the threat that they believe that it poses to their country. So American and Pakistani generals—and diplomats and spies for that matter—generally look at the world with very different priorities. Sometimes they can find common ground for short-term reasons, like fighting communism in Kabul, but generally their strategic views are at odds with each other.

Forty years of cold war diplomacy had left America's relations with both India and Pakistan dysfunctional by the mid-1970s, and the two Indo-Pakistani wars, in 1965 and 1971, had been bad for both bilateral relationships. Seeing South Asia through the prism of the cold war had only made the difficult business of building strong ties to the two rivals harder for the United States. The next decade would see the cold war intensify to its conclusion under President Reagan. Kashmir would fall off the American agenda, a forgotten conflict.

CARTER'S INTERREGNUM

After the scandals of the Nixon administration and the discouraging end to the war in Vietnam, Americans wanted a new face in the White House. When Georgia governor James Carter was chosen to succeed President Ford, he inherited a South Asia in transition. Profound political change was under way in both India and Pakistan. Indira Gandhi had proclaimed a state of emergency in June 1975 in response to a growing wave of protests against her increasingly authoritarian practices and the corruption surrounding her younger son, Sanjay. Opposition leaders were arrested, the press was muzzled, and for the first and only time in India's democratic history the rule of law and freedom of speech were curtailed. Then, as suddenly as she imposed the state of emergency, Indira lifted it in January 1977 and called new elections. She lost. Carter would have a new government headed by Morarji Desai, a Congress party dissident and long-time enemy of Indira, to deal with.

As Carter came to office, Pakistan also was in transition. Zulfikar Bhutto, like Mrs. Gandhi, had become more and more authoritarian in his ways. Mounting protests were met with crackdowns on dissent and increasing reliance on the security services to enforce order. In February 1976, Zulfi appointed a new chief of army staff, General Mohammed Zia ul-Haq, skipping over several more senior officers because he was supremely confident that Zia was a loyal sycophant, totally apolitical and too weak to challenge his control. At dinner parties and in front of foreign guests, Bhutto called Zia his "monkey general."[1] New elections in 1977 were rigged, leading to more protests, and on July 5, 1977, the "monkey general" overthrew Zulfi and became Pakistan's third military dictator. So Carter had a new Pakistani partner as well.

Carter's priority was India. The damage done by Nixon's 1971 tilt toward Pakistan was enormous and required remediation, and the departure of Mrs. Gandhi presented an opportunity. Shortly after Carter's inauguration, the Indian president died (the presidency in India is a largely ceremonial post), and Carter sent his mother, Lillian, to represent him at the funeral. Lillian had served in the Peace Corps in India, and the personal gesture was much appreciated in New Delhi. In January 1978 Carter went to India himself as part of a global trip that would take him to Europe and Iran but not to Pakistan. His deliberate omission of Pakistan from the itinerary, which was favorably received in India, was unprecedented for an American president traveling to South Asia, and it signaled a new U.S. posture. The Delhi Declaration, a result of the summit between Carter and Prime Minister Desai, committed the two great democracies to practice "moral responsibility" in global diplomacy and included a strong commitment to human rights. The visit was tarnished only modestly by an open microphone incident in which Carter was caught complaining about India's nuclear policy to Secretary of State Cyrus Vance. Desai returned the visit in June 1978, when he visited Washington. Carter took the prime minister on an impromptu evening visit to the Lincoln Memorial after the official state dinner, a sign of the warmth that the two had developed.

Their rapprochement was to be short lived. The Iranian revolution and the subsequent hostage crisis came to dominate Carter's presidency. Even his triumphs, the Egyptian-Israeli peace treaty and the Panama Canal treaty, were sidelined by the Iranian crisis. Then, in December 1979, the Soviets invaded Afghanistan. While America saw it as a sign of Soviet imperialism, India was less alarmed. For the Carter team, the moderate Indian reaction was like a "ton of bricks" shattering the goodwill that Carter had sought with Desai.[2] In January 1980 Indira Gandhi swept back into office in a landslide victory in which her party won 350 of 542 seats. Her animus toward the United States had softened during her years out of power, but it had not disappeared. She and Carter would increasingly differ over Pakistan. In the end, Carter's effort to rebuild bridges to India went nowhere. His trip to New Delhi would be the last presidential visit to India for a quarter-century.

Carter had not been pleased by Zia's 1977 coup, which put an end to Pakistan's second experiment in elected government, even if the elections were often tainted. In contrast to Nixon's, his administration was pledged to support democracy and foster human rights. Carter would have been unhappy enough with the coup, code-named Operation Fair Play, but what followed upset him much more. After first promising that new elections would be held in ninety days and releasing Zulfikar Bhutto from detention, Zia changed his mind. Pakistan was too small for two power-hungry leaders. Zia, turning on his nemesis with a vengeance, had Bhutto charged with murder. Carter and many other world leaders appealed to Zia for clemency; Carter himself wrote Zia three letters urging the general to spare his rival. In March 1978 Bhutto was found guilty by a court in Lahore, and more appeals for mercy from Carter followed. Finally, on April 4, 1979, Zulfi was hanged to death. The long, drawn-out trial and appeals process had consumed Pakistani politics for almost two years, and Zulfi's death marked a new low in U.S.-Pakistan relations. Behind the scenes, arguments over Pakistan's developing nuclear program had made matters worse. Carter pressed France and other countries not to provide nuclear technology to Pakistan. Zia, though angered by the American campaign to stop Pakistan's bomb project, was not intimidated.

It got worse. On November 20, 1979, a mob stormed the American embassy in Islamabad, angered by reports that the United States and Israel were secretly supporting the takeover of the Grand Mosque in Mecca, Saudi Arabia, which had been seized by Saudi extremists who believed that the *mahdi,* or redeemer, had arrived. The reports were entirely false. They had been circulated by the new Iranian revolutionary regime, led by Ayatollah Khomeni, which wanted to cause damage to the United States. The demonstrators at the embassy broke into the compound, and the embassy staff, 137 Americans and Pakistanis, locked themselves in a secure vault. The mob set the embassy on fire, and only the bravery of the U.S. marine guards and the embassy staff saved the day. They were able to escape via the roof to safety, but at the cost of two American lives. The crisis at the embassy lasted for hours, and at CIA headquarters a team of analysts watched the drama unfold (I was one of them). At the State Department and the White House, every effort was made to get the Pakistani army to come to the rescue of the embassy, but for hours nothing happened. Zia was touring the city to promote bicycling in Pakistan, and his staff said that they did not want to interrupt him. Finally, Carter got through to the general by telephone. Belatedly, the army sent some helicopters to monitor the scene and then sent troops to regain control.

In the wake of the embassy attack, U.S.-Pakistan relations were at their nadir. Many in the U.S. government believed that Zia had deliberately encouraged the attack and then done nothing to halt it. Carter, more charitably, gave Zia the benefit of the doubt. Then, just when U.S.-Pakistan relations were at rock bottom, the Soviet Union invaded Afghanistan, rescuing the relationship. Carter would have to eat crow and make up with Zia.

THE RUSSIAN BEAR AND ZIA UL-HAQ

Mohammed Zia ul-Haq transformed Pakistan and altered the course of the country's future more than anyone had since Jinnah. Zia can also be rightly called the godfather of the modern global Islamic jihad movement. He was born in Jalandhar (now in India) on August 12, 1924. After joining the British army in India in 1944, he fought with Indian forces in Italy against the Nazis as part of the British Eighth Army. Between 1962 and 1964, he received training as a tank commander in the United States at Fort Leavenworth, Kansas, and he served as a tank commander during Pakistan's 1965 war with India.

In 1967 Zia was posted to Amman, Jordan, as part of a Pakistani military advisory group that was helping Jordan to recover from defeat in the Six-Day War with Israel. Over the next three years, he would distinguish himself in supporting the Hashemite government in its fight with Palestinian guerillas led by Yasir Arafat. Zia helped plan the king's battles with the fedayeen and even commanded some of the Jordanian forces fighting the Palestinians in the civil war that engulfed Jordan in September 1970, the notorious Black September, when King Hussein defeated the Palestinians and drove them out of the kingdom. According to the king's brother, Prince Hassan, Zia became a "friend and confidant of His Majesty, King Hussein. He was a well-respected figure, a professional soldier, and . . . he not only advised on military tactics, he also earned the respect and trust of the *jundis* [soldiers]."[3] Zia probably exceeded his authority as a Pakistani general, but he built a very strong relationship with the Hashemites. His role in Jordan also made him famous at home.[4]

Unlike the earlier generation of Pakistani military dictators, Zia was an Islamist. He aligned himself with the country's Islamic political party, the Jamaat-e-Islami (JeI); he depicted himself as a pious Muslim; and he took steps to Islamize the army. He sought and received the endorsement of Islamic extremists, who enthusiastically praised the new regime.[5] Officers were encouraged to join communal prayers with their troops, and for the first time, promotion boards for officers reviewed their moral and religious behavior in addition to their performance of their normal military duties. The foremost expert on the Pakistani army today, Shuja Nawaz, concludes that "Islamization was the legacy he left Pakistan."[6]

Zia was ambitious. He declared at the height of the Afghan war with the Soviets in the 1980s that

> we have earned the right to have a friendly regime in Afghanistan. We took risks as a frontline state, and we won't permit it to be like it was before, with Indian and Soviet influence there and claims on our territory. It will be a real Islamic state, part of a pan-Islamic revival that will one day win over the Muslims of the Soviet Union; you will see it.[7]

One measure of Islamization under Zia was the growth in the number of Islamic schools (madrassas) in Pakistan. Zia recognized diplomas granted by the madrassas as equivalent to those from universities. The number of such schools grew enormously on Zia's watch, as did their influence throughout the country. In 1971 there were 900 madrassas in Pakistan; by 1988 there were 8,000 official religious schools and another 25,000 unregistered ones.[8] The army's role in Pakistani society also expanded. Ayub Khan had begun a process whereby retiring army officers were given state land in rural areas to improve their retirement pensions and to encourage rural development. Zia expanded that program and also began to give favored officers prime pieces of property in Pakistan's growing urban areas. The practice would continue, and by 1999 the armed forces as a group owned the largest share of urban real estate in Pakistan.[9]

In addition, the Directorate for Inter-Services Intelligence grew. Zia's handpicked choice for director general in 1979 was a Pashtun, Akhtar Abdur Rahman, better known simply as General Akhtar. He hated publicity and the press and avoided being photographed. Akhtar, whom his own subordinates described as "a cold, reserved personality, almost inscrutable, always secretive,"[10] was a gifted intelligence officer, and he knew the Afghan world well.[11] He developed close working ties to many of the Afghan mujahedin leaders, especially fellow Pashtuns, and organized them into political parties to give more legitimacy to their struggle. Akhtar also built strong ISI links to the CIA and the Saudis. He was the first director general of the ISI that I met with.

At Zia's direction, Akhtar vastly expanded the size and strength of the service. According to one estimate, the ISI went from a staff of 2,000 in 1978 to 40,000 employees and a billion-dollar budget by 1988.[12] It came to be seen in Pakistan as omnipotent, listening in on every phone call, planting informants in every village, city block, and public space. Politicians were on its payroll, and its enemies simply disappeared. Much of its growth was designed to keep Zia in power, but much of it was also to wage jihad. As one of Akhtar's deputies would later say, "The ISI was and still is probably the most powerful and influential organization in the country"; he also remarked that Akhtar was "regarded with envy or fear," even by his fellow officers.[13] In short, Zia gave Pakistan an "incendiary mix of despotism and Islamization."[14]

Events outside Pakistan gave Zia more opportunity to Islamize the country. First was the revolution in Iran, Pakistan's western neighbor. In 1978 the Shah's government was toppled in an Islamic revolution that swept Iran and surprised the world, and it had ripples in Pakistan. Pakistan has a large Shia minority, perhaps as many as a quarter of all Pakistanis (Jinnah was one), and the Shia revolution next door heightened sectarian tensions within Pakistan. Iran began supporting Shia dissidents inside Pakistan. At first Zia tried to appease them and bargain with Tehran, but when that failed, he used force. Zia and the ISI supported the growth of anti-Shia Sunni groups like Sipah-e-Sahaba Pakistan (the Army of the Prophet's Companions), which attacked Shia mosques and religious festivities to intimidate the Shia community into quiescence.[15] The Iranian revolution also removed a key American ally in the region. It had seemed to many Cold Warriors that Moscow must have had a hand in the revolution, although in fact it was as surprised as everyone else. The unexpected demise of the Shah's Iran made events in its eastern neighbor, Afghanistan, suddenly seem more important.

Afghanistan had had a very uneasy relationship with Pakistan since 1947. Under the Raj, the border between Afghanistan and British India—the so-called Durand Line—was drawn unilaterally by the British and imposed on the Afghans in 1893. Named after the British officer who drew it, Henry Mortimer Durand, the foreign secretary for India, the line divided ethnic Pashtuns—the dominant ethnic group in Afghanistan—from their fellow Pashtuns in what would become Pakistan. No Afghan government, not even the Taliban, has ever recognized the legitimacy of the line, which stretches for 2,640 kilometers, and Afghanistan pressed for a revision of the border as the British prepared to leave India. When Pakistan refused to change the border, Afghanistan voted against allowing Pakistan a seat in the United Nations. Afghan governments also supported calls for an independent Pashtunistan to be carved out of Pakistan, in effect expanding Afghanistan all the way to the Indus River and even to the Indian Ocean by gobbling up Baluchistan as well.

In 1978, Marxist officers in the Afghan army overthrew the neutralist Afghan government of President Daoud and began to import communist ideology and politics into the country. Large parts of the rural countryside rose in rebellion. Many of the rebels had long had contacts with Pakistan's religious parties, especially the Jamaat-e-Islami, and with the ISI. Zia openly favored the rebels, and Akhtar's ISI began arming and helping them. The Afghan communist government first appealed to Moscow for arms and advisers and then for Russian troops. Initially, Moscow was reluctant to get into what appeared to be a growing civil war and a possible quagmire. But as the situation deteriorated, the Soviet leadership decided that it must intervene to save a client state. On the eve of December 25, 1979, the invasion began: 85,000 Soviet soldiers entered the country, and the borders of the Soviet bloc advanced to Pakistan's western frontier. However, Moscow still showed signs of ambivalence about the project. The Soviets could have put many more troops into the fight if they chose to do so. While they had invaded Czechoslovakia in 1968 with a 250,000-man army, they were fighting in Afghanistan, a much larger and more challenging country, with a smaller force.

Zia immediately turned to Saudi Arabia for help and assistance. The Saudis and Pakistanis had a long history of cooperation; Pakistan received significant aid from Riyadh, and many Pakistani émigré workers were employed in the kingdom, including in the Saudi army, navy, and air force. The Saudis had been worried about the deteriorating situation in Afghanistan even before the Marxist officers took over. During a visit to Riyadh the year before the coup, their intelligence chief, Prince Turki bin Faysal, had warned President Daoud of the communist threat. As the Soviets invaded Afghanistan, Zia dispatched General Akhtar to Riyadh with an urgent message for the king: Zia wanted Saudi assistance to strengthen the mujahedin, the anti-communist rebels in Afghanistan. According to Prince Turki, King Fahd agreed immediately, and the ISI and Turki's General Intelligence Directorate (GID) began cooperating to aid the mujahedin. Saudi money began pouring into the ISI, and Saudi authorities also encouraged private citizens to give money to help in the war against the Soviets and to join the jihad. In addition, the Saudi-Pakistani partnership would soon acquire another partner, the CIA.[16]

Partly in response, Zia dispatched a Pakistani expeditionary force of brigade strength to the kingdom to help it defend itself against its regional enemies. The 12th Khalid bin Waleed Independent Armored Brigade would be stationed in Tabuk, Saudi Arabia, near Israel, for more than six years, from 1982 to 1988. Reinforced, it had 20,000 men under command at its peak, and the Saudis paid all of its costs.[17] With the money from the Saudis and later from the CIA, the ISI was able to begin training Afghans to fight the Soviets more effectively. The ISI set up training camps along the Durand Line, and Afghans began learning more sophisticated tactics and skills to help them wage jihad. The ISI included instructors from Pakistan's own special forces, the Special Services Group (SSG), an elite fighting force within the army.

Zia also turned to Pakistan's other long-time ally, China, and China responded with arms and advisers. By the end of the war, Chinese aid to the Afghans exceeded $400 million and some 300 Chinese advisers had helped train the mujahedin in the ISI camps in Pakistan. A few were trained in camps in China itself.[18] Overall, the ISI had trained at least 80,000 to 90,000 Afghans in its camps.[19] Among the trainees was a young Afghan from Kandahar named Muhammad Omar, who would later found the Taliban. The Afghans were trained either in short ten-day courses or longer three-month courses. Omar was selected for the longer course in 1985. His ISI trainer would later remember Omar as one of his best students.[20]

Supporting the Afghans did not come without costs to Pakistan. First, there were the refugees, about 4 million of whom crossed into Pakistan to escape the war and the communists. Entire cities in Afghanistan were depopulated during the war; for example, especially after the Soviets carpet-bombed much of Kandahar to break a mujahedin rebellion, its population dropped from 250,000 to 25,000. The refugees poured into the poorest parts of Pakistan: the Pashtun-dominated Northwest Frontier Province, the Federally Administered Tribal Areas (FATA), and Baluchistan. The burden of caring for them was an enormous drain on Pakistan. Moreover, with the refugees came a Kalashnikov culture. Every Pashtun man carried an assault rifle. The violence and disrupted lifestyles of the displaced refugees bred a lawlessness in the border regions that undermined traditional tribal authorities and the Pakistani government alike. The opium trade from Afghanistan's large poppy fields added corruption and drug trafficking to the mix.

In addition, the Russians and their Afghan communist allies sought to destabilize Pakistan. The Russian intelligence service, the KGB, and its Afghan client, the KHAD, paid agents to plant bombs in the refugee camps, assassinate mujahedin leaders, and attack the ISI training facilities. They would also try to blow up the arsenals where the ISI stored weapons and ammunition before the supplies got into the mujahedin's hands. (The most successful attack on an arsenal, which came near the end of the war, rocked the entire city of Islamabad; however, it was the work of India, not KHAD.) Soviet aircraft also intentionally strayed into Pakistani air space to intimidate Zia and the ISI, and the Pakistani air force struck back. Dog fights occurred along the border, some of which risked escalating into a mini air war between the Soviet and the Pakistani air force.[21] The Pakistanis were emboldened over time to take the war into the Soviet Union itself. Trained mujahedin units would cross the northern border of Afghanistan to conduct sabotage in Soviet Central Asia, and experts from the SSG would sometimes accompany them on their missions.[22]

At first, however, Zia was very cautious. He knew that the risks of fighting a superpower with the world's largest army were enormous. There was no assurance that Moscow would not invade Pakistan itself or work with its ally, India, to carve up the state. Consequently, for the first few years of the war Zia's orders to the ISI were to heat up the situation in Afghanistan but not to let it boil.[23] Controlling the arms and money going to the mujahedin was the key to keeping the pot simmering just right. The ISI therefore took outside help, money, and arms but was very careful to control how and when the various mujahedin factions received those assets. In the process the ISI could favor some factions over others, and it always favored Pashtuns and Islamic factions at the expense of non-Pashtuns and more moderate elements.[24] The man who actually ran the operation for much of the 1980s was Mohammad Yousaf, the chief of the ISI's Afghan bureau. His two accounts of the war, *Silent Soldier: The Man behind the Afghan Jehad* and *The Bear Trap: Afghanistan's Untold Story,* are the single best pieces on the war from the Pakistani perspective. He describes the pipeline for aid as follows: "As soon as the arms arrived in Pakistan, the CIA's responsibility ended. From then on it was our pipeline, our organization that moved, allocated, and distributed every bullet that the CIA procured."[25]

From the earliest days of the Afghan war, Zia was already planning for the next stage of the jihad, turning east toward India and Kashmir. He turned initially to a political party with which he and the army had long-standing ties, Jamaat-e-Islami. The group had been founded in 1941 by Maulana Syed Abul A'ala Maududi, an Islamist writer who advocated a Muslim state in India and the use of force, or jihad, to get it. Maududi had no sympathy, however, for Jinnah and his independence movement, which he saw as far too secular in outlook. Jamaat-e-Islami wanted an Islamic state. It was an enthusiastic ally of the army in the war against the Bengalis in 1971, a war that helped forge an alliance between the party and jihadists like Zia in the army.[26]

In 1980 Zia met secretly in Rawalpindi with Maulana Abdul Bari—a leader in the Jamaat-e-Islami and a veteran jihadist who had fought in Operation Gibraltar in 1965—to discuss Kashmir. Zia proposed that the JeI begin preparations for jihad in Kashmir and promised that he would use the war against the Soviets as a means to help build the base for a Kashmiri insurgency. In other words, the Afghan war with the Soviets would also be a training ground to build the cadres for another jihad, against India. Zia promised that some of the American assistance that was earmarked for the Afghan jihad would be diverted to the Kashmiri project and that the ISI would help both.[27] Jamaat-e-Islami found, however, that there was resistance among Kashmiris to Zia's promises of support. Having been let down by Pakistan in 1947 and 1965, many were uncertain that they could trust the ISI. So the new jihad took time to develop. A series of clandestine meetings took place between the ISI and Kashmiri militants from Indian-controlled Kashmir. For security reasons, many of the meetings were held in Saudi Arabia. It was easier for an Indian militant leader to travel to the kingdom, often under the cover of performing the hajj, than to go to Pakistan, which would immediately invite the scrutiny of Indian intelligence. Zia and General Akhtar were involved directly in the effort. Finally, in 1983 some Kashmiris began to receive training in the ISI's Afghan camps.[28]

Zia, Akhtar, and the ISI also reached out to other groups in Kashmir, including the Jammu Kashmir Liberation Front (JKLF), which had been founded in 1977 in Birmingham, England, by Kashmiris living in the United Kingdom. However, the JKLF was much more interested in achieving Kashmiri independence than in joining Pakistan. At first it was also reluctant to take ISI help, but Akhtar opened talks with the group in 1984, and by 1987 JKLF militants were attending the ISI training camps. Zia and Akhtar also avidly supported another front in India, the Sikh independence movement, which wanted to create a Sikh state called Khalistan. Sikh grievances dated back to partition, when some Sikhs argued for a third state in South Asia for themselves. When their unrest peaked in the 1980s, Pakistan unsurprisingly became a patron of the Sikh independence movement, which the ISI helped by providing arms and expertise. Zia could not resist the temptation to play in troubled waters.

The Sikh rebellion came to a disastrous climax in June 1984, when activists took control of the Harmandir Sahib—the holiest

Sikh temple, known popularly as the Golden Temple—in Amritsar. Indira Gandhi ordered the Indian army to regain control, but Operation Blue Star turned into a fiasco, in part because the army underestimated the firepower of the militants. After a twenty-four-hour firefight, at least 500 soldiers, militants, and innocent victims were dead; some believe that the casualties were much higher. A low-level insurgency in the Punjab would continue for another decade, with the ISI stoking the flames. It would also take Mrs. Gandhi's life.

REAGAN AND THE AMERICAN CONNECTION

The pro-Soviet coup in Kabul forced Carter to change his view of Pakistan. The country that he had literally flown over in 1978 was now critical to stopping the Soviets. To Carter, shaken by the fall of the Shah of Iran and by the Marxist coup in Kabul, it looked as if Southwest Asia were crumbling into enemy hands. In July 1979, Carter ordered the CIA to provide modest assistance to the rebellion against the communist government in Kabul, six months before the Soviet invasion. The aid was low level, involving mostly propaganda support and very modest amounts of money but no weapons.[29]

The Soviet invasion cemented the change in Washington, and it would lead to a renewal of America's cold war love affair with the Pakistani army and Inter-Services Intelligence. Carter's national security adviser, Zbigniew Brzezinski, traveled to Pakistan after the invasion and offered more assistance for the mujahedin and for Pakistan. When Brzezinski offered $400 million in aid over two years, Zia turned down the offer as "peanuts," a gratuitous insult to Carter, a peanut farmer from Georgia. But Zia allowed the bilateral relationship between the ISI and the Saudis' General Intelligence Directorate to become a trilateral CIA-ISI-GID relationship in which Washington and Riyadh provided matching grants of money and purchased arms and Islamabad handled distribution and training. On January 10, 1980, just fourteen days after the Soviets invaded Kabul, the first CIA-provided arms for the mujahedin arrived in Pakistan via the ISI.[30]

The size of the covert program grew steadily. By 1984 the CIA was providing $250 million dollars annually;[31] at its peak, in 1987 and 1988, the amount reached at least $400 million.[32] Since the program was largely concerned with fundraising and arms procurement, it had very little staff: no more than a hundred people were involved in the Afghan effort, slightly less than half of them at CIA headquarters in Langley, Virginia, the others in Islamabad.[33] Given the enormous consequences of the operation, which helped precipitate the collapse of the Soviet Union and the end of the cold war, it has to be judged one of the most cost-effective federal government programs in history.

One of the most colorful figures in modern American history was associated with the program. Congressman Charlie Wilson, a Democrat from Texas, was an early and enthusiastic supporter of the war effort, the Afghans, and especially Zia. He sat on the key House committees that funded covert operations, and he literally gave the CIA more money than it asked for. He also pushed to get the mujahedin the Stinger, an advanced surface-to-air missile system. Charlie Wilson made close to three dozen trips to the region, stopping in Cairo, Jerusalem, Riyadh, and Islamabad each time to get backing from all of America's key allies. Usually accompanied by a beautiful woman, Charlie flattered the allies, and they flattered him. Zia and Akhtar made him a secret field marshal in the Pakistani army, and Wilson cried when Zia died in August 1988, telling Akhtar's successor, Hamid Gul, that "I have lost my father on this day."[34] Charlie had even planned to get married in Pakistan at one point, and he persuaded Zia to hold an elaborate ceremony in the Khyber Pass with lancers and cavalry. Guests would come from around the world, even from Israel. But the wedding never took place.[35]

Wilson was really a secondary figure in the war, despite the prominence that the movie *Charlie Wilson's War* gave him later. It was Reagan and his spy chief Bill Casey who did the real heavy lifting. Right after they came into office, they offered Zia a new deal, worth $3.5 billion over five years, that included sophisticated F-16 jet fighters to protect Pakistani air space from Russia and India. This time Zia took the offer.

Casey was President Ronald Reagan's hand-picked director of central intelligence (DCI), and he had the president's ear more than any other man in Washington. He had managed Reagan's election victory in 1980 and shared his tough anticommunist views. Reagan made the unprecedented move of making Casey a full member of his cabinet; no DCI before or since has had that status. During World War II, Casey had been involved in supporting underground resistance movements in Nazi-occupied Europe as a member of the CIA's predecessor, the Office of Strategic Services. He was a genuine expert in the art of covert warfare. As director, he supervised America's clandestine war to wear down the Soviet Union and bleed it to death. Afghanistan was at the center of that battle. It was the CIA's war, and the CIA ran policy toward Pakistan (and indirectly India) as a consequence.

Casey traveled repeatedly to Islamabad. On his first visit, Zia ul-Haq had showed him a map of Afghanistan with a red triangle superimposed on it, pointing in the direction of the Indian Ocean, just three hundred miles from the Afghan-Pakistani border. Zia showed the map to many subsequent visitors. Pakistan was the real battlefield, he argued, and Moscow's real objective was access to the Indian Ocean and the Persian Gulf. Zia was determined to keep Moscow from getting a warm-water port on the Indian Ocean, but he also knew that he needed to be careful not to provoke the Russians too much, too soon. As Casey's deputy for operations in Afghanistan would later recount, "Zia was a believer. Without Zia, there would have been no Afghan war, and no Afghan victory."[36]

Zia himself traveled to Washington in December 1982, where, on Pearl Harbor Day, he and Reagan met in the Oval Office. Reagan promised American support against the Soviets. When he raised the issue of Pakistan's nuclear program, Zia assured him that it was only for peaceful purposes and that Pakistan would not "embarrass" America with its nuclear ambitions. "No embarrassment" would become Zia's mantra on the nuclear front, by which he meant that Pakistan would build a bomb but not test it or otherwise be too public about the country's plans for it. Reagan almost certainly left Zia confident that his priority was Afghanistan and that his administration was comfortable with "no embarrassments" on secondary issues. In May 1984, Vice President George Bush went to Islamabad to see the war up front. He too raised the nuclear issue, and he got the same answer. The CIA was asked to brief the Pakistanis on several occasions on what it knew about Pakistan's program, the hope being that the briefings would persuade the Pakistanis to slow down for fear that their program would be discovered and cause "embarrassment." Instead, the briefings simply exposed American methods of collecting intelligence to the Pakistanis. One Pakistani official characterized the briefings as "show and tell" and told his American counterpart that they only encouraged Pakistan to try harder to hide the program.[37]

To satisfy congressional critics of Pakistan's nuclear program, the Reagan administration agreed to abide by a bill requiring annual certification from the president that Pakistan did not have a nuclear bomb. The so-called Pressler amendment, named after Larry Pressler, the Republican senator who sponsored it, was intended to provide a way to keep providing lavish aid to Pakistan, not to prevent it. As long as Casey was DCI, the certifications were certain to be affirmative. In 1986 Casey told the new outgoing chief for Pakistan that the goal was no longer just to bleed the Soviets in Afghanistan, it was to "win the war." A new $4 billion aid package for Pakistan followed.[38] The CIA also began providing Stinger surface-to-air missiles to the ISI for the mujahedin, which challenged the Russian control of the air and provided the Afghans with a critical military advantage.

The nuclear issue refused to stay dormant. In 1984 Pakistan's leading nuclear scientist, A. Q. Khan, who had stolen the plans for the critical centrifuge from the Netherlands, was quoted in an Indian newspaper as saying that the promise that Pakistan's program was only for peaceful purposes was "humbug." The Pakistanis claimed that he was misquoted. The Reagan team escaped embarrassment, but they certainly knew the truth. On a later occasion, Secretary of Defense Frank Carlucci asked Zia directly how he would continue to have the ISI provide arms to the rebels once the Soviets had withdrawn their troops(though not their aid). Moscow had demanded that the CIA and ISI stop providing arms as a precondition to withdrawal, but Washington refused and Islamabad maintained the fiction that it did not supply arms to the mujahedin. Zia replied, "I'll lie to them like I have been lying to them for the past ten years." Carlucci added, "Just like he has been lying to us about the nuclear business."[39]

On August 17, 1988, Zia and Akhtar, who had by then been promoted to chairman of the Joint Chiefs of Staff, and several other senior Pakistani generals as well as the U.S. ambassador to Pakistan, Arnold Raphel, were killed when their C-130 aircraft crashed shortly after takeoff. Raphel's widow was told by American investigators that it was 90 percent certain that the crash was due to a mechanical failure, not sabotage, but immediately suspicions of foul play surfaced.[40] No one ever claimed responsibility, but there are dozens of conspiracy theories about what happened and why.

A thorough and credible investigation has never been conducted. Akhtar's ISI biographer, Yousaf, concluded that "the KGB or KHAD (its Afghan counterpart) had been involved" but that the Americans were eager to see Zia killed now that the jihad was almost over.[41] John Gunther Dean, then the U.S. ambassador to India, accused the Israeli secret service, Mossad, of killing Zia, possibly to stop the Pakistani bomb program.[42] In the most recent study, based on interviews with many of the Pakistani air force officers who investigated the crash, Shuja Nawaz concludes that "many questions still remain" about why the plane crashed and why the investigation of the crash was so incomplete.[43] Like much else in Pakistan's history, this incident remains a mystery. One thing is certain: America does not kill its ambassadors or its allies' leaders.

Casey had died a year before, in May 1987, of a brain tumor at the age of eighty-seven, so the main authors of the war all died before victory was achieved. By then, he and his boss, President Reagan, were engulfed in the Iran-Contra scandal, the secret deal with Iran to trade arms for hostages in Lebanon. In Afghanistan, Casey had presided over the largest CIA covert action program in the agency's history; by the time of his death, its budget had grown from less than $20 million to $400 million.

INDIA AND THE REAGAN YEARS

The Reagan-Casey team focused on the cold war exclusively. Pakistan was an essential ally against Russia; India was at best an afterthought, if not a Soviet ally. Casey, who ran the war in Afghanistan, was uninterested in India. Reagan's primary wish was to avoid Indian interference in Pakistan. So it was a bit of a pleasant surprise that Reagan and Indira Gandhi initially got along together quite well. They met first at a summit of industrialized and developing states in Cancun, Mexico, in October 1981. Their personal chemistry was good, although the two had dramatically different policy views. In July 1982 Indira came to Washington, her first visit since the dark days of 1971. Again the dynamic between the two leaders was positive, but the good vibrations masked very serious differences, especially over Pakistan as Zia stepped up interference in Kashmir and Punjab.

In April 1984 Indian forces took control of most of the Siachen Glacier in northern Kashmir. (*Siachen* translates as "place of roses," but it is in fact a frozen river of ice at the top of the world.) Operation Cloud Messenger was intended to preempt a Pakistani effort to seize the glacier, but it also sent a signal to Zia that Indira was not to be trifled with. Pakistan responded by trying to seize back the wasteland, and a bloody war for control of the glacier began that lasts to this day. More soldiers die from exposure to the harsh elements there than from combat; in April 2012, 135 Pakistani soldiers and civilians died in one avalanche alone. For two poor countries, it is a monumental waste of resources.

On October 31, 1984, Indira Gandhi was assassinated by two of her bodyguards, Sikhs who were angered by her bloody military operation in Amritsar (Operation Blue Star). Her son, Rajiv, became prime minister. Her daughter-in-law, Sonia Gandhi, was with Indira in her last moments and accompanied her body to the hospital. The investigation of the assassination did not find evidence of Pakistani involvement, but many in South Asia assume that the assassins had connections to the ISI and/or the CIA. A prominent Pakistani author, Tariq Ali, has written a clever screen play suggesting such a conspiracy.[44]

Rajiv had planned to be an airline pilot and met his Italian wife while studying in the United Kingdom. On the death of his brother Sanjay, he was propelled into politics, despite the fact that he was reluctant to take up a political career and Sonia was very much against it. He would prove to be a shadow of his mother as prime minister, lacking her sharp, decisive edge, but he probably also had less her animosity toward the United States. The two leaders, Reagan and Rajiv, would separately call for a world without nuclear weapons during their political careers, but they did not make that goal part of the bilateral relationship. Reagan invited Rajiv to the White House in June 1985. The personal relationship between Reagan and Rajiv, like that between Reagan and Indira Gandhi, was positive, but little of substance followed, aside from a visit to India by Secretary of Defense Caspar Weinberger in October 1986. Shortly after his visit, the first of an American secretary of defense to India, a major crisis erupted between India and Pakistan.

Rajiv authorized a large military exercise along the Pakistan border in the fall of 1986, code-named Operation Brass Tacks. He may have intended it to discourage further Pakistani activity in Punjab among the Sikhs, but he may not have fully understood the likely impact of the exercise in Pakistan. His army commander, General Krishnaswamy Sundarji, may have had more ambitious motives, perhaps hoping that the exercise would provoke a response that would allow India to destroy Pakistan's nascent nuclear program as Israel had destroyed Iraq's program in 1981. Sundarji would later write a novel making the case that Indian decisionmaking on nuclear issues was muddled and ill informed and that the army should be given a greater voice in strategic planning.[45] Whatever India's motives—and they were clearly muddled—the deployment in January 1987 of two armored divisions, one mechanized division, and six infantry divisions along the border with lots of supporting air power prompted a major Pakistani response.

Both sides' militaries were deployed in dangerous postures. In Washington, the CIA was warning that war was possible. Reagan and Casey feared that an Indo-Pakistani war would only play into the hands of the Soviets and undermine the Afghan war. Washington urged restraint on both sides. Fortunately, cooler heads prevailed, and Zia and Rajiv backed away from conflict. Zia accepted an invitation to attend a cricket match in Jaipur, India, in February, and the meeting in the stands between Zia and Rajiv lowered tensions considerably. Not for the last time, cricket diplomacy offered a way to avoid potential disaster in the subcontinent.[46]

Rajiv made a second visit to Washington in the fall of 1987, but once again the visit was more show than substance. He lost his bid for reelection in December 1989. By then Reagan had left the Oval Office and Vice President George Bush was elected president in his place. Reagan had decisively tilted the United States toward Zia and Pakistan during his tenure; together the two had won the war in Afghanistan and set the stage for the collapse of the Union of Soviet Socialist Republics and the end of the cold war. Yet Reagan ignored the Kashmir issue entirely. The American-Pakistani alliance had been built on sand, with a time bomb, Pakistan's nuclear program, ticking beneath the surface. It exploded on Bush's watch.

CHAPTER FIVE

FROM CRISIS TO CRISIS: BUSH AND CLINTON

THE OFFICE OF the deputy national security adviser to the president of the United States is tiny. In many American homes, the walk-in closets are larger. But in the White House, proximity is power, and the deputy sits near his boss, the national security adviser to the president, who has a much more spacious, lavish office in the corner of the West Wing directly across from the Oval Office. In the fall of 1991, the deputy national security adviser was Robert Gates, a career CIA officer who had been chosen by Brent Scowcroft to be his deputy in 1989. Gates was meeting with General Sunith Francis Rodrigues, chief of army staff of the Indian army. I was the note taker for the meeting. General Rodrigues—an Indian soldier of Portuguese descent who was a graduate of the Royal College of Defence Studies in London (formerly the Imperial War College)—had been decorated for his service in the 1971 war with Pakistan and had become commander of the Indian army in June 1990. He was visiting Washington to improve military-to-military relations between India and the United States.

After welcoming Rodrigues, Gates began to urge that India sign the Treaty on the Non-Proliferation of Nuclear Weapons (NPT) and keep its nuclear program strictly peaceful. Rodrigues interrupted Gates almost immediately, leaning toward him across his desk in the cramped office and asking, "Why are you reading me these talking points? This is the only message we ever hear from Americans," he said. "You speak about the importance of the NPT and want us to give up the nuclear option. America is the only country ever to use the bomb on an enemy, and you have built thousands of them. Yet you tell us not to do what you have done! And you turn a blind eye to Israel's possession of nuclear weapons and its refusal to sign the NPT! And you give Pakistan the combat aircraft, F-16s, to deliver its nuclear attack on our cities!"

In essence, Rodrigues's argument was about the fairness of the post–World War II world order. The five victors in the war are all nuclear weapons states, with their rights to the bomb institutionalized in the Treaty on the Non-Proliferation of Nuclear Weapons (Nuclear Non-Proliferation Treaty) and in their permanent seats on the UN Security Council. Other states, like India, were expected to accept second-tier status and to forgo nuclear weapons. India, which did not exist as a state in 1945, when the United Nations was created and the modern order established, found that policy to be both hypocritical and unfair. As the world's largest democracy, it feels that it has a right to be on the Security Council; in fact, many Indians argue that they have more right to a seat than their former colonial masters, Britain and France. The general was simply more passionate in his denunciation of the new world order than the mostly soft-spoken Indian diplomats.

Bob Gates is a cool customer, and he did not lose his composure. He knew his message was not going to be well received. It had been America's message to India and Pakistan for more than a decade; I had heard it and the responses to it over and over again. From the end of the war against the Soviets in Afghanistan until 9/11, the nuclear issue had dominated American diplomacy in South Asia. It came to dominate the bilateral agenda and sometimes forced every other issue off the menu at high-level meetings. Nonproliferation was the centerpiece of American policy to deal with India and Pakistan. Two presidencies were dominated by the nonproliferation issue, those of George H. W. Bush and Bill Clinton, despite their efforts to broaden the discussion.

And the policy largely failed. America proved powerless to stop India and Pakistan; both tested devices in May 1998 and blew their way into the nuclear club. But America did help prevent the two from using their nuclear arsenals against each other. From 1990 to 2000 India and Pakistan lurched from crisis to crisis, fighting one small war and almost going to war several other times. In each crisis, Washington would be a key player, keeping the worst—nuclear war in South Asia—from happening.

BUSH PREOCCUPIED; PAKISTAN BETRAYED AGAIN

George Bush was better prepared for the foreign policy challenges of the new post–cold war world than almost any other president. He had been director of the CIA, ambassador to China and to the United Nations, and vice president of the country; as vice president, he had visited South Asia in May 1984. He was well traveled and knew almost every world leader. America was indeed fortunate to have such an experienced hand in the Oval Office. The world was transformed on his watch, and he guided America through the transformation with great skill. The Soviet army left Afghanistan on February 15, 1989. Shortly after it began leaving, the Warsaw Pact nations in Eastern Europe crumbled along with the Berlin Wall. The cold war was over, and within three years the Soviet Union had vanished. At the same time, there was major unrest in China and Iraq invaded Kuwait, an action that was followed by a UN–sanctioned war to liberate the emirate. Given all the global change it is not surprising that South Asia got only limited attention from the Bush White House. No member of his cabinet visited South Asia in the first two years of his term. Vice President Dan Quayle made one short visit to India in May 1991 for the funeral of Rajiv Gandhi; Bush himself never went. In his memoirs, written with his brilliant national security adviser Brent Scowcroft, India is mentioned only once and Pakistan not at all.

India also was changing. After Rajiv lost his bid for reelection in December 1989, a coalition Indian government was formed, led by V. P. Singh. Since 1971 New Delhi had looked to Moscow as its most important foreign friend, and now, as the Soviet Union collapsed, India struggled to find its foreign policy ground. The Indian economy was badly damaged by the loss of Russian markets and then by the rise in oil prices brought on by the war in Kuwait. Spare parts for India's Soviet-supplied jets, tanks, and other equipment became hard to acquire in the confusion surrounding the breakup of the USSR. Most important, Zia's investment in building an insurgency in Kashmir had finally paid off. A major insurrection against Indian rule erupted in 1989, and soon the Indian government was confronted with angry young Kashmiri Muslims, backed by the ISI, who were fighting for their freedom.

After Zia's death, Pakistan too was in turmoil. The army chose not to put forward a new military dictator and to allow elections instead. Just after Bush's election victory in November 1988, Pakistanis voted for a new prime minister. The contest was between two leaders who would dominate Pakistani elections for the next quarter-century; indeed, they were the only two serious candidates on the top of the Pakistani ballot for the next quarter-century. The loser in 1988 was the army's preferred candidate, Nawaz Sharif, a Punjabi industrialist who had been groomed by Zia to be a future leader. Benazir Bhutto, Zulfikar Bhutto's daughter, was the winner. At thirty-five years of age, she became the first woman elected to run Pakistan. A Harvard graduate, she knew America better than any Pakistani leader before or since. She later said that her four years at Harvard were the happiest of her life, and that was almost certainly true. When she was a child, her father was arrested, tortured, and hanged. She herself spent six years either under house arrest or in prison. For a time she was in solitary confinement in a windowless cell in the Sindh desert, which she described in her first memoir as an "oven." In 1984 Zia finally let her go into exile, but the next year her brother Shahnawaz was poisoned in Nice, France, allegedly by an agent sent by Zia. In 1987, a year before her election, she married Asif Ali Zardari, a wealthy businessman with a reputation for corruption and ruthlessness. Her other brother, Murtaza, died in Karachi in 1996 in a shootout with the police; her own niece suspects that her husband was responsible.[1]

Benazir and Bush met early into their new jobs in February 1989, at the funeral of the emperor of Japan in Tokyo. Bush was impressed by the young prime minister and eager to continue America's entente with Pakistan to help it make the transition into a stable, healthy democracy. Benazir was invited to the White House for the first state visit of a foreign leader during the Bush administration, and when she arrived in early June 1989, finishing the Afghan project started by Reagan and Zia was at the top of the agenda. Bush welcomed Benazir publicly by praising that joint effort, but he stressed that "the job is not done."[2] The war in Afghanistan was expected to end quickly, with the Russians leaving. The CIA and ISI expected that the communist government in Kabul would then collapse quickly and that afterward America and Pakistan would help install a new government in Kabul to help bring stability to South Asia. It did not work out that way.

The largest supply depot for the arms used in ISI's war in Afghanistan was located just outside Rawalpindi at the Ojhri ammunition storage facility. On April 10, 1988, it was racked by a massive explosion. Ten thousand tons of arms and ammunition were expended in a massive series of rippling explosions.[3] While most of the arms were for the Afghan mujahedin, the ISI had used the same site to store equipment for the Kashmiri jihad. More than a hundred people died in the disaster, including five ISI officers. In 2012 two former Indian officers told me that it was their service that sabotaged the facility to punish Pakistan for helping the Kashmiri and Sikh rebels. The Indian intelligence service believed that the destruction of the stockpile would set back the ISI Kashmir campaign and cripple the ISI.[4] That did not work out as planned either.

In Srinagar, the capital of Indian Kashmir, the crowds blamed India and riots broke out, the opening salvo in what would become a rapidly building insurgency against the presence of the Indian army.[5] It was a harbinger of how Zia's jihad would now spread east, as he had always wanted. Among his last acts before his death, in 1988 Zia ordered the ISI to step up support for the Kashmiri insurgency. Benazir inherited from Zia two jihads along with an army and an ISI that were outside her control and deeply suspicious of her. She in turn was deeply suspicious of the ISI and the army, which she despised from her years in prison and in exile after her father's execution. She felt her election victory had come despite a concerted effort by the ISI, Jamaat-e-Islami, and Osama bin Laden to back her opponent, Nawaz Sharif, and defeat her.[6] After she was in office, the ISI told her that the mujahedin would sweep to victory quickly once the last Soviet soldier left Afghanistan in 1989, and the CIA gave President Bush the same estimate.[7] However, the communist government in Kabul, which did not fall from power until 1992, would actually outlive the Union of Soviet Socialist Republics.

One reason was a strategic miscalculation by the new ISI director, Hamid Gul. Gul decided that because the Soviets were gone, the mujahedin should shift from guerilla to conventional warfare. The first target would be the city of Jalalabad, on the road from the Khyber Pass to Kabul. The American ambassador to Pakistan, Robert Oakley, endorsed the idea. The siege that followed was a terrible mistake. The Afghan communist army held off the mujahedin, and the stalemate led to bitter recriminations within the mujahedin factions. After the debacle, Bhutto engineered Gul's removal from the ISI leadership, firing him just before her visit to Washington. Gul would go on to be a public advocate for the Taliban, the Kashmiri insurgency, and Osama bin Laden. After 9/11, he would claim that the attacks were the work of the Israeli intelligence service, the Mossad, and an excuse for the American intervention in Afghanistan.[8] Just before her assassination in 2007, Bhutto claimed that he was plotting her murder.[9]

While the Afghan insurgency stalled, the Kashmiri insurgency blossomed, much of it the result of indigenous Kashmiri anger at years of heavy-handed oppression by India. In 1988, 1989, and 1990, the bottled-up anger of the Kashmiri Muslim population exploded into riots and violence, incidents of which rose from 390 in 1988 to 2,100 in 1989 and to almost 4,000 in 1990.[10] Hafiz Saeed's Lashkar-e-Tayyiba began setting up its infrastructure inside Kashmir, and its camps in Afghanistan and Pakistan trained hundreds of militants;[11] according to one estimate, 200,000 militants went through its training camps in the ensuing two decades.[12] The ISI had to play catch-up to regain control of the movement. The insurgency was dominated at first by the Jammu Kashmir Liberation Front, which was dangerously independent of the ISI. Zia's clients, the Jamaat-e-Islami and Lashkar-e-Tayyiba, were still relatively small players struggling to expand their sphere of influence. Indeed, "what the ISI wanted to prevent, above all else, was the creation of a separate state in Kashmir that would include both the Pakistani and Indian controlled sections of Kashmir, which was precisely the JKLF's goal."[13] As many as 180 different splinter groups sprouted up in Kashmir to fight the Indians, and the fracturing of the insurgents ultimately helped the ISI regain control of the insurgency. The ISI moved quickly to support the dozens of new groups, which the JKLF had found very difficult to control, and gradually moved to isolate the JKLF and take over. It set up an umbrella group, Hizbul Mujahedin, to unite the pro-Pakistan elements and then cut off aid to the JKLF. The JKLF tried to appeal directly to Benazir to overrule the ISI, but the ISI blocked any communications between the insurgents and the prime minister. The insurgent factions began to fight not only the Indians but each other, and the infighting became violent. In the end, the ISI succeeded in gaining effective control of the militants, although it never fully controlled all elements of the insurgency.[14]

Some of the ISI's insurgents would become famous figures in their own right. Perhaps the best example is Muhammad Ilyas

Kashmiri. Born in Kashmir on February 10, 1964, he joined the Afghan war against the Soviets in the 1980s. Kashmiri trained in the ISI border camps in North Waziristan; according to some accounts, he received training with the elite Special Services Group of the Pakistani army. He was involved in several years of combat, in which he lost an eye and a finger. After the defeat of the Soviets, Kashmiri turned his attention to his homeland, where, with ISI assistance, he formed a militant group known as the 313 Brigade, a unit that made itself famous by harassing and attacking the Indian army. In 1991, he was captured and spent two years in an Indian prison before escaping.

In 1994, Kashmiri took the war into India proper. A team of his men kidnapped several Western tourists and held them for ransom in a safe house near New Delhi, demanding the release of a senior Kashmiri militant, Maulana Masood Azhar, who had been arrested in Kashmir early in the year. The Indian army tracked down the band and raided the house, but Kashmiri escaped. His campaigns in Kashmir made him a hero in the ISI. In 2000, he brought the severed head of an Indian soldier to ISI headquarters in Islamabad. On several occasions, both General Pervez Musharraf, the dictator of Pakistan at the time, and Lieutenant General Mahmud Ahmed, then head of the ISI, personally thanked him for his accomplishments in the jihad.[15]

The growing tension in Kashmir exacerbated Indo-Pakistani tensions. By August 1989 India was reinforcing its already large troop presence in the province to suppress the unrest, using a very heavy hand. Indian troops engaged in massive and sustained human rights violations against the Kashmiri people, and hundreds died in extra-legal killings; even more disappeared with no explanation. The brutal Indian response just encouraged more violence and desperation. New Delhi accused Islamabad of helping the insurgents. In December 1989, Pakistan responded with a massive military exercise, deploying 200,000 ground troops and virtually the entire Pakistani air force in a display of its might and determination.[16]

The rhetoric heated up on both sides. On March 13, 1990, Benazir Bhutto said that Pakistan would fight for a "thousand years" to free Kashmir, and the two countries seemed to be heading toward war. To calm the waters, President Bush dispatched deputy national security adviser Robert Gates and Richard Haass, the senior director for Near East and South Asia affairs on the National Security Council, to the region; however, even before their trip in May, tensions began to abate. At no point did either India or Pakistan actually put their nuclear weapons on alert or start the nuclear countdown, so the crisis never got to the boiling point. But it was sufficiently alarming that Bush felt that he had to send Gates. It would be not be the first or the last time that the two countries seemed to be heading toward war because of Pakistan-based terrorism.[17]

After the crisis faded, the army and Pakistan's president, Ghulam Ishaq Khan, moved to oust Benazir Bhutto from office, alleging corruption. New elections were held, and the ISI worked actively to help elect Nawaz Sharif, the Zia protégé whom Bhutto had defeated earlier. According to Husain Haqqani, Pakistan's future ambassador to the United States, Hamid Gul, a former ISI chief, ran the anti-Bhutto campaign for the army. The campaign included allegations that Bhutto had "strong Zionist links" and was too pro-American.[18] Bhutto's suspicions of what the ISI and the army would do to her proved later to be all too accurate.

Before Sharif took office, the bottom fell out of the U.S.-Pakistan relationship. The spring 1990 crisis and the Gates-Haass trip to the region had contributed to the growing sense in Washington that Pakistan had the bomb; after all, why was Bush worried about a possible nuclear exchange in South Asia if Pakistan did not have the capability? In October 1990, President Bush reported to Congress that he could not certify that Pakistan was abiding by U.S. legislative requirements not to cross the nuclear threshold—saying, in effect, that Pakistan had the bomb. Under the Pressler amendment, all U.S. foreign assistance to Pakistan had to be halted immediately.

Even equipment paid for, like F-16 fighter jets, could not be delivered. Pakistanis argued that the United States just did not need their country any longer because the Soviets were in retreat. Many, if not most, felt then and now that the United States used the nuclear issue as a means to dispense with helping Pakistan; after all, they claimed (correctly), Washington had known of Pakistan's nuclear ambitions under Zia but pretended that the country had not gone over the threshold. Others would say that the Afghan war had provided Zia with crucial cover in Washington to build the bomb without American sanctions. A. Q. Khan, for example, has said that he urged Zia to test a bomb in 1984 but that Zia told him to wait while the war continued. As Khan concluded, "had the Afghan war not taken place, we would not have been able to make the bomb as early as we did given the U.S. and European pressure on our program."[19]

Sharif, the new prime minister, thus found himself inheriting the two jihads but without the support of the United States that Zia and Benazir had enjoyed. Sharif was very dependent on the ISI and the army as well as the religious parties for his position. Some former ISI officers have even alleged that Sharif reached out to Osama bin Laden in early 1990 for assistance and secretly met with bin Laden in Saudi Arabia, where he had returned after the withdrawal of the Soviets from Afghanistan.[20] However, those accusations have not been proven; they probably were part of a later smear campaign against Nawaz that occurred after the army broke with him in 1999. Sharif's new ISI commander was Lieutenant General Javid Nasir, a self-proclaimed Islamist who was very eager to prosecute the wars east and west.

The Afghan war came to a climax in April 1992, when a key Uzbek commander in the communist army, Abdul Rashid Dostum, broke ranks and defected with his supporters to the mujahedin. The communist government collapsed quickly from within, and Kabul finally fell to the mujahedin. After twelve years it appeared that Zia's jihad had triumphed, but it was an empty triumph. The mujahedin fell to fighting among themselves, and the brutal and bloody civil war that followed continues until today. Pakistan found itself backing its major clients in the mujahedin, especially Gulbuddin Hekmatyar's primarily Pashtun group, against the other mujahedin factions, especially that led by Ahmad Shah Massoud, a Tajik, and Dostum's Uzbek faction. The civil war was incredibly complex, with players often switching sides, and much violence was directed against civilians. Afghanistan was descending into anarchy, hardly the vision of a Pakistani ally that could provide strategic depth for Islamabad against India. And by now, the Kashmir war was a stalemate. India had a half-million men in the province, and while violence levels had peaked, they remained high.

Pakistani politics then turned to another of the mysteries in the nation's history. The chief of army staff, General Asif Nawaz, suddenly died on January 8, 1993. His wife suggested that he had been poisoned and that Prime Minister Nawaz Sharif may have been part of the conspiracy to kill him. Asif Nawaz had taken command determined to get the army out of politics. In his first order of the day, he said that it was time for the army to return to the business of being a professional military and to allow the democratic process to work, and he tried to persuade Nawaz Sharif and Benazir Bhutto to reconcile for the good of the nation.[21] Asif also was concerned by the deteriorating security situation in the country's only port, Karachi, where sectarian violence was getting out of control, and he was increasingly said to be concerned that the prime minister was not up to the job. His mysterious death has never been fully explained, but it would usher in yet another change at the top.[22] Nawaz Sharif was removed by the president for corruption, just as Benazir had been, and for failure to investigate Asif's mysterious death adequately, and new elections were held in 1993.

By 1993, Bush was no longer president; Bill Clinton had defeated him in the 1992 elections. During the campaign, Clinton had stressed domestic issues—"It's the economy stupid"—not foreign policy. Bush had done a superb job of managing most of

America's foreign policy challenges in the transition from the end of the cold war to the era that followed. South Asia, however, had not been one of his strong points. For perhaps understandable reasons, he had largely neglected India altogether. India was pre-occupied with itself—with its economic crisis, with the collapse of its Soviet friendship treaty, and with forming a stable government. Bush had hoped to build a new relationship with Pakistan, but his courtship of Benazir Bhutto failed when she could not control the ISI and the jihadi monster that America had helped to create. But Bush, Gates, and Haass had kept the region from nuclear disaster.

CLINTON'S FIRST TERM

Although Clinton was elected for his stance on domestic issues, he was fascinated by India, and he believed that India was certain to be a major global player in the twenty-first century. His emphasis on economics helped him to see better than his predecessors that India was bound to prosper once it allowed its entrepreneurs the freedom to invest and develop. The star of the Indian government in the early 1990s was Manmohan Singh, who served as finance minister from June 1991 to May 1996. In those five years he trans-formed the Indian economy by opening it up to outside investment and reducing, though but not eliminating, government regulations and controls. Singh was born in what would become Pakistani Punjab into a Sikh family that moved to India after partition. He was educated at Cambridge and Oxford. On opposite sides of the globe, both Singh and Clinton were trying to transform their country's economy, and Clinton followed Singh's economic poli-cies closely during his first term in the White House. Clinton was eager to build a new partnership with New Delhi and became more interested as he watched Singh open up and transform India.

Clinton's fascination with India went back to his student days at Oxford in the late 1960s, according to his friend and confi-dant Strobe Talbott. His interest in India and South Asia con-tinued when he became governor of Arkansas, a poor Southern state. Clinton was intrigued by the experiments in microcredit in Bangladesh conducted by Muhammad Yunus (a future winner of the Nobel Peace Prize), for example, and tried to import them to Arkansas. When he became president in 1993, Clinton focused on domestic issues, but from his very first days in office, he looked forward to a trip to India. In March 1995 his wife, Hillary, traveled to the subcontinent, and her report on the trip only increased his interest.[23] But once again, Pakistan was a more pressing immediate concern. The president believed that the Pressler amendment was profoundly unfair. The United States was not only refusing to deliver the F-16s, it would not refund the money that Pakistan had paid for them. On top of that, the United States was charging Pakistan the cost of storing and maintaining them at an American air force base. To Clinton all of this seemed like overkill. When Benazir Bhutto was reelected to office in the fall of 1993, Clinton invited her to Washington. When she arrived in April 1995, she found a receptive Clinton.

It was unfair for the United States to sanction Pakistan by both freezing delivery of the F-16s and refusing to return the money that Pakistan paid for them, but the president's hands were tied. The Pressler amendment was very clear: once the president no longer certified that Pakistan did not have the bomb, it was illegal to provide any assistance to Pakistan and, according to government lawyers, even returning its money was a violation of the law of the land. Although Clinton sympathized with the prime minister in private and even in public, she went home largely empty handed. A single-minded preoccupation with nuclear nonproliferation had locked the U.S. government in a position in which it could not help the struggling democracy in Pakistan, and it was losing the effort to block the development of nuclear weapons.

One member of the president's cabinet who was especially outraged by the situation was his secretary of defense, William Perry. Perry believed strongly that nuclear war was a real possibility in South Asia—indeed, over time, a probability. A student of nuclear planning and decisionmaking, Perry was intensely frustrated that the United States was doing little to reduce the likelihood of catastrophe while it stuck to stale talking points to lecture India and Pakistan, as Gates had done with Rodrigues. Perry was especially eager to change American policy and undo the Pressler amendment after the CIA detected preparations for a nuclear test in India in December 1995. The CIA's warning was leaked to the *New York Times,* and Clinton's ambassador in New Delhi, Frank Wisner, used the leak to persuade India not to test. However, it was a close call with bringing the bomb out of the closet and into the open in a dramatic nuclear test.

As secretary of defense, Perry could not change the law or abandon American arms control policy, but he could try to develop richer and more extensive military-to-military relations with India and Pakistan. With encouragement from the White House during Clinton's first term, Perry brought senior defense officials from the Pentagon together with their Indian and Pakistani counterparts on a regular basis in separate bilateral forums held both in Washington and in New Delhi and Islamabad. It was a first in U.S.-Indian relations and a partial warming of U.S.–Pakistani relations. Perry traveled to the region in January 1995 to put his personal stamp on the process and outlined his thinking in a speech later that month. He began by stressing the importance of security in South Asia, noting that India and Pakistan had fought three wars before each acquired nuclear capability. He argued that "a fourth India-Pakistan war would not be just a tragedy—it could be a catastrophe." To avert it, the United States needed to engage the militaries of both states to encourage restraint. With India, "it was a matter of building a defense relationship almost from scratch." He quoted a letter from John Kenneth Galbraith to President Kennedy in 1962 in which he stated that "politics is not the art of the possible, rather it consists of choosing between the disastrous and the unpalatable."[24] Perry was convinced that South Asia was headed toward nuclear disaster if the United States did not take action to end Indo-Pakistani tensions; sooner or later, the nuclear nightmare would explode. Perry tasked me, as his deputy assistant secretary of defense for the Near East and South Asia, with helping to build new ties between New Delhi and Islamabad.

Perry energetically lobbied on Capitol Hill for some relief from the Pressler amendment. He was joined by Robin Raphel, the first assistant secretary of state for South Asia affairs, a position that had been created at the behest of Congress at the end of the Bush administration. Bush and his secretary of state, James Baker, were against creating a separate bureau for South Asia, but Bush was unwilling to use the veto to stop it. The Perry-Raphel team got limited relief for Pakistan when Congress passed the Brown amendment, named for Hank Brown, a Republican senator from Colorado, which allowed some assistance, including economic aid and equipment such as naval patrol aircraft. However, the amendment did not touch on the most toxic issue, the F-16s. India's supporters on the Hill fought even the small steps that Brown had supported.

Benazir Bhutto also pushed the administration to recognize the new government in Afghanistan. The civil war between the mujahedin factions finally produced a new player, the Taliban, an extreme Muslim movement for law and order. The Taliban—translated literally as "students"—emerged suddenly in Kandahar province, in southern Afghanistan, born of the frustration of Pashtuns who were sick and tired of endless feuding among the warlords. Led by Mullah Omar, the group dispensed quick justice based on Islamic and Pashtun law and practices. The ISI quickly saw the power of the new movement. The ISI had ties with Mullah Omar going back to his training in ISI camps during the war against the Soviets. A Taliban-run Afghanistan would end the chaos next door, stabilize Pakistan's western border, and open trade and transit routes to Central Asia, a new market for Pakistan. With ISI help, the Taliban expanded rapidly in southern Afghanistan in 1994, capturing Kandahar and moving to the outskirts of Kabul. Benazir agreed to support the ISI on this issue even though ideologically, the Taliban were her enemy. In 1995 Benazir Bhutto pushed Clinton to reopen the American embassy in Kabul and recognize the Taliban as the legitimate government of the country. Her request was, of course, deeply ironic in that as a progressive woman in politics who was a fighter for women's rights, she represented much of what the Taliban hated. Clinton held back recognition, influenced by Hillary Clinton, who was hearing alarming reports about the fate of women in the new regime: schools were being shut to girls, women were being fired from their jobs, and justice was gender biased. Benazir's second term in office did not last long. On November 6, 1996, the president again dismissed her government. Once again, the choice on the ballot was the same as it had been twice before. This time Nawaz Sharif beat Bhutto, winning the February 1997 elections.

At the start of his second term in office, Clinton had little to show for four years of effort in South Asia. India and America were still estranged, and Pakistan and America were at odds over nuclear weapons, Afghanistan, and the aging F-16 aircraft.

1998: THE YEAR OF CHANGE

Clinton's second inauguration in 1997 also marked the fiftieth birthday of both India and Pakistan. During those fifty years, however, American diplomacy had produced little in the way of enduring relationships with the two powers of the subcontinent. Bill Clinton was determined to do better, and his second term should rightly be marked as the turning point in the American encounter with South Asia and with India in particular. Ironically, it would be decisions made in New Delhi about testing nuclear weapons that would make change between Washington and New Delhi possible. It was Clinton's genius to recognize that in adversity, opportunity beckoned.

Engagement with South Asia began slowly in Clinton's second term. While the president was more focused on advancing the stalled Middle East peace process and the ongoing crises in Iraq and the Balkans, he decided to make South Asia a priority for his annual trip to New York for the UN General Assembly. World leaders gather there every September, each giving a speech to the assembly and having side meetings with other world leaders. For an American president, it is an easy way to see a lot of foreign leaders without having to deal with the protocol of White House visits. Clinton had decided to see both Pakistan's prime minister, Nawaz Sharif, and India's prime minister, I. K. Gujral. I was the note taker for both sessions.

It was Clinton's first face-to-face meeting with Nawaz Sharif, and they got along fine. Clinton repeated his irritation with the constraints of the Pressler amendment, vowed to try to do more to remove it, and urged Sharif to control the proliferation of nuclear technology from Pakistan. The president said that he hoped to visit Pakistan during his second term. It was also Clinton's first meeting with Gujral, who had just come into office. Gujral had written a book on Indian foreign policy that advocated building better ties to the country's neighbors, and Clinton hoped that in him he would find a kindred spirit. The soft-spoken Gujral was famously prone to speak in a very low voice, but that day he outdid himself. It was very difficult to understand him. Clinton leaned in closer to hear, and I leaned over the president, all to no avail. When the meeting was over, the president turned to me and said that he looked forward to reading the memorandum of the conversation to find out what the prime minister had said. He was disappointed. I couldn't hear Gujral either.

The summitry in New York set the stage for a follow-on trip to the region by Clinton's ambassador to the UN, Bill Richardson, in April 1998. In the interim, Gujral lost in an election to the Bharatiya Janata Party (BJP), or Indian People's Party, in early 1998. The BJP, India's second-largest party, stands politically to the right of the Congress Party, its traditional rival. It is often labeled a Hindu nationalist party, a title that it rejects, and it is frequently criticized as excessively nationalist and anti-Muslim. Fortunately, the State Department's intelligence staff included a real expert on the BJP, Walter Anderson, who would be invaluable in the next couple of years as an adviser on the party. At the White House, I had urged Clinton and Sandy Berger, his national security adviser, to follow the BJP's progress closely. I warned that a BJP government might be difficult to work with given the party's background and its promises over the years to develop a more muscular nuclear policy. At the National Security Council's 1998 New Year's retreat, I predicted that the BJP would probably win the February elections and proceed to challenge the global nonproliferation regime by openly developing a nuclear weapons arsenal. That said, I did not anticipate just how quickly the new government, led by Prime Minister Atal Behari Vajpayee, would move to test India's nuclear weapons once in office.

Richardson's trip became a reconnaissance mission to determine the intentions of the new BJP-led coalition government in New Delhi. In addition to Richardson, the new assistant secretary for South Asia, Karl (Rick) Inderfurth was on the trip. Rick had served on Carter's National Security Council and had traveled with Carter in 1978 on his last trip as president to New Delhi. More recently, he had been in New York as Madeleine Albright's deputy at the UN during Clinton's first term. After a stopover in Bangladesh, the Richardson team arrived in New Delhi on April 14, 1998. Vajpayee proved to be almost as soft spoken as Gujral. Vajpayee had been prime minister briefly once before, for thirteen days in 1996 when the BJP came in first in an election but could not form a stable coalition. He had also served as foreign minister in the Desai government in the 1970s. He was experienced and rightly regarded as one of the most thoughtful and moderate voices in the BJP. He assured Richardson that India was not intent on making any dangerous changes in its foreign policy and that he looked forward to working with Clinton. The Indian message was that no surprises were in the works and that the BJP would carefully study its options regarding the bomb.

At the end of a long day of talks with officials of the new government, an additional meeting was put on our calendar on short notice, without any press coverage. Jaswant Singh, Vajpayee's close aide and confidant, came to Roosevelt House, the ambassador's residence, to call on us. His message was simple: India wanted a good relationship with America, and the prime minister wanted a direct channel to the White House. Singh suggested that he and I should be that channel. If any issue arose that needed urgent direct attention from Vajpayee and Clinton, the two of us could speak immediately to get messages to our bosses. It seemed to be an important gesture that would reassure those who were worried about the BJP's intentions. Richardson went on to Islamabad and Kabul next.

Then, on May 11, 1998, less than a month later, India tested three nuclear weapons in the Rajasthan desert at Pokhran. On May 13, it tested two more. The U.S. intelligence community was caught completely off guard. The CIA would later conclude after a post-mortem that it also had been misled by Indian officials, who had engaged in careful deceptive practices at the test facility, having learned about American intelligence collection capabilities from the 1995 episode in which Ambassador Wisner had stopped a planned Indian test after it was leaked by the *New York Times*. Most work was done at night, and preparations for the test were skillfully covered up by the time that U.S. satellites scanned the site. None-theless, local residents knew something was amiss, and a small Canadian Sikh newsletter reported that test preparations were under way, but no one noticed. Vajpayee and Singh had pulled off a diplomatic and intelligence coup and surprised the world with five underground nuclear tests. The era of nuclear ambiguity in South Asia was over.

Clinton was furious at India, the CIA, and everyone else. The tests tied his hands. Under existing legislation, he had no choice but to impose harsh sanctions on India. Aid would be cut off and military-to-military ties broken, and Washington would have to vote against loans to India at the World Bank and other interna-tional financial institutions. He was especially upset because one of the signature accomplishments of his first term was the conclusion of the Comprehensive Test Ban Treaty (CTBT), which, on September 26, 1996, he had been the first world leader to sign. JFK had started on the road to the CTBT in 1963, and Clinton rightly regarded it as a major step toward making the world safer. Now it was in deep trouble, and rather than planning a trip to South Asia, he was imposing tough sanctions on India.

The Indians justified their tests by pointing to China, not Pakistan. They reminded the world that they had been attacked by China in 1962 and that China had tested its bomb in 1965. As recently as 1987, there had been another flare-up on the border at Wangdung Ridge, where each deployed 60,000 troops in an uneasy standoff.[25] In the first visit to China by an Indian prime minister since the 1962 war, Rajiv Gandhi had traveled to Beijing the next year to try to reduce tensions. Negotiations to permanently settle the border conflict began in 1991, but it still is not resolved. By putting its test in the context of its relations with China, India was arguing that it was a major global power in the league of the P5, the permanent members of the UN Security Council. For its part, the Security Council unanimously condemned the test on June 6, 1998, in Resolution 1172. The resolution demanded no further tests, a halt to development of nuclear-capable ballistic missiles, and a halt to production of fissile material for weapons. It encouraged India and Pakistan to address "the root causes of the tensions between them, including Kashmir."[26]

By then Pakistan had followed India's lead. It was virtually certain that Islamabad would do so, but the Clinton team tried to head it off. Deputy Secretary of State Strobe Talbott was given the mission impossible assignment. Strobe, Rick, and I flew to Pakistan on the airplane of CENTOM's commander, General Anthony Zinni. It was then the oldest aircraft in the U.S. air force, and the trip from Tampa took forever. Sharif and his cabinet were in turmoil. The Pakistani media and elite wanted an immediate, powerful response to India's tests. The scientists, including A. Q. Khan, were pushing for permission to test. The Foreign Ministry was screaming for tests. Only the chief of army staff, General Karamat, was cool-headed, but he knew that Sharif had no choice but to test or lose all credibility at home, so there was no reason to be excited. Foreign Minister Gohar Ayub told Talbott that "now that India has barged its way into becoming the world's sixth nuclear power, it will not stop there. It will force itself into permanent membership of the UN Security Council."[27]

The forlorn hope of the Talbott team was to offer Sharif billions in new economic and military aid, a promise to get the F-16s released from Pressler prison, international support, and a state visit to the White House with all the panoply possible. Sharif asked for American arbitration of the Kashmir dispute and a promise that Clinton would visit only Pakistan, not India. Before we had left Islamabad for the flight back to Tampa, he had told the army and scientists to test. They did so on May 28 and 30, after briefly floating a warning that Israel and India were planning a surprise attack on Pakistan's nuclear facilities. That was just smokescreen for what Sharif announced as a "New Clear Vision" for Pakistan!

THE TALBOTT MISSION

What came next was the most serious and substantive American engagement with South Asia to that point. For the next two years, South Asia, especially India but also Pakistan, went to the top of the American presidential agenda as never before or since. The effort failed to achieve its stated goals; it did not implement Resolution 1172, for example. But what it did do was to transform American-Indian relations profoundly. Clinton got what he wanted, a new day in America's relations with India, though not the way that he wanted it.

Strobe Talbott led the Clinton effort. As an old friend, he had a direct line to the president, but he worked carefully to keep Berger and Secretary of State Madeleine Albright fully in the loop. Over the course of the next two and a half years, Strobe met with his

Indian counterpart, Jaswant Singh, fourteen times at ten locations in seven countries on three continents. As he has written in his artful memoir, the dialogue added up to "the most intense and prolonged set of exchanges ever between American and Indian officials."[28] There was a parallel effort with Pakistan, but, as events unfolded, it never gained the same traction. The Indians had initiated the dialogue through an indirect approach to me by an American expert on nuclear issues, George Perkovich, who had traveled to India after the tests as part of the research for his masterful study on Indian nuclear decisionmaking. He interviewed Singh, who stressed that now that India had tested its nuclear capability, it would observe a unilateral moratorium on further tests and wanted to talk to the White House about the Comprehensive Test Ban Treaty. Perkovich asked me whether Singh would be received positively; I replied that he would. Tempers were still hot, but Clinton wanted to get back to business. Singh came to Washington shortly afterward for the first round of talks, right after Resolution 1172 was adopted. The two diplomats found each other to be not just counterparts but intriguing partners. They set a tone for the dialogue that followed that was serious and straightforward and that also emphasized trying to understand each country's individual needs and policies. Lectures were kept to a minimum; conversation was encouraged. After the June meeting in Washington, the two diplomats and their teams met in Frankfurt, Germany, on July 9, 1998, and then in New Delhi on July 20.

Strobe pocketed the unilateral moratorium and pressed India to take several steps to underscore its restraint in the nuclear field. Some were relatively easy, such as taking steps to ensure that Indian nuclear technology did not end up in the hands of third parties. That was a huge problem with Pakistan, which was selling its expertise to almost any buyer, from North Korea to Iran. India had a much better, almost perfect, track record. On this issue, Strobe was pushing on an open door, but the effort to get India to sign and ratify the CTBT would be much harder. To do so would look like an admission of error on India's part, and it would prevent India from conducting further tests to develop more sophisticated bombs. Neither the United States nor any of the other permanent members of the UN Security Council could claim the moral high ground on this issue. The United States had conducted 1,054 nuclear tests, using 1,151 devices (some tests used multiple devices), before halting; Russia had done so 715 times; France, 210 times; and China and the United Kingdom, 45 times each. (France and the United Kingdom had tested in countries other than their own—France in Algeria, and Britain in Australia.) India argued that the P5 were guilty of gross hypocrisy, but Jaswant said that Vajpayee wanted to find a way for India to sign and adhere to the treaty. He repeatedly suggested that it was primarily a problem of timing and domestic sensitivities, but it was hard to tell whether he was stalling or genuinely trying. He probably was doing both.

In August 1998 the whole issue was transformed. On August 7, 1998, al Qaeda terrorists simultaneously exploded truck bombs at the American embassies in Dar es Salaam, Tanzania, and Nairobi, Kenya. In Tanzania 212 died and 4,000 were wounded; in Kenya 11 died and 85 were wounded. The majority of the casualties were Africans, but twelve Americans died. In just one morning, al Qaeda went to the top of the American national security agenda. The trail led directly to Pakistan.

Literally, "al Qaeda" means "the base" in Arabic. It can refer to a physical facility, such as a camp, or it can refer to a concept, a narrative, or an idea that is the basis of something else. In this case, it refers to all of those things, but especially to the basis of global jihad. Founded by Osama bin Laden, a wealthy scion of one of the richest families in the world, al Qaeda has been based in Afghanistan and Pakistan since its foundation. The world's first truly global terrorist organization, it still commits acts of violence around the globe. Its first big assault on America took place at the U.S. embassies in East Africa.

Bin Laden had been an early recruit in the war against the Soviet Union; he first traveled to Pakistan in 1980. From the beginning of his jihad he was a known quantity to the ISI. He had helped found Lashkar-e-Tayyiba with the ISI, and he worked closely with it in the 1980s to help the mujahedin. As discussed, the ISI was preoccupied with keeping control of the war against the Soviets in Afghanistan; it did not let anything happen in the mujahedin camps that it did not want to happen. When the siege of Jalalabad failed in 1989, bin Laden went home to Saudi Arabia. He returned in 1996 from self-imposed exile in the Sudan. The ISI introduced bin Laden to its new proxy in Afghanistan, the Taliban, which provided him a safe haven. By 1998, al Qaeda was a state within a state in Afghanistan, a guest of the Taliban.[29] It operated its own training bases and a special entry and exit facility at Kabul airport, and its members traveled the country with distinctive license plates and identification papers.

The Indians were quick to connect the dots. Jaswant Singh came to Washington in August after the embassy bombings in Africa. He reminded Strobe that India had warned America in the 1980s that the war in Afghanistan was creating a "Frankenstein monster" composed of Afghan Pashtun Islamists, Muslim extremists from around the world, and the ISI. America needed to recognize that "the United States and India were on the same side in the war on terrorism—by which he meant that we should be allies against Pakistan."[30] Clinton and Talbott resisted the idea of ganging up on Pakistan, and Singh was probably not all that eager for a showdown either. But America's priority with Pakistan changed profoundly in August 1998, from counterproliferation to counterterrorism. The key to eliminating al Qaeda was shutting down its base in Afghanistan. The United States had tried to get the Taliban to do that when the Richardson team traveled to Islamabad, Kabul, and Sheberghan in northern Afghanistan to persuade the Taliban to hand bin Laden over to the Saudis or to the United States. In Islamabad they had pressed Nawaz Sharif to use Pakistan's leverage to get the Taliban to restrain bin Laden and shut down his terror gang, but Sharif offered only to help arrange meetings in Kabul with the Taliban. When Richardson met with the Taliban's second in command at the presidential palace in Kabul, he asked that bin Laden be turned over to the Saudis and pressed to have the al Qaeda state within a state shut down. The Taliban leadership was entirely negative. So, after the embassy bombings, the president tried two approaches, military and diplomatic.

A cruise missile strike, part of the military response, narrowly missed killing bin Laden on August 21, 1998, at a training camp in Afghanistan; a group of ISI officers were killed instead. The fact that the ISI was at a camp where bin Laden was visiting two weeks after the twin embassy bombings confirmed U.S. suspicions of the close links between Pakistani intelligence and al Qaeda.[31] Pakistan was not given any advance knowledge of the strike, although it was arranged for the vice chairman of the Joint Chiefs of Staff, Admiral Joe Ralston, to be in Rawalpindi as the missiles entered Pakistani territory en route to Afghanistan so that he could tell General Karamat that they were not incoming Indian missiles and so avoid inadvertently causing a war with India.

Diplomatic efforts included getting the United Nations, which had immediately condemned the embassy attacks, to demand that the Taliban take action to halt terrorist activity from its territory. In December 1998 the UN passed Resolution 1214, demanding that the Taliban take action to bring bin Laden to justice and close down al Qaeda. All states were encouraged to press the Taliban to act—a clear message to Pakistan, which provided the Taliban with free oil, thousands of recruits, and hundreds of ISI and army advisers for its military. To add to the pressure on Pakistan, Clinton invited Sharif to the United States. They met first in September 1998 at the UN General Assembly in New York and then again on December 3 at the White House. In both meetings Clinton pressed hard for Pakistan to get the Taliban to act against bin Laden. During the Oval Office visit, he had a sweetener: after eight years, the Department of Justice had concluded that Pakistan was right about the F-16s and that America should return the money that Pakistan had paid for them. The Department of Justice provided $324 million from a claims fund, and the Department of Agriculture provided $140 million in free wheat over two years to make up the difference. It was not an elegant solution to the F-16 imbroglio, but Sharif took it. He did nothing to bring the Taliban to shut down al Qaeda.

Talbott made another trip to India and Pakistan in January 1999. In India, the CTBT was still top priority; in Pakistan, it took back seat to al Qaeda. It was an unproductive trip. The crisis in Kosovo soon overwhelmed U.S. diplomacy for the next six months. Strobe and Jaswant had only one meeting in this period, in Moscow in May 1999, which was entirely unproductive. Just as the Talbott effort looked to be out of gas, Pakistan took the subcontinent to the brink of catastrophe.

THE KARGIL WAR

Bill Clinton had another encounter with Nawaz Sharif in February 1999. Both were in Amman, Jordan, for the funeral of King Hussein, one of the great men of the twentieth century. The king had been a good friend of America and Pakistan. I engineered a meeting between Clinton and Sharif in a stairwell just outside the kitchen during a reception hosted by Hussein's son, King Abdullah II. Again the president pressed Sharif on al Qaeda, but Sharif was more focused on an upcoming visit to Pakistan by Indian prime minister Vajpayee, who was going to take a bus from India to Lahore to open a new direct transportation link across the border—and possibly a new beginning in relations between India and Pakistan.

The Lahore dialogue between Sharif and Vajpayee brought a bright moment of hope to South Asia. The BJP leader talked of the "spirit of Lahore" as the beginning of a new day for the two rivals. In Amman, Clinton had encouraged Sharif to be receptive and to do all he could to make the visit a success, and Sharif did indeed play the role of a welcoming and encouraging host. The Lahore meeting was a significant step forward, and it seemed to open the door to further dialogue and expansion of trade and transit links.

However, Sharif's new chief of army staff, General Pervez Musharraf, was not on the same track. Musharraf had come to Pakistan from New Delhi in the great migration following partition. In the army, he was a hawk's hawk on India. Like General Rodrigues, Musharraf graduated from Britain's prestigious Royal College of Defence Studies, its premier military academy. At the academy Musharraf was remembered for being full of plans for how to win Pakistan's next war with India. In 1999 he tried, taking the subcontinent to the edge of Armageddon.

Musharraf's plan was to exploit a traditional stand-down in operations along the northern front line of divided Kashmir province to create a fait accompli that would force India to the bargaining table on Pakistani terms. Just north of the town of Kargil, the line of control, or cease-fire line, between the two armies is located in high mountains and ridges. In what had been the practice for half a century, every winter the armies pulled their frontline troops back from their advance posts to avoid placing the men in extreme weather conditions; in the spring, the troops returned. Musharraf chose to cheat instead, sending his troops under the command of 10th Corps commander Mahmud Ahmed into the empty Indian positions. They moved deeper and deeper, undiscovered, and ended up taking 500 square miles of Indian-occupied Kashmir. The Pakistani troops moved sufficiently forward that they were overlooking a crucial highway, Route 1, which linked the capital, Srinagar, to the easternmost parts of Kashmir, including the disputed Siachen Glacier. By controlling the heights overlooking the highway, Pakistan not only gained territory but also could cut the supply line for much of India's army in Kashmir. Musharraf apparently gambled that India would sue for peace and agree to negotiations on the status of the province. He was much influenced by India's successful grab of Siachen fifteen years before, which he regarded as a humiliation requiring redress and as a precedent for his own action.

The problem was that Musharraf did not have a plan B or a fallback option if India refused to give in. If the Indians decided not to talk and to fight instead, they could try to storm the occupied heights or open a new front somewhere else to take pressure off their Kargil positions. In short, India could widen the war. If it did, then Pakistan would find itself facing a broader military campaign and blamed for starting a dangerous new conflict. And that is what happened.

Former Pakistani heads of state, including Zia and Benazir, had previously rejected such risky plans for precisely that reason. A big unknown about the 1999 Kargil war is how much Prime Minister Sharif knew about Musharraf's plans before General Ahmed implemented them. After the fact, Sharif and Musharraf, who came to despise each other, disagreed about what the prime minister was told. It is unlikely that Musharraf told him nothing but equally unlikely that he expressed concern about the possibility that the plan would end in disaster since Musharraf fully expected a glorious success. Even today he still argues that it could have worked out fine if Sharif had not lost his nerve. The full truth may never be known.

Part of the Pakistani plan was to use a cover for the attack, claiming that the advancing forces north of Kargil were Kashmiri mujahedin fighting for their rights. That was pure propaganda. If there were any mujahedin at Kargil, they were not in the lead. Pakistani troops from the Northern Light Infantry, a regiment composed of natives of the area, were the main combatants. A thorough study of the battle by a team of experts from the United States, India, and Pakistan concluded in 2009 that the Pakistani forces were not mujahedin and that Pakistan was supremely confident of victory. Their conclusion is that "the false optimism of the architects of the Kargil intrusion, colored by the illusion of a cheap victory, was not only the main driver of the operation and hence the crisis; it was also the cause of Pakistan's most damaging military defeat since the loss of East Pakistan in December 1971."[32]

The Indians were caught completely by surprise, and so were the CIA and the U.S. government. The success of the Lahore meeting had created an unwarranted sense of optimism. Musharraf used what became a false dawn of a new day to cover his preparations.

But he had completely miscalculated the Indian response. Once the Vajpayee government was fully briefed on the military situation by the commander of the army, General V. P. Malik, it ordered a counteroffensive at the point of the attack. Malik organized a brilliant series of assaults on the Pakistani position. He also brought in air power, and Indian jets began attacking the Pakistani position, a move that Musharraf and Ahmed had not properly anticipated. Malik also prepared to broaden the war. He ordered his forces elsewhere in Kashmir and along the border with Pakistan itself to be ready to expand the conflict if his assaults did not produce results. According to his memoir of the war, in mid-June 1999 he told Vajpayee that if "we could not throw the intruders out from Kargil, the military would have no alternative but to cross the international border or the LoC." Malik visited every corps headquarters along the border with Pakistan to prepare them all. On June 18 he warned all of his commanders to "be prepared for escalation—sudden or gradual—along the LoC or the international border and be prepared to go to declared war at short notice."[33]

The Indians took other measures as well. The Indian brigade usually deployed in the Andaman and Nicobar Islands in the Bay of Bengal was moved to the west coast of India and prepared for an amphibious landing in Pakistan. The Indian navy concentrated in the Arabian Sea and began aggressive patrols that threatened to blockade the port of Karachi and cut off Pakistan's oil imports. The navy was so aggressive that Pakistan's navy began providing escorts for oil tankers, and Malik had to caution the admirals "not to start a full-scale conventional war before all three services were ready." As Malik recounts it in his memoirs, "the juggernaut was moving steadily."[34]

In Washington, Clinton followed the war with alarm. Talbott and his team went from shuttle negotiations to crisis management. Naturally, given the tests in 1998, the nuclear issue and the risk of a broader war were uppermost on the president's mind. Some have suggested after the fact that Washington was too fixated on the nuclear issue. Perhaps that was true, but Clinton would have been justifiably worried about the risk of escalation. He was reminded of how World War I had escalated from a terrorist attack in the Balkans into a global war in less than a month, and he worried, of course, that the Kargil war could go nuclear. On June 16 Sandy Berger, the national security adviser, met with his Indian counterpart, Brajesh Mishra. According to Malik, Mishra informed Berger that "India would not be able to continue with its policy of 'restraint' for long and that our military forces could not be kept on a leash any longer."[35] Berger got the message. Washington went on full alert. The administration's public statements, which made it clear from the beginning that Clinton blamed Pakistan for starting a dangerous conflict, now demanded an unconditional Pakistani withdrawal to the line of control.

For the first time ever in a Pakistani-Indian conflict, the United States was unequivocally and publicly siding with India. Islamabad was devastated, and New Delhi could hardly believe it. When the Indian ambassador called on me in the White House to make sure, I told him that the United States was fully behind India. Jaswant Singh later wrote that "this was perhaps the first-ever articulation of an unambiguous stand by the U.S."[36] Clinton urged Sharif to pull back and sent the commander of CENTCOM, General Zinni, to Islamabad with the message. Panicked, Sharif tried to secure Chinese support for Pakistan's position. Beijing received him in late June but gave no promise of support. Pakistan's so-called "all-weather friend" (so called in contrast with the United States and its "betrayals") would not help, and Sharif was left with nothing. Other countries, including the United Kingdom, firmly backed the U.S. demands. Pakistan must pull back unconditionally. Sharif called the White House and asked to come to Washington for an immediate meeting with Clinton. Clinton's response was clear: if Sharif came to Washington, he would have to announce a complete and unconditional withdrawal to the LoC; if not, Pakistan would be fully blamed for starting a war. Sharif, now desperate, came on July 4, 1999.

The two leaders met that morning at Blair House, the official guest house of the executive mansion. I was the third person in the room for the entire summit.[37] Clinton later read my account and sent me a handwritten note confirming its accuracy; Sharif also privately confirmed every point with me. Before the two leaders met, the "President's Daily Brief," the CIA's daily report to the president, had delivered alarming news to the Clinton team, which was gathered in the Oval Office to get ready to see Sharif. As Talbott later recounted, intelligence indicated that "Pakistan might be preparing its nuclear forces for deployment." Among the team preparing to see Sharif "there was a sense of vast and nearly unprecedented peril."[38] Some would argue later that the danger was not really that serious. Musharraf, in his memoir, argued that nothing unusual was under way in the Pakistani nuclear forces.[39] Moreover, he claimed that Pakistani forces were still fully in control of the main heights above Kargil. Indian commentators also tended to diminish the risk. Some have noted that Clinton never mentioned the intelligence to Vajpayee, which is true. Clinton hoped that by the time that he and Vajpayee talked later in the day, Sharif would have backed down and agreed to withdraw from Kargil; he saw no reason to alarm New Delhi further. Both Jaswant Singh, then foreign minister, and General Malik note in their accounts that on its own India had detected unusual activity in Pakistan's missile forces. Singh says that they saw evidence of Pakistan "operationalizing its nuclear missiles,"[40] and Malik refers to "intelligence reports about the Tilla Ranges being readied for possible launching of missiles." According to Malik, the Indian army "considered it prudent to take some protective measures. Accordingly some of our missile assets were dispersed and relocated."[41]

Clinton confronted Sharif directly with his concerns about the nuclear menace when the two met alone (with me as the only note taker) the morning of July 4. Clinton said that he was worried that India and Pakistan were taking a horrible risk: getting into an escalation of the conflict similar to the one that the Soviet Union and the United States stumbled into during the Cuban missile crisis in 1962. He asked Sharif whether he knew how far along his military was in preparing for nuclear conflict. Sharif was evasive. Clinton pressed harder: "Do you recognize what even one nuclear bomb would mean?" As Talbott recalls, "Sharif finished the sentence: '. . . it would be a catastrophe.'"[42] Clinton was now very direct. He gave Sharif a choice. If he would announce the immediate withdrawal of all Pakistani forces to a position behind the LoC, the United States would support resumption of the Lahore process between India and Pakistan and urge India to allow the withdrawal to proceed. If not, America would blame Pakistan for starting a war that could end in nuclear disaster. On top of that, Clinton would blame Pakistan for assisting Osama bin Laden and other terrorists. In his memoirs, Clinton notes that on July 4, 1999, he also signed an executive order placing sanctions on the Taliban and freezing its assets. The direct message was to Kabul, but the indirect message was to Pakistan's army, the Taliban's and al Qaeda's protector.[43]

Sharif very reluctantly agreed to withdraw, knowing that he would be castigated at home for giving up Pakistan's territorial gains with nothing to show for it. Musharraf immediately began a whispering campaign that labeled Sharif a coward, and the move to oust Sharif began. Benazir Bhutto later put it well when she wrote that the outcome of the Kargil war "was the most humiliating moment for the military since the fall of Dacca. A blame game started, and it was just a matter of time as to who would move first against the other."[44] The Indians were delighted with the outcome, although they were also confident by July 4 that their army had the situation well in hand and that Operation Vijay (Victory) had triumphed. As Malik later wrote, the Blair House summit was a fundamental turning point in U.S.-India relations.[45] A few weeks later, on a visit to New Delhi, I was delighted to see large models of the White House on display in public parks, celebrating America's intervention on India's side in the Kargil war.

CLINTON'S VISIT TO SOUTH ASIA

The Kargil war and the Blair House summit marked the beginning of a new era in American diplomacy with India and Pakistan. Before Kargil, America was preoccupied with trying to keep India and Pakistan first from acquiring the bomb, then from testing it, and then from further developing their nuclear arsenals. After Kargil, America was much more focused on trying to keep them from ever using the arsenals that they were building. In part, Clinton had little choice. The Republicans in the Senate voted against ratification of the Comprehensive Test Ban Treaty on October 13, 1999. I was in New Delhi a few days later, and it was clear that once the U.S. Senate had rejected the treaty, Vajpayee was no longer seriously considering having India sign it.

Clinton recognized that the Kargil war allowed him to skip over the nonproliferation dispute at long last and do what he wanted to do: open a new chapter in America's relationship with India. He had also been seared by the experience of the war, and he was determined to try to do more to persuade India and Pakistan that if they remained focused on their rivalry, they would sooner or later go over the edge. The intelligence community sent the president a National Intelligence Estimate (NIE) in the winter of 1999–2000 that concluded that the chances for a full-scale war in South Asia had increased further because of the nuclear tests and the Kargil conflict. In February 2000, John McLaughlin, deputy director of the Central Intelligence Agency, briefed the president in depth on the nuclear arsenals of India and Pakistan based on the draft NIE. The NIE concluded that the chance of war between India and Pakistan within the next few years was 50-50.[46]

Clinton's trip to South Asia in March 2000 was the first by an American president in a quarter of a century. He visited Bangladesh, India, and Pakistan. In India he spent five days traveling across the country, and he was cheered by enormous crowds. He delivered an eloquent message to the Indian parliament that called for nuclear restraint but also pushed for a new era in Indo-American relations. He traveled across the subcontinent, visiting Dacca, New Delhi, Hyderabad, Mumbai, and Jaipur. As he put it, "Somewhat to my surprise, I got a grand reception. Indians were as eager as I was for our long estrangement to end."[47] A series of agreements on environmental, trade, health, and other substantive issues were signed, and the two leaders committed to meeting regularly to follow up. Later that year, Vajpayee came to the White House for a state visit.

The Pakistan stop was much briefer, only a few hours. Sharif had fired Musharraf in October 1999 while he was visiting Sri Lanka. Musharraf refused to be fired and staged a coup, literally from the air, as his plane was returning from Colombo to Karachi. Sharif was arrested and jailed. General Ahmed, the 10th Corps commander, became director general of the ISI, and Musharraf became Pakistan's fourth military dictator. The United States cut off any remaining ties between the two militaries, as required by law in the wake of a military ouster of an elected government. In the meeting between Musharraf and Clinton in Islamabad, the two disagreed on virtually every issue. Clinton pressed especially for Pakistan to take action on al Qaeda, but he was rebuffed. On only one issue did Musharraf suggest some willingness to compromise: he thought Sharif should not be executed. After a good deal more behind-the-scenes American effort and intricate diplomacy involving Prince Bandar of Saudi Arabia; Pakistan's new ambassador, Maleha Lodhi; and me, Sharif was sent into exile in Saudi Arabia.

By the start of the twenty-first century, American diplomacy had helped manage two major crises in South Asia in less than a decade: the spring 1990 near-war experience under Bush and the Kargil mini-war in 1999 under Clinton. It had also dealt with the dangerous days in May 1998 surrounding the nuclear tests. After much effort, thanks largely to Talbott and Clinton on one side and Singh and Vajpayee on the other, America and India were poised to end their decades of estrangement. U.S. relations with Pakistan, however, were again at a very low ebb.

CHAPTER SIX

BUSH, MUSH, AND SONIA

PRESIDENT GEORGE W. BUSH was a man in a hurry, pacing the Treaty Room of the White House. The Treaty Room, on the second floor of the mansion, is a private study for the president; a large painting hanging there depicts President Lincoln, General Grant, General Sherman, and Admiral Porter in a meeting in early 1865 to decide the final offensive campaigns of the Civil War. The room is usually a place of refuge, but on that day the usually relaxed president was agitated. He was eager to get the war started. On September 11, 2001, al Qaeda had destroyed the Twin Towers of the World Trade Center and attacked the Pentagon. Now it was October 7, almost a month later, and the American military response was set to begin in Afghanistan. The government of Afghanistan—the Taliban and its leader, Mullah Omar—had refused to hand over Osama bin Laden and the al Qaeda leadership. America was poised to invade Afghanistan, a landlocked country on the opposite side of the planet, with a handful of CIA officers and the U.S. air force.

A short list had been prepared by the National Security Council of key foreign leaders who were to get a heads-up call from the president just before the military campaign was to begin. I was with the president in the Treaty Room when he called Crown Prince Abdullah, the de facto ruler of Saudi Arabia since his half-brother

King Fahd suffered a stroke in 1995. Saudi Arabia was one of only three countries—Pakistan and the United Arab Emirates were the others—that had diplomatic relations with the Taliban, and Osama bin Laden was, of course, a Saudi. The conversation with the crown prince was short. The president informed him that America and a coalition of allies including the United Kingdom, Canada, and Australia were about to begin air strikes on Taliban targets in Kabul, Kandahar, and other locations. He did not tell the prince that CIA teams were already on the ground, working with the Northern Alliance, the Taliban's enemy, to help locate targets for the strikes. Bush did ask for Saudi support for the operation, especially in getting Pakistan to break its long-standing ties to the Taliban and al Qaeda completely. Abdullah promised Saudi support and assistance. The president thanked him and closed the call quickly.

The war that he was so eager to get started became the longest in American history. Begun with a lightning campaign, it would turn into a stalemate. The Taliban were evicted from Afghanistan within a few months but then gradually regained their footing in Pakistan, with the help of Pakistan's Inter-Services Intelligence. Within five years, they again controlled much of the eastern and southern parts of the country.

At the start of a new millennium, George W. Bush became the forty-third president of the United States. His new team called him "43" to differentiate him from his father, called "41," who had been the forty-first president. However, there were many other differences between the very experienced elder Bush and his son. During the election campaign, 43 could not name the president of Pakistan when asked by a journalist. In office he would fail to take note of the growing threat of catastrophic terror based in South Asia until it literally smashed into America on 9/11. He would then fail to bring the perpetrators of the attack to justice, allowing them to hide for years in Pakistan. He would be lied to by the Pakistani dictator, Pervez Musharraf, whose name Bush did not know when he was a candidate. But Bush did shut down Pakistan's proliferation of nuclear technology to a host of bad actors, from Libya to North Korea.

Bush would also preside over a significant further improvement in America's relationship with India. He would sign a landmark civil nuclear power treaty and shepherd it through Congress, something that probably only a Republican could have done. Like his father and Clinton, Bush would help prevent nuclear war in South Asia by helping to defuse another Indo-Pakistani crisis. Like Clinton, he would have a very successful visit to India. He would forge a partnership with a new Indian leadership, led by Rajiv Gandhi's Italian widow, Sonia Gandhi, who had become the head of the Congress Party.[1] Bush usually tried to reject any policy that Clinton had pursued, but on India he outdid his predecessor in looking for ways to build strong ties between the United States and India.

To those in the National Security Council, the change was apparent from the first days of the new administration. After decades of including South Asia in the Near East office—the responsibility of the senior director for Near East and South Asia affairs, who was also a special assistant to the president—South Asia was moved into the East Asia office. Or at least most of it was; Afghanistan was forgotten for a couple of months during the reorganization. It was unclear whether it would stay with the Near East office or move to the East Asia office. When I and my counterpart for East Asia asked for guidance, we were told to wait for the arrival of Zalmay Khalilzad, an Afghan American who would have responsibility for the Afghan portfolio when he came to the White House staff in a few months. Unfortunately, Afghanistan and al Qaeda were not waiting for Zal.

MUSHARRAF AND THE "WAR ON TERRORISM"

Pakistan's fourth military dictator was born in New Delhi in August 1943. His family fled to Pakistan in August 1947, and from 1949 to 1957 they lived in Turkey, where his father was a diplomat and the young Musharraf learned Turkish. In 1961, at the age of eighteen, he entered the prestigious Kakul Military Academy, in Abbottabad, Pakistan. He served with distinction in the 1965 and 1971 wars, fought with the elite Special Services Group (SSG) on the Siachen Glacier in 1987, but played no role in the war against the Soviets. In 1990–1991 he attended the Royal College of Defence Studies in London. Upon his return to Pakistan, he was involved in supporting the Taliban in Afghanistan. Sharif picked him over several more senior officers to be chief of army staff because Sharif thought that Musharraf was apolitical and unlikely to be a threat. Just as Zulfikar Bhutto had been wrong about Zia ul-Haq, Sharif was wrong about Musharraf. Two weeks after ousting Sharif on October 13, 1999, Musharraf traveled to Saudi Arabia to secure Saudi support for his new regime and then visited the United Arab Emirates. With their backing, he felt confident enough to challenge India again. His partner in the Kargil war, General Mahmud Ahmed, became the new director general of the ISI.

On Christmas Eve 1999, five terrorists hijacked Air India flight 814 in Katmandu, Nepal. They were Pakistanis from Harakat ul-Mujahedin (HuM), a group long supported by bin Laden; it was a HuM camp that bin Laden was visiting in Afghanistan when Clinton's cruise missiles failed to kill him. The airplane refueled in Amritsar, Lahore, and Dubai before it finally landed at Kandahar on Christmas Day for negotiations with India on the terms for release of the hostages. The hijackers told the captain, "Fly slowly, fly carefully, there is no hurry. We have to give India a millennium gift."[2] In fact, there was a bomb in the cargo hold of the plane that had been smuggled on in Nepal and was timed to go off at midnight on December 31, 1999.[3] One passenger was murdered by the terrorists, a young man who had just been married. His bride was widowed on her honeymoon.

The airport in Kandahar was controlled by the Taliban. Al Qaeda had an office at the airport, as the 9/11 Commission later reported. Osama bin Laden was behind the scenes, directing the plot and the negotiations.[4] The ISI had helped the terrorists hijack the plane by assisting them with getting weapons in Nepal. The Indian government also reported that the hijackers were in constant contact by satellite phone with ISI headquarters in Rawalpindi.[5] The terrorist cabal demanded the release of three Kashmiri terrorist leaders held in India: Maulana Masood Azhar (the senior Kashmiri militant whose release Ilyas Kashmiri had also demanded in the 1994 Delhi kidnappings referred to in chapter 5), Ahmed Omar Saeed Sheikh, and Mushtaq Ahmed Zargar. India's foreign minister, Jaswant Singh, flew to Kandahar to arrange a deal to free the hostages.[6] After the exchange, the ISI took the three terrorists to Pakistan, where they did a fundraising tour for a new terrorist group that Azhar had founded, Jaish-e-Mohammad. Saeed would later be implicated in the murder of the American journalist Daniel Pearl. Jaswant would later rightly call the episode the "dress rehearsal" for 9/11.

The first American delegation to visit Islamabad after Musharraf's coup in 1999 was led by Assistant Secretary of State Inderfurth, who pressed General Mahmud Ahmed and the ISI to track down and arrest a Saudi al Qaeda operative known as Abu Zubaydah, who was involved in another millennium plot in Jordan and a third in California. The CIA believed that Zubaydah was in Peshawar and operating openly for al Qaeda. William Milam, the U.S. ambassador to Pakistan at the time, later said that Mahmud turned Inderfurth down, claiming that the ISI did not know where Zubaydah was. In fact, as Milam put it, "The ISI just turned a blind eye to his activities, even though everyone knew where he was." Zubaydah was helping ISI recruit and vet Kashmiri militants and sending them to al Qaeda training camps in Afghanistan.[7]

By the summer of 2001, the CIA was receiving multiple reports that a major al Qaeda attack was coming. George Tenet, who was then director of central intelligence, recalled later that "threat information poured in, almost from every nook and cranny of the planet."[8] In July he met with Condoleezza Rice, Bush's new national security adviser, and told her that the CIA expected a "spectacular" attack designed to cause mass casualties through multiple and simultaneous attacks.[9] On August 6, 2001, the "President's Daily Brief" included an article entitled "Bin Ladin Determined to Strike in the U.S." Tenet traveled to Texas, where Bush was on a month-long vacation, to brief him face to face on the gathering storm.

The CIA had been briefing Bush on the al Qaeda threat since he won the Republican nomination for president in 2000. Ben Bonk, the deputy director of the agency's Counter Terrorism Center, traveled to Texas then with the message that al Qaeda was the top terrorist threat to the United States, that it was intent on mounting a catastrophic attack, and that it was seeking chemical or biological weapons to do so. After the election Sandy Berger, the national security adviser, told his successor, Condoleezza Rice, the same thing: that al Qaeda was the country's greatest national security threat.[10]

But the new administration was slow to react. The Principals Committee of the National Security Council did not hold a meeting on the al Qaeda threat until just before 9/11. When Berger had been national security adviser, in periods of high terrorist threat, such as during the Air India hijacking, he had held daily meetings of the principals to ensure maximum interagency cooperation and information sharing. In the summer of 2001, no such meetings took place. The warnings from the CIA and other counterterrorism experts got louder and louder, but the White House was complacent.

If the CIA was getting so much warning that a massive al Qaeda attack was in the works in 2001, then the ISI must also have had knowledge of the preparations. After all, the ISI had officers throughout Afghanistan and met regularly with those at the highest levels of the Taliban, including Mullah Omar. The ISI was closely tied with al Qaeda, as the Air India operation demonstrated. Their friends, such as Harakat ul-Mujahedin, were training with the al Qaeda operatives. Nonetheless, no warning came from the ISI; instead, General Ahmed, ISI's director general, came to Washington on September 9, 2001, to press Tenet and the Bush team to reduce the sanctions on the Taliban and Pakistan. When Tenet had lunch with Ahmed that afternoon, Tenet pressed for action against Omar and bin Laden. Ahmed defended Omar, saying that he was just a "man who wanted only the best for the Afghan people." Tenet remembers that he was "immovable when it came to the Taliban and al Qaeda."[11] Ahmed shared no intelligence of any impending al Qaeda attack with Tenet.[12]

Three days later, after the attacks on the Twin Towers and the Pentagon, Ahmed was given an ultimatum by Deputy Secretary of State Richard Armitage. Pakistan was either with America or against it. It must immediately give the U.S. air force access to its bases for military operations against the Taliban, withdraw all its support (experts, oil, and everything else) from the Taliban, and cooperate in the hunt for al Qaeda. If not, the United States would treat Pakistan as a state sponsor of terrorism and an enemy. Ahmed took the message home to Musharraf. General Ahmed later complained bitterly to the new U.S. ambassador to Pakistan, Wendy Chamberlin, that Armitage had been very rude in the meeting.

Chamberlin followed up Armitage's meeting with Ahmed with a meeting with Musharraf. After an hour of pressing, Musharraf agreed to support the United States. Pakistan would allow U.S. aircraft to overfly its territory to strike targets in Afghanistan as long as they did not fly from India, and the United States could use Pakistani airbases for emergency landings and station a few personnel at a base to deconflict flight operations so that Pakistani and American aircraft did not clash. Musharraf insisted that there could be no Indian role in the Afghan war or in the government that would follow the Taliban; he also said that while Pakistan would assist in capturing al Qaeda operatives who fled into Pakistan, there could be no operations against Pakistani citizens, meaning that Lashkar-e-Tayyiba and other Pakistani groups were off limits to counterterrorism operations.[13]

Mahmud Ahmed was sent to Kandahar upon his return from Washington to convince Mullah Omar that the world had changed and that bin Laden was a liability. The two met alone; Mahmud ordered the rest of the Pakistani delegation to stay outside. What they said remains unknown. Mahmud later told Shuja Nawaz that he felt that he could not press Omar to hand over a fellow Muslim. Even if Mahmud tried to convince Omar to hand over bin Laden, he failed, perhaps because his heart was not in the mission. He may have told him to hang tough and fight.[14] Mahmud told a senior intelligence officer that he found it distasteful to betray the Taliban to America given the American betrayals of Pakistan and the Pressler amendment.[15] It is most likely that Mahmud made his argument half-heartedly because he did not want to abandon the course that the Pakistan army and ISI had been on for over a decade in Afghanistan.

Musharraf fired his protégé Mahmud. It was a brave decision: Mahmud had been his partner at Kargil and was responsible, as 10th Corps commander during the coup, for his coming to power in the first place. However, Musharraf knew that Mahmud was not ready to do what Musharraf felt was essential: move toward the Americans or be isolated as a friend of terrorists. In his memoirs, Musharraf relates that he "war gamed" what would happen if Pakistan stayed with the Taliban. His war game showed that India would be the major beneficiary and that Pakistan's nuclear arsenal would be at risk. "Our military forces would be destroyed . . . and the security of our strategic assets would be jeopardized. We did not want to lose or damage the military parity that we had achieved with India by becoming a nuclear weapons state," Musharraf wrote.[16]

Musharraf put it succinctly. Pakistani policy derived from Pakistan's concerns about India. There would be no role for India in the Afghan war, and Pakistan would temporarily sacrifice its terrorist pawns if necessary to save its nuclear arsenal. "The ultimate question that confronted me was whether it was in our national interest to destroy ourselves for the Taliban. Were they worth committing suicide over? The answer was a resounding no."[17] Years later Musharraf told me that it was an agonizing decision for him, especially as he knew that many of his fellow officers would not like it.[18] Musharraf immediately cut off supplies to the Taliban army and evacuated the Pakistani advisers with the Taliban; many were air lifted out of northern Afghanistan from Kunduz. The impact on the cohesion of the Taliban forces was devastating, and they rapidly collapsed under the weight of U.S. air power and a revitalized Northern Alliance, which had CIA support and money. The Islàmic Emirate of Afghanistan, which had taken six years to build, collapsed in less than three months. The United States had intervened in the Afghan civil war and tilted the balance decisively against the Pashtuns.

The defeated Taliban fighters were ordered by Mullah Omar to scatter and avoid further direct confrontation with the enemy while they regrouped. Many just went home. The leadership and the hard core fled south from Kandahar into Pakistan. Most relocated in Baluchistan, around the city of Quetta, where Omar himself settled and began rebuilding the Taliban in exile, with critical assistance from Pakistan.[19] Without Pakistan's help, the Taliban would never have recovered. A NATO study published in 2012 that was based on more than 27,000 interrogations of 4,000 captured Taliban, al Qaeda, and other fighters in Afghanistan concluded that ISI support has been critical to the survival and revival of the Taliban since 2001, just as it was critical to the Taliban's conquest of Afghanistan in the 1990s. Even today "the ISI is thoroughly aware of Taliban activities and the whereabouts of all senior Taliban personnel."[20] A central player in this relationship, NATO concluded, remains Hamid Gul, the former director general of the ISI.

The Bush White House paid little attention to the Taliban after 2001. The CIA's chief officer in Islamabad was never told to make apprehending Mullah Omar or his associates a high priority.[21] A $10 million reward was offered for information on Omar's whereabouts, but no serious effort to find him was made. The ISI, however, knew where to find him all along. Once Bush began the war in Iraq, resources became even slimmer for fighting the Afghan war and the Taliban. As one study by the U.S. Army War College concludes, once preparations were made to invade Iraq, "the impact of the shift in focus and resources from Afghanistan to operations in Iraq cannot be overstated. Under-resourced from the beginning, the campaign in Afghanistan now fell to a distant second place."[22] The undersecretary for resources in the Bush Pentagon, Dov Zakheim, later wrote a book about how the war was systematically under-resourced by the Bush team, as did Bush's ambassador to Kabul, Ron Neuman.[23]

Bin Laden and his deputy, Ayman al-Zawahiri, also escaped from the allies. Again, there was a tragic lack of attention to the hunt for bin Laden in the last days of 2001. A comprehensive study of the failure to catch bin Laden, based on extensive interviews with all the Americans involved, concludes that the White House failed to provide clear guidance to the military that capturing or killing bin Laden was a top priority.[24] Bin Laden went into hiding for the next decade. After escaping to Pakistan, he moved back to Afghanistan in 2002 to remote Kunar province, a longtime al Qaeda stronghold. In 2003 he moved back to Pakistan, first to Peshawar and then to Haripur in 2004. Two of his wives and some of his children were with him during this exodus. Another wife and some children were in Iran, under Iranian detention of some kind. In 2005 a property was acquired by al Qaeda to build a more permanent hideout in Abbottabad, a small city about thirty miles north of Islamabad and the home of the Kakul Military Academy, Musharraf's alma mater.[25]

The new hideout was less than a mile from the academy, putting it within the military security zone that surrounds the school. Abbottabad was named for a British general, Sir John Abbot, who founded the city as a cantonment for the British East India Company's army in January 1853. Abbot was very fond of the location, which he later wrote "seemed like a dream." Ayub Khan was born nearby. After partition, the Pakistani army took it over, and three regiments call it home. It is one of the most secure military zones in the country, so much so that the first Chinese-Pakistani military counterterrorism exercise was held there in December 2006, about a year after bin Laden moved in. The Kakul academy is central to the Pakistani officer corps: future corps commanders and chiefs of army staff start their careers in Kakul.

Bin Ladin's hideout was considerably larger than most of the other homes in the area and had walls varying from twelve to eighteen feet in height to prevent outside observation of the interior. It was known in the neighborhood as the "Waziristan house," a reference to the district along the Afghan border where al Qaeda has most of its training facilities. Bin Laden and al Qaeda practiced excellent operational security—no surprise since he knew that he was the CIA's number-one target and the most wanted man in history. All communication with the outside world was done through one courier, Abu Ahmed al-Kuwaiti, a Pakistani who had lived in Kuwait. Al-Kuwaiti relied on an extensive support network to help maintain the hideout and keep bin Laden in communication with his global jihadist network. Although bin Laden was a recluse, he was very active in overseeing al Qaeda's activities and in putting out propaganda messages.

According to the *New York Times*, telephone numbers found in the hideout when U.S. Navy SEALs finally found and killed bin Laden on May 1, 2011, suggest that the support network included Harakat ul-Mujahedin, the group that hijacked the Indian airliner in 1999. Its leader, Fazlur Rehman Khalil, lives openly in a suburb of Islamabad and works very closely with the ISI.[26] In the summer of 2010, bin Laden and Khalil reportedly even had dinner together in one of the al Qaeda leader's rare trips beyond his hideout.[27]

Pakistan did help the CIA find other important al Qaeda figures after 2001, including Abu Zubaydah, who was captured in a Lashkar-e-Tayyiba safehouse, and Khalid Sheikh Mohammed, who was the tactical commander of the 9/11 hijackers. Mohammed was found in Rawalpindi, the military capital of Pakistan and home of the general headquarters of the Pakistani army. But the number and rate of captures steadily declined after 2004, dropping to almost nothing by 2008.

Bush acknowledges in his memoirs that his relationship with Musharraf was troubled. As the president looked back, he noted that "over time it became clear (to me) that Musharraf either would not or could not fulfill all his promises. Part of the problem was Pakistan's obsession with India. In almost every conversation we had, Musharraf accused India of wrongdoing."[28] But the most dangerous crisis of the Bush administration in South Asia was the result of Pakistani wrongdoing.

INDIA AND PAKISTAN AT THE BRINK OF WAR

While bin Laden was escaping from Tora Bora into Pakistan, a squad of five terrorists invaded the Indian parliament's grounds in New Delhi on December 13, 2001. A forty-five-minute gun battle followed, in which nine policemen and parliament staff were killed. The terrorists had hoped to get inside the building and kill as many senior Indian politicians as possible. Fortunately, both houses of parliament had just adjourned, but 200 members were still inside, along with several senior cabinet ministers. It was an outrageous attack. Indian intelligence soon identified the plot as the work of Lashkar-e-Tayyiba (LeT) and Jaish-e-Mohammad (JeM), operating together. India demanded that Musharraf immediately crack down on both and arrest their leadership. When Musharraf procrastinated, India mobilized for war.

The timing of the attack may well have been linked to the hunt for bin Laden. By creating a crisis on Pakistan's eastern border, LeT and JeM forced Pakistan to withdraw troops from its western border and the Durand Line; any hope of finding bin Laden or Zawahiri or blocking their escape was thus lost. The mastermind of the New Delhi attack was Ghazi Baba, the JeM's India operations commander, who had been deeply involved with bin Laden in the Indian airlines hijacking.[29] The ISI's role in the attack on India's parliament remains a subject of intense debate. Musharraf, whose memoirs are unusually chatty about most issues, is curiously silent on this one. He did tell Ambassador Chamberlain soon after the attack that intelligence work was often a "dirty" business, but he did not elaborate.[30]

Five days after the attack, on December 18, 2001, Prime Minister Vajpayee announced the start of Operation Parakram (Operation Valor) and the mobilization of Indian military forces to compel Pakistan to turn over twenty top terrorist leaders. More than 800,000 Indian army troops deployed along the border, air force units forward deployed to advance bases near Pakistan, and the Indian Eastern Fleet in the Bay of Bengal was moved to the Arabian Sea to unite with the Western Fleet to prepare to attack Karachi and blockade Pakistan.

The United States and United Kingdom moved quickly to try to avert Armageddon. London was especially concerned that war was imminent, a war that would vastly complicate the Afghan operation and benefit al Qaeda. It would also cause enormous human and material damage, even if it could be kept from going nuclear. The British pushed the Americans to get involved in trying to stop disaster. The British ambassador to India told me later that he thought that the chance of war was at least 50-50. According to one participant, the interagency daily meetings in the Cabinet Office Briefing Room (nicknamed COBRA) at the Foreign and Commonwealth Office in London were calculating wind speeds to measure radiation dispersal and trying to estimate the number of civilian casualties if nuclear weapons were detonated. One American estimate put the estimated deaths in a nuclear war at 12 million.[31]

The American ambassador to India, Robert Blackwill, also saw the danger in the crisis. Blackwill was a close adviser to President Bush during the election campaign and transition, and his mission was to build a strong relationship between India and America. From the start of the Afghanistan war, Blackwill was worried that Bush and Washington were being taken in by Musharraf and tilting too much toward Pakistan. The day after the attack on parliament,

Blackwill went to the site of the firefight and publicly described the attack as "no different in its objectives from the terror attack in the U.S. on September 11th," thus equating it with 9/11.[32] Most Indians saw it the same way.

Secretary of State Colin Powell and his deputy, Richard Armitage, were reluctant to put it in those terms because doing so implied that India was justified to use force in retaliation, as America had in Afghanistan. However, they moved quickly to press Musharraf to take action against LeT and JeM and to urge New Delhi to avoid military action. On January 12, 2002, at U.S. prompting, Musharraf gave a speech in which he promised that Pakistan would not be a base for terror. He banned five terrorist groups, including LeT and JeM, but reiterated Pakistan's commitment to the Kashmiri cause. In practice, the two terrorist groups simply changed their names. No serious crackdown followed the speech, but it did reduce the tension. India and Pakistan remained mobilized for war.

In February tensions worsened when a train filled with Hindu pilgrims was attacked by a Muslim mob in the Bharatiya Janata Party–run state of Gujarat. A fire started, and at least fifty-eight Hindus burned to death. Anti-Muslim riots followed, and hundreds of Muslims in the state were killed. The sectarian violence only fueled the perception that the subcontinent was on the verge of disaster. On May 14, 2002, the second peak of the so-called Twin Peaks Crisis occurred when another major terrorist attack, in which the families of Indian soldiers were killed, took place in Kashmir (the attack on parliament had been the first peak). India again threatened military action, and Musharraf gave another speech. On May 30, 2002, Washington and London announced a drawdown of their nonessential diplomatic personnel in both countries and issued travel advisories to their citizens that India and Pakistan were in danger of going to war. At the same time, in an unrelated occurrence, an article that I had written on the Kargil war and its possible nuclear dimension was published by the Center for the Advanced Study of India and got front-page attention in the *Washington Post* and *London Times*. The saga of the Blair House meeting added to the sense of danger that was so vivid in the spring of 2002, reminding readers that Pakistan and India had only narrowly escaped a wider war in 1999.

Some experts have argued that the travel advisories and media attention pushed the Indian business community to tell Vajpayee to avoid conflict and ease tensions. Major Indian corporate leaders could see that the war scare was bad for business and discouraged investment. One expert has argued that the American and British travel advisories "effectively dramatized the economic disruption that would be caused by war. Business leaders worked to bring an understanding to government leaders of the wide potential for economic damage inherent in precipitous cross-border attacks."[33] As it was, the Indian mobilization cost New Delhi at least $2 billion.[34] It finally stood down in October. Powell and Armitage both later told me that they thought that war was a very real danger and that if it began, it would go to the brink of nuclear war, if not over. Their cool-headed actions (backed by Bush and Rice in the White House) probably helped save the lives of countless innocents. Vajpayee, of course, had made the really hard decisions and chosen the path of restraint. For a second time, the Indian prime minister had proven himself a great leader.

But India was humiliated by the crisis. None of the wanted twenty terrorists were turned over, the crackdown on LeT and JeM was a farce, and the mobilization had failed to intimidate Pakistan and Musharraf. The Pakistani army felt that its nuclear weapons had worked to deter India, and they had. President Bush had built closer ties to Vajpayee in the crisis and with Blackwill's help now began looking for a way to cement a closer relationship. Again, nuclear issues would be the driving force behind the effort.

THE NUCLEAR DEAL

Like his father, Bush devotes very little attention to India in his memoir, *Decision Points*—less than a paragraph out of 481 pages.

That is puzzling because he fashioned a very significant deal with India that all but ended decades of American-Indian wrangling over nuclear issues, granted India special status as a nuclear weapons state outside the Nuclear Non-Proliferation Treaty (NPT), and opened the door for stronger ties between the two democracies.

The U.S.-India Civil Nuclear Agreement was a landmark in American-Indian relations. The nuclear issue would no longer be a source of constant friction between Washington and New Delhi; there would be no more Gates-Rodrigues shouting matches. The first framework for the deal was announced in a joint statement on July 18, 2005, during Prime Minister Singh's visit to Washington. The essence of the deal was to put some Indian nuclear reactors under an international safeguard and inspection regime while others would remain available for military use and production of fissile material. In return, India would be able to purchase nuclear reactors and technology from the United States and other countries. India would be given a de facto waiver for testing nuclear weapons and for not signing the Nuclear Non-Proliferation Treaty, which it regards as unfair and unbalanced. Since the Bush team did not support the Comprehensive Test Ban Treaty, India was not asked to sign and ratify it either. Congress would later warn that renewed tests could scupper the deal, but India has at least formally kept its options open.

Singh negotiated the deal with Bush, but the real decisionmaker in New Delhi was Sonia Gandhi, Rajiv's widow. Sonia is without question the power behind the throne. She has led the Congress Party as its president since 1998, and she engineered its surprise electoral victory in 2004 and its even more stunning victory in 2008. She now is the longest-serving president of the party in its 125-year history. She is also the chair of the ruling coalition. India's economy has grown on her watch, allowing hundreds of millions to escape grinding poverty; modest economic reforms have been introduced; and a civilian nuclear power agreement was concluded with the United States. Relations with rival Pakistan have modestly improved despite the November 2008 terrorist attack on Mumbai, the worst terrorist incident in the world since 9/11. Sonia probably deserves most of the credit for restraining India from a military response to the Mumbai attack and giving diplomacy a chance.

She was born Edvige Antonia Albina Maino in the province of Veneto in Italy on December 9, 1946, and grew up in a modest village in the Piedmont near Torino. Her father was a Mussolini supporter who had fought with the Italian army on the Eastern Front with the Nazis in World War II. She remains a Catholic but celebrates Hindu festivals and traditions. In 1965 she met her future husband in Cambridge, England, where he was enrolled at university and she was studying English and waiting tables in a Greek restaurant to make ends meet. By all accounts, theirs was a true romance. Rajiv became prime minister in 1984 after his mother, Indira Gandhi, was assassinated by her Sikh bodyguards; Rajiv himself was assassinated in 1991 by a female Tamil terrorist.[35]

The murders of her mother-in-law and husband affected Sonia tremendously. She was very close to Indira, and some suggest that she now tries to look like her role model. Security precautions taken for her have been intensive since Rajiv's death. I remember changing cars twice when visiting her bungalow in New Delhi in 1998; although the vehicles were part of her own security detachment, apparently even they were not judged to be secure enough from possible terrorist tampering. At first reluctant to take power, Sonia finally agreed. Now power seems to come naturally to this remarkable woman.

In March 2006, Bush made a trip to the subcontinent, spending four days in India and then one night in Pakistan. On the way to New Delhi he stopped briefly in Kabul to promise America's long-term support for Afghan democracy, making Bush the first American president to visit Afghanistan since Eisenhower. It was more than four years after the war that he had started had begun. He was hailed in India for accepting India's nuclear status. In Pakistan there was intense disappointment that India had gotten a nuclear deal but that none was in the works for Pakistan, even though India had started the nuclear arms race in South Asia. For Pakistanis, it was yet another American betrayal.

Bush and Singh signed the civil nuclear agreement during Bush's visit to New Delhi. The process of ratification of the agreement was complex; it required the approval of both the Indian parliament and Congress and the approval of the multinational organizations that oversee the NPT process. There was considerable opposition to the agreement in India and the United States, but by the end of 2008 the legislative processes in both countries were complete. In the United States it helped that it was a presidential election year and no candidate wanted to alienate Indian-American voters, who were enthusiastic about the agreement. Barack Obama and John McCain both voted for the deal in the Senate. So did Hillary Clinton.

The International Atomic Energy Agency (IAEA) and the Nuclear Suppliers Group (NSG) also had to approve the agreements and implement the inspection regime for the civilian reactors. That process also was prolonged, but the IAEA approved the safeguards agreement on August 1, 2008, and the NSG provided a waiver on September 6, 2008, to allow India full access to civilian nuclear technology and fuel from other countries despite not being a signatory of the NPT. The deal was a considerable achievement for the Bush team, and it enhanced the president's popularity in India enormously. Nonproliferation and arms control advocates were much less enamored of the deal, which many labeled a dangerous precedent for other countries to follow. Pakistan, as noted, was one of the critics. Pakistanis argued that India had been given special treatment by the United States, IAEA, and NSG and that Pakistan should be offered a similar agreement. Pakistan's case, however, was weak. Unlike India, which has a stellar record of nonproliferation, Pakistan was burdened by its long history of exporting dangerous nuclear technology to other countries, including Iran, North Korea, and Libya.

George Bush could also rightly claim a major role in shutting down the worst excesses of Pakistan's nuclear bazaar. The man that most Pakistanis believe is the father of the Pakistani bomb, A. Q. Khan, was the central actor in Pakistan's proliferation activities. He had given Iran its first centrifuges and had been a key player in North Korea's nuclear development, receiving in return access to North Korea's medium-range missile technology, which it has copied and used to produce the Ghauri missile. The CIA uncovered an A. Q. Khan plan to provide nuclear technology, including the design for a bomb, to Libya in 2003. CIA director Tenet confronted Musharraf with the evidence of Pakistani proliferation to Libya and Iran in a one-on-one meeting in New York on September 24, 2003, in which Tenet told Musharraf that Khan "is betraying your country and has stolen some of your nation's most sensitive secrets."[36] It was fiction; Khan worked for Musharraf. But it was a way out for Musharraf and the army. Pretending that Khan was a lone wolf offered Musharraf a face-saving way of shutting down the bazaar and blaming it all on one bad man instead of the nation. All of the responsibility for decades of Pakistani help to North Korea and Iran in developing their nuclear programs and now for help to Libya could be placed on Khan.

Musharraf seized the opening. Khan was put under house arrest and forced to confess on Pakistani television that he had exceeded the authority of his position. Pakistan stopped providing help to Libya, which dismantled its nuclear program. But no one was given access to Khan; neither the CIA nor the International Atomic Energy Agency was allowed to question him about his decades of doing business with North Korea and Iran (and perhaps Syria and Saudi Arabia). After Musharraf resigned in 2008, Khan reappeared and began putting out his version of the story. Khan says that he was authorized to carry out all the nuclear technology transfers by officials at the highest levels of the Pakistani state, starting with Zulfi and Zia and including Musharraf. Benazir Bhutto, he says, not only sanctioned his deal with North Korea to trade nuclear technology for missile technology, she actually help negotiate it and carried key files from Islamabad to Pyongyang.[37] He was no rogue operator but a bureaucrat working for the government, trading nuclear secrets for technological help from other states.

Khan probably was both. He did act on the orders of the army and the state, and he probably operated as a loner as well. The details may never come out because the Pakistani military does not want to expose them to outside scrutiny. For the Bush administration, the fiction of a nuclear pirate helped resolve a troubling problem that might have derailed the budding rapprochement between Bush and "Mush," as the Pakistani dictator was increasingly nicknamed in Pakistan. But Khan's activities also provided a perfect and legitimate excuse for why the United States could not offer a civil nuclear power deal to Pakistan.

The Bush administration did very little to press Musharraf to allow a return to democracy after his coup. The administration complained half-heartedly when he rigged elections in 2002 that endorsed his rule, even when the elections produced the first provincial governments dominated by Islamist parties in Pakistani history. The key provinces bordering Afghanistan, Baluchistan and the Northwest Frontier Province, both elected local governments that were very sympathetic to the Taliban, largely because the ISI helped tilt the electoral playing field in that direction to weaken the major secular political parties that backed Benazir Bhutto and Nawaz Sharif. The supporters of Benazir and Nawaz pressed the United States to push Musharraf to allow their leaders to come home and compete in the political process. That would mean that Musharraf would have to promise that they would not be arrested for alleged past corruption or, in Sharif's case, for allegedly trying to kill Musharraf by forcing his plane to land outside of Pakistan. Musharraf had no intention of letting his sworn political foes back into Pakistan, and Bush put no pressure on him to do so. Since Benazir's Pakistan People's Party (PPP) and Sharif's Pakistan Muslim League (PML) still dominated the political process at the grassroots level and would certainly do very well in any reasonably open elections, Musharraf could not afford to let them come home.

So, in the eyes of a growing number of Pakistanis, Bush was all for democracy except in the second-largest Muslim country in the world, their homeland. There, Bush wanted to keep a military dictator in office indefinitely. Bush's ambassador in Islamabad, Ryan Crocker, told the press that "there is no dictatorship in Pakistan" and that the country was fast heading toward "true democracy" under Musharraf.[38] The hypocrisy drove more Pakistanis to hate America and some to support the jihad.

When Musharraf's regime began to unravel in 2007, Bush stood by his man. According to well-informed insiders, some in the White House, including Vice President Cheney, argued behind the scenes that Musharraf was like the Shah of Iran, a strong man who was needed to prevent an Islamic revolution. Bush should not throw Musharraf under the bus, as they alleged Jimmy Carter had done with the shah. Instead of calls for the rule of law and an independent judiciary, the administration urged patience and compromise. It did criticize Musharraf, but only reluctantly, when he imposed martial law in November 2007. Finally, it began to support the idea of trying to soften the face of military rule in Pakistan by arranging a shotgun wedding of Musharraf and Benazir. In this marriage of mutual foes, Bhutto would return to Pakistan to serve as prime minister and run domestic affairs while Musharraf would remain president and control national security affairs. Encouraged by the White House, Musharraf met secretly with Benazir in Dubai to see whether they could reach a deal, and the two began to think that they might be able to do so. Benazir saw a chance to return home, have the corruption charges against her and her husband dropped, and compete for power. Musharraf was very reluctant but was also increasingly desperate to hold on to power.

It was a foolish idea. The two could not really share power, and domestic and external issues could not be so easily separated.

Musharraf was especially opposed to giving up his uniform because being chief of army staff was the real source of his power, and Bhutto knew that she would not really run the country if he remained chief of army staff. I said so at the time. I told *The New York Times* in October 2007 that "this backroom deal is going to explode in our face," arguing that "Ms. Bhutto and Mr. Musharraf detest each other, and the concept that they can somehow work collaboratively is a real stretch."[39] Nawaz Sharif opposed the deal for an obvious reason: it left him on the outside. He demanded fair treatment: if Bhutto could come home, he should be able to do the same. Because Sharif was certain to push for Musharraf's impeachment for the 1999 coup if he returned, the Bush team did not like that idea at all. So the deal to broker a little democracy was actually a barrier to real democratic reform.

Bhutto returned to Karachi on October 18, 2007, and was almost killed in an assassination attempt that evening while she was traveling among hundreds of thousands of adoring PPP followers to her home. She was murdered two months later, on December 27, 2007, while attending a political rally in Rawalpindi in the same square where Liaquat Ali Khan was murdered in 1951. The elections that followed in 2008 were relatively free and fair and brought her husband, Asif Ali Zardari, to power. At his request, the United Nations was asked to do an inquiry into the "facts and circumstances of the assassination" of Benazir Bhutto. The result is a fascinating document and analysis of Pakistan's political system and the links between the army and the jihadists.

The UN concludes that the assassination was probably planned by al Qaeda and its Pakistani Taliban allies, who recruited a fifteen-year-old suicide bomber to kill Bhutto. An al Qaeda spokesman claimed credit for the murder, saying, "We have terminated the most precious American asset" in Pakistan.[40] The UN investigators point a finger in particular at the notorious al Qaeda operative Ilyas Kashmiri, discussed earlier, as a possible mastermind.[41] The report notes that Bhutto represented everything that the jihad hated: she was a woman in politics, educated in the West, who advocated a harsh crackdown on the jihadist movement in Pakistan. The report notes that many saw her as a Shia as well because her mother and husband were Shia.[42]

A more damaging conclusion of the UN inquiry, however, is that the Musharraf government did far too little to protect Benazir despite her repeated requests and then deliberately and effectively took action to make a thorough investigation of the crime impossible. With adequate protection, the report says, "Ms. Bhutto's assassination could have been prevented." Instead, the Musharraf government denied her the normal security arrangements made for any VIP in Pakistan, even after the first attack in Karachi. The cover-up was even worse. The crime scene was immediately washed down by fire hoses to remove forensic evidence, no proper autopsy was conducted, and "high-ranking Pakistani government authorities obstructed access to military and intelligence sources" to impede the inquiry.[43] The UN report concludes that the ISI played a key role in the cover-up and intimidated the Pakistani police from doing their job. It may even have been quietly encouraging the assassins through former officials who had well-known contacts with the extremists. Before her death, Benazir had alleged that former ISI officials, including former director general Hamid Gul, were plotting her demise with al Qaeda.[44]

Musharraf lost office within a year. President Bush had tried to arrange a political deal to save the Musharraf regime but saw that deal blow up in its face. After eight years of dealing with Musharraf, the United States did not have Osama bin Laden or Mullah Omar, had not slowed the growth of Pakistan's nuclear arsenal, and had lost the faith of the Pakistani people by supporting a dictator for too long. Musharraf went into exile in London. In 2011 he was charged by Pakistan's judiciary with conspiracy to murder Benazir Bhutto and an arrest warrant was issued for him. Treason charges have also been filed against him in Pakistan. At least for now, he cannot go home again.

By the time that Musharraf left Pakistan, Bush was leaving the White House. His record in dealing with South Asia was very mixed. His India policy had been a great success. Indians genuinely appreciated his efforts to defuse the 2001–02 Twin Peaks crisis, and the nuclear deal was well received in India once it was clearly explained and understood. Pakistanis have a different view. They believe that Bush shortchanged democracy in their country. Although Pakistan received more aid from Bush than any previous president had provided, approval ratings for the United States were at an all-time low when he left office.

CHAPTER SEVEN

OBAMA AND SOUTH ASIA

THE PRINCIPALS COMMITTEE of the National Security Council is chaired by the president. On March 20, 2009, in the White House Situation Room, Barack Obama was chairing the committee's last meeting on his new strategy for Afghanistan and Pakistan; later he was to give a nationally televised speech laying out his thinking to the American people. As the chairman of the strategic review of policy toward Afghanistan and Pakistan, a job that the president had personally asked me to do, I opened the meeting with a few key points that summarized my thoughts on the issue. Obama sat at one end of the long table in the Sit Room; I sat at the other end. Around the table were Vice President Joe Biden; Secretary of State Hillary Clinton; Secretary of Defense Bob Gates; Jim Jones, national security adviser; Dennis Blair, director of national intelligence; Leon Panetta, director of central intelligence; Susan Rice, U.S. ambassador to the United Nations; Admiral Mike Mullen, chairman of the Joint Chiefs of Staff; Jim Steinberg, deputy secretary of state; Tom Donilon, deputy national security adviser; Ambassador Richard Holbrooke, special adviser on Pakistan and Afghanistan; and Michele Flournoy, undersecretary of defense. Aides sat along the back.

I had already spent hours with the president and the principals going over the details of the 40-page top secret review, its 20 principal recommendations, and its more than 140 sub-recommendations. During the previous two days I had been traveling to and from California with the president on Air Force One so that he and I could discuss the review and the options together, in depth. This meeting was the last chance to present the big picture and emphasize the most critical points for the president and his cabinet.

Obama had inherited a disaster in Afghanistan and Pakistan. Due to the failure of the Bush administration to provide adequate resources for conducting the war in Afghanistan and its misplaced faith in the U.S. alliance with Musharraf, the war against the Taliban was being lost and al Qaeda was under little or no pressure in Pakistan. The United States and its NATO allies and non-NATO partners in Afghanistan faced the real possibility of catastrophic defeat. In the summer of 2009, General Stanley McChrystal, Obama's new commander in Afghanistan, conducted an intensive review of the war effort. The resulting report was devastating. It concluded, as did my report, that the war was being lost, but because the McChrystal report was done in the field, it provided far more detail on just how badly the situation was deteriorating. The report was leaked to the media and widely disseminated. At the same time, a new study came out that showed how thoroughly the Afghan war had been under-resourced for seven years. It was written by Dov Zakheim, who had been in charge of resource management at the Pentagon during the Bush administration.[1]

The dust had barely settled in Mumbai from what had been the worst terrorist attack since 9/11, and the United States and its European partners now faced the danger of a revived al Qaeda. Obama was also confronted with the worst economic crisis in the country's history since 1929, a collapsing automobile industry, and a banking system that was on the verge of failure. And America was still bogged down in an unnecessary war in Iraq that consumed resources, including drones, that were needed in Afghanistan.

My message to the NSC principals could be summarized in three points. First, the threat of al Qaeda was real and urgent. Al Qaeda's core group in Pakistan—al Qaeda al Umm, or Mother al Qaeda—was under little or no pressure from the Pakistani authorities; it was deeply embedded in a syndicate of like-minded jihadist groups such as Lashkar-e-Tayyiba (LeT) and the Taliban; and it was intent on striking America and its allies, including Europe, Israel, and Australia. Al Qaeda and its sympathizers were exploiting Pakistan's weaknesses and its ambivalence about the global jihad. Our urgent goal, therefore, had to be to disrupt, dismantle, and destroy al Qaeda.

Second, Pakistan was the key to attaining our objectives in South Asia, and it was thwarting achievement of our goals. Its behavior—or, more specifically, the behavior and policies of the Pakistani army and the Inter-Services Intelligence Directorate—was our biggest problem. The complex relationship that the army had with terrorist groups was a difficult and critical challenge to our interests (Admiral Mullen interjected that this was the "heart of the matter"). However, there was no easy or simple solution to the question of how to change Pakistani behavior. Pakistan's polices were rooted in its obsession with India, which went back six decades, and Pakistan, with the fastest-growing nuclear arsenal in the world, had considerable leverage in Afghanistan due to geography, demography, and history. Only the synergy produced by both pressure and inducements would have a chance of changing Pakistani behavior in the right direction, and even then it might not succeed. We had to try to change Pakistani behavior, but we also had to unilaterally protect our interests in spite of Pakistani obstruction of our efforts.

Third and most important, the game changer in South Asia for the United States was the Pakistani-Indian relationship. The rivalry between the two big powers in the subcontinent was the most important driver in the region's politics and security, and managing that rivalry was the key to U.S. success in the region. Failure to get it right could lead to disaster—a war between two nuclear states. Getting it right, nurturing rapprochement between Islamabad and New Delhi, could open the door to fundamental change in the entire region, producing a self-fulfilling virtuous circle of peace and prosperity. Significant improvement in relations between the two main players in the subcontinent would erode the power of both the Pakistani hard-liners in the army and the ISI and their jihadist partners and free Pakistani politics from the dysfunctional paralysis that has stymied the development of the country's democracy. To succeed, the administration needed to put its emphasis on this aspect of the problem, as the president and I had agreed two days before. All the key principals around the table also agreed on this approach. Most of the conversation then focused on how to provide the resources necessary for waging the war in Afghanistan. At the request of the White House press spokesman, after Obama announced his new strategy on the evening of March 27, 2009, I repeated virtually all of my points on national television when Charlie Rose interviewed me on his program late that night. My father was thrilled; he was a big fan of the show.

Unfortunately, Obama had already made a serious error in addressing the challenge in South Asia in the weeks between his election and inauguration. Rather than crafting an approach to the region as a whole, an integrated South Asian policy, he had agreed to a proposal from Richard Holbrooke, former U.S. ambassador to the United Nations, to appoint a special representative for Afghanistan and Pakistan as the administration's point person for the region. AFPAK, as Holbrooke called his new strategy, was designed to recognize that Pakistan was essential to any Afghanistan policy and to resolving the war; what it failed to do was to recognize that India was the key to any change in Pakistan. Holbrooke had been appointed special representative in order to give him a key role in the administration; he wanted to be secretary of state, but Hillary Clinton got that job and this was his consolation prize. He could have been made assistant secretary for South Asia, but he had already been an assistant secretary years before and that would have seemed too small a role for one of America's most successful diplomats. Appointing a special representative was an understandable rookie mistake; with little experience in the executive branch of government, the president did not realize that bad organization would inevitably bring poor policy implementation and incoherent policy analysis.

During the transition the president had briefly flirted with the idea of a bigger bureaucratic role for a special representative that would include Kashmir, and he hinted at that in a press interview. The Indians hated the idea, which to them suggested a crude trade of their interests in Kashmir for Pakistani help with Afghanistan and counterterrorism efforts. That was never Obama's intention. But the Indians made clear in public and in private that they did not want to be part of AFPAK or Holbrooke's agenda. When Holbrooke later tried to involve the Indians in his diplomacy, they were suspicious and kept him at arm's length.

Shortly after his inauguration and Holbooke's appointment, the president had called to ask me to chair an urgent review of U.S. policy on Afghanistan and Pakistan, with a special emphasis on the al Qaeda threat. He needed the complete review before the next NATO summit, scheduled for early April 2009 in Strasbourg, France—only sixty days away. In Washington, two months is very little time to coordinate any interagency undertaking; most of the time would be spent in high-level meetings to review the proposed strategy for dealing with Pakistan and Afghanistan, which would have to be conceived and articulated quickly by a small group of experts. Fortunately, we were able to draw on several reviews of the situation that had been done at the end of the Bush administration, and I was fortunate in having excellent aides to draft the paper. The president met his deadline, and he presented the results of the review in a speech to the nation on March 27, 2009. He did not talk about the centrality of the India-Pakistan issue for diplomatic reasons—it would not go down well in New Delhi—but it was at the heart of the review's conclusions. However, it was not built into the bureaucracy now tasked with seeking to implement the strategy, which was a serious design flaw.

It might have worked better if the president and Holbrooke had gotten along; unfortunately, they didn't. Holbrooke had a long-standing reputation for being strong willed and difficult to work with, and the president found him to be pompous and self-absorbed. He did not invite Holbrooke on Air Force One to Los Angeles in March and—much more important—he did not invite him on Air Force One the following December, when Obama made his first visit to Afghanistan as president. The second omission sent a message to everyone: the president did not have confidence in his special representative. Early on Holbrooke was tasked with managing the Afghan presidential election in 2009 to ensure that it was a credible process; instead, President Hamid Karzai had engaged in massive vote fraud, counting more than a million false ballots in his favor. Karzai got away with it. Rightly or wrongly, Holbrooke was blamed in the White House for the debacle. Holbrooke also was an enthusiastic supporter of nation building in Afghanistan and Pakistan, encouraging a surge of civilian experts to come to both countries to undertake projects that Obama increasingly began to doubt would work.

Within months of his inauguration, Obama's South Asia team was riven by internal rivalries and backstabbing. Obama's first two commanders on the ground in Afghanistan were removed before their tour of duty was over. The second, Stanley McChrystal, was fired for an interview that his staff had given to *Rolling Stone* magazine during a night of drinking in Paris in which they disparaged Holbrooke, Biden, and the administration. Rumors that Holbrooke would be fired kept appearing until his death in December 2010. It was a sad end to a very distinguished career, and it distracted attention from the many important contributions that he had made to American diplomacy in Afghanistan and Pakistan. Much of the infighting and squabbling was reported in the media, especially by one of Washington's most famous journalists, Bob Woodward, in his book *Obama's Wars* in 2010.[2] It was no way to fight a war.

PAKISTAN AND AL QAEDA

Despite all the self-inflicted damage from poor organization and personality differences, the Obama team did have considerable success in working toward its principal goal in South Asia, which Obama announced in his March 27, 2009, speech: the destruction of al Qaeda in Pakistan. There the White House was focused and organized. Obama recognized immediately after taking office that the hunt for Osama bin Laden had gone stale; the trail was cold as a glacier. Obama's chief of staff, Rahm Emanuel, who had opposed the Holbrooke appointment, asked me on my second day of conducting the White House review of policy on Afghanistan and Pakistan why we did not know where bin Laden was hiding. I told him that we didn't know because no one was in charge of finding him. The Bush administration had taken its eye off the ball in searching for bin Laden in late 2001, and the hunt had never recovered.[3] Obama gave the job to Leon Panetta, his director of central intelligence. In the White House, the overall counterterrorism mission was given to John Brennan, a friend and colleague of mine from the CIA who had been a great help to me when I was writing my first book, *The Search for Al Qaeda,* in 2008. The president, who had rightly decided that he needed a good sheriff to lead the posse, picked two, one inside the White House and one at the CIA.

The threat was indeed urgent. Al Qaeda had planned an attack in September 2009 on the New York City subway system, the nation's largest, which is used by more than 5 million riders every day. The successful al Qaeda attacks on metro systems in Europe—in Madrid in 2003 and London in 2005—were to be outdone by three suicide bombers blowing themselves up during rush hour on the eighth anniversary of 9/11. Three American citizens, Najibullah Zazi, Zarein Ahmedzay, and Adis Medunjanin, had traveled to Pakistan in 2008 to join the Afghan Taliban and fight in Afghanistan. The Taliban instead gave them over to al Qaeda, which persuaded them to conduct a "martyrdom" mission in New York and taught them how to make the explosives needed for the attack. Their al Qaeda trainer was Rashid Rauf, a British citizen of Pakistani origin, who had been a key player in the attack on the British underground in July 2005. He was also deeply involved in a plot in 2006 to blow up several passenger jets en route from Heathrow Airport near London to cities in the United States and Canada; that plot was foiled by British intelligence. Briefly arrested in Pakistan after the plot was detected, he escaped from an ISI prison, almost certainly with inside help. He then trained Zazi and his team. Fortunately, the FBI and the New York Police Department were tracking the three would-be terrorists in a joint counter-terrorism mission code-named Operation Highrise, and they were arrested before they could conduct their attack. They have since been convicted of attempted murder.[4]

In December 2009 another al Qaeda attack was narrowly averted. A Nigerian named Umar Farouk Abdulmutallab approached al Qaeda's cell in Yemen, where he was recruited to conduct a martyrdom operation by Anwar al-Awlaki, an American citizen of Yemeni descent. A Saudi bomb maker for al Qaeda named Ibrahim al-Asiri built a bomb that could be concealed in a terrorist's underwear to thwart airport security measures. Abdulmutallab boarded a Northwest Airlines flight from Amsterdam on Christmas Day but failed to detonate the bomb as the plane descended over Ontario into Detroit. Osama bin Laden issued an audio message a few days later from his hideout in Abbottabad, promising that more such attacks would follow until America ceased all aid to Israel.[5] Obama told his staff, "We dodged a bullet, but just barely."[6]

Then, in May 2010, a Pakistani named Faisal Shahzad left a car bomb in the heart of Times Square in New York City with the fuse set to blow up. Shahzad was a naturalized American citizen who came from a prominent family in Pakistan; his father was an air vice marshal in the Pakistani air force. He had been trained to build the bomb by al Qaeda's ally in Pakistan, the Taliban, but proved to be a poor student. His bomb did not explode, and he was arrested at JFK Airport trying to escape to Pakistan. He later made clear that he was inspired to try to attack America by reading Abdullah Azzam's books and by his hero Abu Musab al-Zarqawi, the Jordanian leader of al Qaeda in Iraq.

By 2010 Obama had already ordered a significant escalation in drone attacks on al Qaeda targets in Pakistan's Federally Administered Tribal Areas (FATA), a largely ungoverned space in the border region whose autonomy dated from the Raj. The Bush administration had begun drone attacks in the FATA in 2007, and at first it provided the ISI with advance warning of the attacks and their targets. However, every lethal mission failed to achieve its goal, so the decision was made not to give the ISI advance notice any longer. By the end of the Bush administration, there had been forty lethal drone attacks, almost all in Pakistan. Within the first three and a half years of the Obama administration, there had been more than 300 attacks, 85 percent in Pakistan.[7] Drone attacks in Pakistan increased from 7 in 2007 to 33 in 2008, 54 in 2009, 118 in 2010, 70 in 2011, and at least 50 in the first nine months of 2012.[8] Significant al Qaeda figures were killed in the operations, including Rashid Rauf, Ilyas Kashmiri, and many more.

At first the drones flew from air bases in Afghanistan and Pakistan. Musharraf had allowed use of a Pakistani base, but it was closed down in 2011 when Pakistanis demanded an end to the use of their soil for drone attacks inside their territory. So the base in Afghanistan became the only one close enough to the targets, in effect making it crucial for American intelligence operations against al Qaeda and its allies in Pakistan. In addition to the many lethal drone operations in the FATA, there were many more nonlethal intelligence collection missions to monitor activity both inside and outside the FATA—for example, in Abbottabad.

The focused use of the drones in Pakistan disrupted and dismantled the al Qaeda network in the country. It became increasingly difficult to train and dispatch terrorists like the Operation Highrise team; it was just too dangerous. For the first time since al Qaeda retreated into Pakistan after 2001, the terrorist group was under sustained and serious attack. It fought back hard. On December 30, 2009, a Jordanian al Qaeda operative posing as a double agent for the Jordanian intelligence service was set to be debriefed at a CIA forward operating base in Afghanistan near the Pakistani border. He was allegedly about to reveal the location of bin Laden's deputy, Ayman al-Zawahiri, to the CIA. Instead, once inside, he blew himself up, killing seven CIA officers and his Jordanian handler. It was the second-most-lethal day in CIA history.[9]

But in 2011, thanks to good intelligence work, the CIA finally found the trail to bin Laden's hideout. The breakthrough was a result of focused information gathering and painstaking data analysis, more Agatha Christie than Ian Fleming. Even so, the most that the CIA could tell Obama in April 2011 was that there was a 50-50 chance that bin Laden was hiding in the Abbottabad lair. The president gave the order to pull the trigger, and bin Laden was dead and buried on May 2, 2011.

From the day that the CIA became focused on Abbottabad, Obama had decided that he could not trust the Pakistanis with information about the hideout. No Pakistani official was given any advance warning that the United States suspected that bin Laden was hiding in the Abbottabad complex or that it intended to send commandoes to find and either capture or kill him. During months of surveillance of the compound and preparation for the SEAL operation, Pakistan was kept completely in the dark. It was an extraordinary decision. Since 2001 Pakistani leaders from former president Pervez Musharraf to current president Ali Asif Zardari and General Ashfaq Kayani, the chief of army staff and the real power in the country, had promised again and again to help America fight al Qaeda. To help them do so, the United States had given Pakistan almost $25 billion in aid since 9/11 and sold the army huge amounts of new equipment, including eighteen new F-16s.[10]

Now, at the moment of truth, the American president correctly judged that he could not trust the Pakistanis with vital information on the location of al Qaeda's top leader. Obama's decision spoke volumes about America's real attitude toward its Pakistani partner.

Abbottabad is not an ordinary city. Pakistan's first military dictator, Field Marshal Ayub Khan, was born very close to Abbottabad. It is the home of the Pakistan Military Academy–Kakul, the Pakistani equivalent of West Point or Sandhurst. Several regiments of the army call it home. Pakistani military helicopters routinely flew over bin Laden's lair, ferrying the senior command of the Pakistani army in and out of the academy, while bin Laden paced the roof.[11] In 2006 the commandant of the Kakul academy was General Nadeem Taj, a close confidant of Musharraf, whom Taj had accompanied on an official visit to Sri Lanka in October 1999. While they were on the flight home, Prime Minister Nawaz Sharif fired Musharraf from his job as chief of army staff, and Taj helped Musharraf engineer a coup from the plane. Taj was also with Musharraf when Musharraf survived an assassination attempt in December 2003. For his loyalty, Taj was appointed director general of military intelligence in 2003 and commandant of Kakul in 2006. So he was the man in charge when bin Laden set up his hideout.

In late 2007 Taj was promoted again, to director general of Inter-Services Intelligence, the top intelligence job in the country, replacing General Kayani, who was moved up to be chief of army staff. On Taj's watch, the drone campaign to kill al Qaeda leaders in Pakistan was expanded by President George Bush, but the targets consistently escaped because they were warned of the impending attacks. Since at the time the ISI was given advance notice of drone operations, it was not hard to determine where the leaks came from. Then, in December 2007, former prime minister Benazir Bhutto was assassinated in Rawalpindi. A UN investigation later concluded that the ISI deliberately destroyed vital forensic evidence that would have assisted in finding those responsible. When in 2008 the Indian Embassy in Kabul was attacked by the

Afghan Taliban, the United States determined that the attack had been ordered by the ISI.

Under heavy pressure from the Bush team to move Taj out of ISI, Kayani promoted him again in October 2008, making him commander of the XXX Corps, one of the most important positions in the Pakistani army, and one of the dozen men who control the army. Taj was too powerful and well connected to be moved any other way. A month later, ten Pakistani terrorists attacked the Indian city of Mumbai, killing dozens, including six Americans. The attack was planned and partly funded by the ISI during the tenures of both Kayani and Taj as director general of the intelligence service.

Pakistanis have wondered from the moment that the SEAL raid became public knowledge what their army and intelligence services knew about bin Laden's location. No one believes that President Zardari knew anything; he is powerless and clueless about the ISI's activities. Officially, the ISI says that it too was clueless and knew nothing, but many Pakistanis find that hard to believe. Four days after the raid, for example, an op-ed entitled "The Emperors' Clothes" in the influential newspaper *Dawn* stated, "As the initial shock and disbelief wears off, there is a deep, deep sense of unease here. Did they know he was here? . . . They knew. They knew he was there. And they knew they could get away with it."[12]

But no one really knows. One senior Pakistani official told me that bin Laden's presence in Abbottabad was just a "freak coincidence."[13] Perhaps the ISI was clueless and negligent in looking for bin Laden. Maybe Musharraf, Kayani, and Taj were just incompetent. They had been warned to look in Abbottabad. In 2006, in his own memoirs, Musharraf wrote that they knew that al Qaeda was hiding key leaders in the city. The Afghan intelligence chief, Amrullah Saleh, says that he told Musharraf in a meeting in Pakistan in 2006 that bin Laden was hiding in the area around Abbottabad. According to Saleh, in response to the news Musharraf "banged the table and said am I president of a banana republic? How can you tell me bin Laden is hiding in a settled area of Pakistan?"[14] After the SEAL raid, Musharraf told the media that he remembered jogging by the house that bin Laden was hiding in when he visited the academy.

In early 2011 an Indonesian terrorist, Umar Patek, was arrested in Abbottabad by the ISI. Patek had been the mastermind of the 2002 bombing of nightclubs in Bali, in which more than 200 people were killed. According to Indonesian intelligence experts, he went to Abbottabad in 2011 looking for al Qaeda contacts to help him rebuild the Indonesian terrorist underground and train operatives in Pakistan. He may or may not have been looking specifically for bin Laden; the sources are uncertain whether Patek knew that bin Laden was there or just that some senior al Qaeda officials were there. One of bin Laden's wives actually found bin Laden in Abbottabad; she had gone into exile in Iran in 2001 but was reunited with her husband in either late 2010 or early 2011. If she could find bin Laden's house, why did not the ISI? The question haunts U.S.-Pakistan relations.[15]

The Abbottabad raid and the drone war made it virtually impossible for Obama to develop a strong relationship with Pakistan's leaders. He tried hard. In the first two years of his administration he pushed his cabinet to try to find common ground with Pakistan. Secretary of State Clinton, Secretary of Defense Gates, Joint Chiefs of Staff chairman Mullen, and special representative Holbrooke made numerous visits to Islamabad. The message was that America and Pakistan faced a common threat from al Qaeda and Islamic extremism and that they should work together to defeat their common foe. That meant pressing the Afghan Taliban to accept a cease-fire and negotiate, attacking al Qaeda together, and cracking down on groups like Lashkar-e-Tayyiba. Behind the message was a major increase in economic assistance to Pakistan. The so-called Kerry-Lugar bill, named after its Democratic and Republican sponsors in the Senate, promised $1.5 billion in economic aid each year for five years. The original bill promised a ten-year commitment and an annual $1 billion bonus if the president could certify that Pakistan was a democratic government, but those ideas died in legislative wrangling. The bill that passed was intended to provide tangible support to those in Pakistan who agreed that the country needed to stop abetting terror or, worse, actively colluding with terrorists.

Some in Islamabad agreed. President Zardari understood from the start that the jihadists and their generals were his enemies; they had, after all, killed his wife. His ambassador in Washington, Husain Haqqani, understood the common threat and the perfidious role of the ISI; he had written about it extensively before becoming ambassador, and he tried hard to make the U.S.-Pakistan relationship work for both.[16] The terrorists went after their critics. The governor of the Punjab, Salmaan Taseer, was assassinated by his own security guard in January 2011 for his outspoken opposition to extremism and his criticism of the ISI. Obama sent a letter to Zardari in November 2009 urging that their two countries take a joint approach to fighting the extremists, who "plan attacks against targets in Pakistan, the region, and beyond." He got back an answer written by the ISI that spoke of dark plots by India in Afghanistan "in which neighboring intelligence agencies are using Afghan soil to perpetrate violence in Pakistan."[17] Indeed, the real power remained with the army and the ISI. When the president met with Kayani in the Roosevelt Room of the White House on October 20, 2010, he got a fourteen-page memo from the general that labeled America "intrusive and overbearing." The memo claimed that America was "causing and maintaining a controlled chaos in Pakistan. The real aim of U.S. strategy is to de-nuclearize Pakistan."[18]

Despite the best efforts of Obama and Zardari, a series of incidents damaged the U.S.-Pakistan relationship. In early 2011 an American security guard, Raymond Davis, killed two Pakistanis in Lahore and was arrested for their deaths. Washington claimed that he should be given diplomatic immunity; the Pakistani press said that he was a CIA operative. In the end, Ambassador Haqqani negotiated his release. Then came the bin Laden raid. The Pakistani air force scrambled two F-16s to chase the SEALs' helicopters, one of which was carrying bin Laden's body, on their way back to Afghanistan, but it was too late. The army was deeply humiliated that it had failed to defend Pakistan's air space and territorial integrity.[19] A Pakistani American claimed that Haqqani had sought American help after the raid to prevent an army coup against Zardari.[20] Summoned home by the ISI, Haqqani was driven from office and barely escaped with his life.

On November 26, 2011, American aircraft fired on Pakistani soldiers supporting the Afghan Taliban along the Durand Line and killed two dozen in a major airstrike. Pakistan demanded an apology and cut off the use of Pakistani territory to resupply NATO forces in Afghanistan. When Obama took office, more than 80 percent of NATO supplies in Afghanistan arrived via Pakistan, almost all through Karachi. He ordered a major effort to diversify the supply route and bring in more supplies from the north. The Pakistani aid cut-off therefore was not a fatal blow to the alliance, although it raised the cost of the logistical supply line considerably (by $100 million a month) by forcing near-total reliance on the northern supply route, via Russia and Uzbekistan. To try to reset the relationship, Obama invited Zardari to the NATO summit in Chicago in May 2012. But Zardari could not deliver a reopening of the supply line, and he demanded an apology for the November firefight. Obama and Zardari barely exchanged greetings in Chicago; the relationship was all but broken. In July, after Secretary Clinton said that she was "sorry" for the November incident, the Pakistanis finally reopened the Karachi-Kabul road.

Hafiz Saeed, the head of Lashkar-e-Tayyiba and the mastermind of the Mumbai attacks, was put on the American most-wanted list with a $10 million reward on his head. He was not hiding from justice, however; he remained the ISI's darling and a friend of the generals. Instead, he often mocked America on Pakistani television, and in large rallies across Pakistan, he called for an end to the drone war, a complete cut-off of bilateral relations with America, and support for the "liberation" of all Muslims in India through jihad. He also led prayers mourning the loss of Osama bin Laden the Friday after his death.

Saeed's evident immunity from prosecution symbolizes the challenges that America faces in Pakistan. Despite overwhelming evidence of his culpability in the murder of dozens of innocents, including American citizens, in many terror attacks and despite repeated American demands that he be brought to justice, Pakistan still provides him not just a safe haven but also active support and assistance. Obama had made real and tangible progress in the fight against al Qaeda, progress that made Americans safer, but he had not changed Pakistani behavior. Nor did the drone war significantly affect the rest of the groups in the syndicate, such as Lashkar-e-Tayyiba. For Americans, the drones and the Abbottabad raid were essential means of self-defense, all the more important because Pakistan itself seemed unwilling to take the action needed to fight terrorism. Afghanistan had become a U.S. base for fighting terrorists in Pakistan.

For Pakistanis the picture was different. The drones and the SEAL raid were constant intrusions into their territory without their foreknowledge or approval. That Musharraf had privately agreed to the drones back in 2007 was irrelevant; by 2012, he was a traitor and an outcast. In a review of policy toward America, the parliament demanded an end to the drone attacks, and polls showed animosity toward the United States at record levels. One poll in June 2012 showed 74 percent of Pakistanis regarded America as an "enemy," and in the Punjab the level rose to 85 percent. In contrast, 90 percent saw China as a friend. The drones were seen by 94 percent as killing far too many innocents despite American claims that they were highly selective and killed very few innocents.[21] One observer summed it up this way: "It was the drones, beyond any other real or imagined provocation, that inflamed Pakistani emotions against the United States. Their psychological impact on society was so disproportionate that the CIA might as well have dropped an atom bomb on Karachi's Fatima Jinnah Avenue during rush hour."[22]

OBAMA AND INDIA

It was no accident that the first foreign trip by Leon Panetta, Obama's new director of central intelligence, was to India. It was a highly symbolic and significant gesture. It not only showed solidarity with India just after the Mumbai attacks, it also showed the ISI that the CIA was looking elsewhere for allies in South Asia. Obama wanted to send a signal to both India and Pakistan that it was a new day in Washington. More trips followed. On November 24, 2009, Prime Minister Singh became the first foreign leader to make a state visit to the Obama White House; the visit called for the highest level of protocol and a state dinner at the White House, the first such dinner for the Obama family.

Obama himself traveled to India and Afghanistan in November 2010. He decided not to visit Pakistan on that trip, promising to go in 2011 instead. He visited New Delhi, Mumbai, and Kabul. In Mumbai the president and the first lady paid an emotional tribute to the victims of the 26/11 terror attack. During the trip Obama decided to announce American support for giving India a permanent seat at the UN Security Council. It was a major advance in the U.S. position, which had long advocated Security Council reform but had never argued explicitly to include India in the Security Council. It was further recognition that America not only understood that India was on the path to great power status but welcomed India's inclusion in the elite circle of top global players.

Of course, the news did not go down well in Pakistan. Nor was it welcomed in China, which has the power to veto Security Council reform. Some critics in the United States dismissed it as a hollow gesture; others have since noted that even after Obama's announcement, India voted with the United States in the UN General Assembly in 2011 only 33 percent of the time.[23] The criticism missed the point. Like his two predecessors, Obama was coming to grips with the inevitable rise of India and seeking to position America in the best way possible to take advantage of it.

Arms sales to and military-to-military exchanges with India also increased on Obama's watch. Secretary of Defense Gates and his successor, Secretary Panetta, both visited New Delhi. Like Obama, Panetta skipped visiting Pakistan while flying to India and Afghanistan; he said that his patience with Pakistani support for terrorism had reached its limits. By 2012 the United States and India were holding fifty annual military training exercises. But India was careful in its military dealings with Washington. It purchased C-130J and C-17A heavy lift transport aircraft but not advanced fighter aircraft. When India held a multiyear competition to select a new fighter aircraft for its air force—a deal worth tens of billions of dollars—the two American jets, the F-16 and the F-18, lost out in the first round and France won the award.[24] Memories of 1965 and 1971 remain vivid in the Ministry of Defense, where America is not considered a reliable supplier of lethal military equipment in a crisis. Should there be another war with Pakistan, which almost all Indian military planners believe is all but inevitable, New Delhi does not want to have to rely on Washington to resupply key combat equipment.

Increasingly, India looked to Israel as its primary source of advanced military technology. Arms sales grew annually, to $1.5 billion by 2006, and have stayed around that level since then. Israel has helped to upgrade India's jet fighter fleet, sold India advanced airborne early warning aircraft, and worked with India on satellite imagery technology. President Clinton had encouraged the start of the Israeli-Indian military entente in 2000 during his visit to New Delhi and at the Camp David peace summit with Prime Minister Ehud Barak.

Counterterrorism cooperation also increased in the wake of the Mumbai attacks. Panetta's 2009 visit to New Delhi was followed by trips by other senior U.S. security officials, including the secretary of homeland security and the director of the FBI.

Lashkar-e-Tayyiba and the investigation of the Mumbai attacks became priorities for the American counterterrorism community. The United States worked jointly with India on the investigation of David Headley's role in the massacre and in the apprehension of the LeT's mastermind, Abu Jindal, in Saudi Arabia. Headley and his partner were prosecuted in Chicago in high-profile trials. In 2012, after first listing Hafiz Saeed as an al Qaeda accomplice, the United States publicly offered a $10 million bounty for him and for information leading to his arrest. India welcomed the decision. After decades of cool relations between the two countries' security services, the change was important and significant.

There were other significant successes in thwarting Lashkar-e-Tayyiba. In 2009 a plot to attack the American, British, and Indian embassies in Dacca, Bangladesh, was foiled by effective counterterrorism cooperation. A much more elaborate LeT plot in October 2010 to attack the Nineteenth Commonwealth Games in New Delhi also was disrupted and prevented by good counterterrorism work. If the plot had succeeded, it might have been even bigger than the 2008 Mumbai attack.[25]

But there was little discussion about India's troubled neighbor Pakistan and what India could do to try to help change Pakistani behavior. For example, in the joint communiqué issued in June 2012 after the third round of the U.S.-India Strategic Dialogue, an annual summit chaired by Secretary Clinton and her Indian counterpart to review all facets of the bilateral relationship, Pakistan is mentioned only once, in passing. Afghanistan is mentioned seventeen times.[26] The biggest challenge facing both India and America in South Asia barely received any public attention in their dialogue. In private, of course, there was more discussion about Pakistan and shared irritation at its continued role in sponsoring and abetting terror. But those conversations did not translate into a strategy on how to leverage India's strengths to influence Pakistani behavior. The U.S.-India dialogue suffered from malaise—lots of soaring rhetoric, but less substance.

It would, of course, have been a difficult dialogue under even the best of circumstances. After Mumbai, it was even more difficult, but it was also even more vital. The United States did welcome the cautious resumption of political dialogue between India and Pakistan in 2009 and the visit of President Zardari to India in 2012. It also supported discussion of modest steps to increase trade between the two countries and open more transportation links. But Obama's approach in his first term was cautious and small. Perhaps he remained trapped in the AFPAK paradigm and ill served by a bureaucracy focused almost exclusively on the Afghanistan imbroglio. He had a wealth of other problems on his plate, given the state of the American economy and the legacy of two wars; nevertheless, it was not a policy designed to alter the game in South Asia.

CHAPTER EIGHT

PROMOTING GAME CHANGE IN SOUTH ASIA

THE THAR DESERT of Rajasthan, an arid wasteland astride the Indian and Pakistani border, is a forbidding place. In the summer, it can be as hot as any spot on earth. Fortunately, I was staying the night near Jodhpur in a hotel that was once a maharaja's palace. My delegation, from the United Kingdom's Royal College of Defence Studies, was visiting the subcontinent for a month in September 2002, and on this particular day we were guests at an advanced Indian air force jet fighter base. After a tour of the MiG-29 jets on the tarmac, we had a briefing and lunch with the pilots. The crisis over the attack on the Indian parliament was now nearly nine months old. More than 1 million Indian and Pakistani troops were deployed along the border, eyeball to eyeball, expecting war.

The pilots were frustrated. They had been preparing for war for nine months now, and they were ready. As professionals, they were eager to do their job. But the order never came, and a month later they would be told to stand down. As we talked to them, it was clear that they understood that a war with Pakistan would not be a simple or clean affair. They all agreed that it could go nuclear, although most argued that it probably would not. When asked who would win, they were all in agreement, of course. India would prevail rapidly, bringing Pakistan to its knees. Pakistan would be forced to finally abandon any claims to Kashmir and to stop sponsoring terrorism. Would the Pakistani army accept a crushing defeat and not use its bombs, my mates and I asked? Perhaps not, they responded, but India could absorb the cost of a nuclear strike and hit back even harder. From the Thar Desert to Fort Williams in Kolkata, the Indian military academy in Pune, and military headquarters in New Delhi, we heard the same argument: India cannot let Pakistan get away with terrorism; it must pay a price. Nonetheless, in 2002, Pakistan got away with it.

When the Royal College team met with General Musharraf in Rawalpindi a couple of weeks later, his tone was triumphant. A graduate of the college himself, he was eager to talk with members of the current class. When asked how it was possible for Pakistani terrorists to attack the very heart of Indian democracy in New Delhi, Musharraf was evasive, saying only that such clandestine affairs are always complicated. But his main message was simple: Pakistan had prevailed in the year-long crisis after the New Delhi attack. India had been forced to back down; Pakistan's deterrent had worked. His implicit message also was simple: if it chose, Pakistan could do it and get away with it again.

The stakes in South Asia are huge. There is a very real chance of another Mumbai or Kargil. There is the risk of nuclear war. There is also the potential for one and half billion people to live a better life and create a zone of economic prosperity and democracy unrivaled on the planet. South Asians will determine which path they follow; Americans will be mostly observers. But the United States can help.

America would be wise to first organize itself properly to deal with South Asia. Poor organization has been a consistent problem for decades. South Asia was the stepchild of the Near East until Congress forced the first Bush administration to set up a separate bureau in the State Department in 1992. The second Bush administration then tried to merge it into East Asia, inadvertently leaving Afghanistan homeless. The Obama team partitioned the subcontinent again, splitting Afghanistan and Pakistan from India. The right answer, which is also a simple one, is to see the region as a whole and create an organizational structure that does the same. A South Asia bureau should be created in the National Security Council, and the rest of the executive branch, including the uniformed military services, should be instructed to follow suit. A new Indian Ocean command should be created to make sure that the U.S. military—the largest part of the American national security apparatus with the biggest throw weight in policy formulation outside the White House—has a holistic view of South Asia. With the right bureaucracy in place to plan, analyze, and implement strategy, the United States can then turn to substantive policy matters.

Today South Asia is at a unique moment in its history. India is more prosperous and democratic than ever before; it is growing rapidly, and its democracy is deeply ingrained in the national psyche. A military coup in New Delhi is unthinkable. Hundreds of millions of Indians are escaping dire poverty, and hundreds of millions more are becoming middle-class consumers. Despite a recent slowdown in its economic growth rate, in the new millennium India is certain to be one of the most important countries in the world, as it was for so much of human history.

Pakistan's progress has been less certain but nonetheless important and impressive. Despite all the odds, President Zardari has survived as a democratically elected leader, the first elected Pakistani head of state to serve a full term in office. Although behind the scenes the army wields excessive power and influence and controls the national security agenda, it has not been able to oust Zardari or to convince Pakistanis that the generals should rule again. A coup is still a real danger, especially if it brings back a twenty-first century version of Mohammed Zia ul-Haq, but it is by no means inevitable. Pakistan's economy is not consistently growing as fast as India's, but it has shown some promise.

A wealth of good books about Pakistan's future have been published in the last several years, with some arguing that Pakistan is a failing state and others maintaining that the case for the collapse of Pakistan is overstated.[1] In any event, there are good reasons to be concerned about its future. Violence, terrorism, and political assassinations have become all too common. The civil-military relationship is poisonous. The ISI's flirtation with terrorists has made Pakistan the terrorism capital of the world; it was no accident that Osama bin Laden spent the last decade of his life in Pakistan. According to the Pakistani government, since 9/11 almost 45,000 Pakistanis, including 7,000 soldiers, have died in terrorism-related violence, defined to include sectarian and ethnic terrorism in Pakistan's major cities and borderlands. Much of the violence has taken place in the major cities of Karachi, Lahore, and Islamabad. While there was one suicide bombing in Pakistan before 9/11, there have been more than 300 since.[2]

Pakistanis themselves are increasingly fed up with the political gridlock that has stymied the country's progress for years. In a sense, every national election in Pakistan since 1988 has had the same two candidates: Nawaz Sharif and Benazir Bhutto, or her husband as a stand-in. The lack of choice is frustrating, and one consequence is the increasing search for an alternative. The country's former star cricket player, Imran Khan, has attracted huge interest recently as a possible alternative.[3] Even A. Q. Khan is considering some kind of political future as well, sensing the desire for change in the country.

But Pakistan is not falling apart like Somalia or Syria. The instruments of state power, though corrupt, are still strong. The army and the intelligence services are not likely to collapse in the foreseeable future, nor is the Pakistan Taliban likely to defeat them in battle. A more realistic danger is another coup. It might be a soft one, without tanks in the streets, done largely behind the scenes. If the next coup were to be led by a general in the mold of Zia ul-Haq, it could mean the transformation of Pakistan into a jihadist state. That would be a global nightmare.

In addition, another small war or another big terrorist attack, like Kargil or Mumbai, could spiral out of control all too easily, precipitating disaster. India and Pakistan's track record since independence shows that they have gone from one crisis to the next. True, they have not fought a major war since 1971, but they went to the brink in 1987, 1990, 1999, 2001, 2002, and 2008. The two countries are certainly well armed for war. India has the world's largest volunteer army, with 1,300,000 active duty personnel and another 1 million reserve personnel; its air force has 127,000 personnel and operates almost 1,400 aircraft; and its navy is one of the few true blue-water fleets in the world capable of projecting power. India is also the world's largest importer of arms today, accounting for almost 10 percent of global arms purchases. Pakistan, with a much smaller demographic and economic base, is stretched to keep up, but it has the seventh-largest military in the world. The army has an active duty force of 700,000 men; the air force has 65,000 full-time personnel and operates 550 combat aircraft and many more transport and training aircraft.[4] Both countries spend an enormous amount of their national wealth on their military. For two countries facing huge challenges of poverty and unemployment, it is a tragedy to spend so much on preparing for war.

They also spend precious resources on their nuclear deterrents. How large their respective arsenals are is a closely guarded secret in both New Delhi and Islamabad. Estimates by various think tanks vary; a safe estimate would put both at no less than a hundred weapons each. Pakistan's arsenal, the fastest growing in the world today, may be twice that size. Both countries can deliver their weapons by aircraft and missiles. Pakistan's Ghauri missiles, based on a North Korean design, can strike all of India's major cities. India's Agni missile, which was tested in May 2012, flew deep into the Indian Ocean; it can reach all of Pakistan and as far as Beijing. Both are now developing naval delivery systems. India, which already has a nuclear-powered submarine, launched in 2009, has plans to build four more, and it has practiced with leased Russian-supplied nuclear submarines extensively in the past. Pakistan set up a new naval strategic forces command and is developing tactical nuclear weapons.[5] It also is building three more Chinese-supplied plutonium reactors to increase its arsenal even faster.[6]

Some have argued that the possession of nuclear weapons now has created a more or less stable balance of terror that will preclude Armageddon in South Asia. That argument, which was part of Musharraf's message to the Royal College group, suggests that just as America and the Soviet Union fought a cold war but never a hot war because of their mutually assured destruction, India and Pakistan, though rivals, will not engage in a nuclear war; they are not suicidal. This argument may prove true over time, but that is an uncertain bet. America and the Soviet Union came very close to nuclear war more than once. The worst scare occurred during the Cuban missile crisis in 1962, when, according to new research, nuclear war was only narrowly averted;[7] however, there were other crises, in Germany and the Middle East, that also threatened conflict between the two superpowers. If John Kennedy had listened to his generals and diplomats in 1962, the world would have been incinerated. Almost all of them recommended invading Cuba, and it is now known that if the United States had done so, the Russians would have used nuclear weapons to defend the island.

Unlike America and the Soviet Union, India and Pakistan are not separated by the Arctic Ocean. There is no buffer of frozen water between them; they confront each other every day along a long, disputed border. While the border area has been more stable since the end of the Twin Peaks crisis, it remains a source of friction. Pakistani or Indian nuclear-tipped missiles would arrive on target in a matter of a few minutes from launch to explosion. There would be no time for using a hot line to phone the other leader, let alone for reflection or discussion.

Moreover, the subcontinent is home to a wealth of terrorists eager to provoke war between India and Pakistan. The Mumbai attack in 2008 demonstrated that most dramatically. The 2000 attack on the Indian parliament was also a vivid warning that there are those in Pakistan who seek a nuclear confrontation to realize their twisted dream of destroying the Indian union. Al Qaeda, Lashkar-e-Tayyiba, and a host of others want war in South Asia, and they have the ability to create a provocation, a casus belli, as did the Serbian terrorists who started World War I. The events of 1914 were very much on Bill Clinton's mind at Blair House in 1999; he worried about the danger of escalation—how terrorists could reignite an already dangerous conflict to create disaster. The subcontinent's terrorists also long to gain direct control of Pakistan's nuclear weapons. George Tenet, a former director of central intelligence, discussed in his memoirs repeated efforts by al Qaeda to acquire nuclear weapons.[8] The terrorist organizations in Pakistan have repeatedly attacked military installations where the country's nuclear weapons are stored. One observer sagely noted that "Al Qaeda and other militant groups are known to be desperate to get their hands on fissile material or an assembled warhead. As Pakistan is apparently increasing its arsenal as fast as it can and investing in smaller and more easily waylaid weapons, the risks are mounting." At least six nuclear sites have been targets of militant attacks in recent years.[9]

The United States has played a key role in all of the recent crises in averting the worst and helping to keep the peace. From Reagan in the Brass Tacks crisis to George H. W. Bush in the 1990 war scare, Clinton in Kargil, George Bush in 2001 and 2002, and George Bush and Obama in 2008, American presidents have been key intermediaries in helping to keep conflict limited and contained. Some scholars have even argued that the United States now has the equivalent of a "playbook" for conflict management in South Asia.[10] They are right; the United States does know how to manage a crisis. But that isn't enough. South Asia is playing Russian roulette, with war as a possible outcome. So far India and Pakistan have fired empty chambers in their revolvers, but it is all too likely that sooner or later, that will end. When the next crisis comes, it will be harder than ever for an Indian prime minister to argue that diplomacy will lead Pakistan to put pressure on the terrorists; it has failed too many times. The next time that it does, the American play book could be useless.

At the heart of the matter is Pakistan's twin sense of vulnerability and unfulfilled aspirations. Pakistan is a state that is unsatisfied with its borders and living next to a much-bigger rival. Indeed, Pakistan's longest borders with its two largest neighbors are unsettled and unrecognized by those neighbors. It is really remarkable that in the twenty-first century such a large country still has two disputed borders, and that fact explains in part why the military has been such a dominant player in the country's politics. Pakistani generals can make a convincing case that the country faces serious national security threats on multiple fronts and therefore must devote much of its budget to preparing for war. Of course, for decades the generals have made Pakistan's problems worse by supporting terrorism and schemes like the 1999 Kargil war and Operation Gibraltar, the plot to seize Kashmir in 1965. They also have used the excuse of national security to justify creating a state within the state that is beyond the reach of civil authority and the rule of law. That does not change the fact that Pakistan needs to find a peaceful resolution of its border disputes.

One way to begin to resolve Pakistan's border situation would be to encourage more cross-border trade and transit. Since 1947 and especially since 1965, there has been little trade between India and Pakistan and transit between the two has been limited and difficult. For two countries that share a subcontinent, their interaction is minimal. There are occasional joint sporting events, usually cricket matches, and a good many informal academic discussions, but while both are useful endeavors, they are unlikely to change the dynamics of South Asian politics. The goodwill generated by a cricket game in which both prime ministers are cheering in the stands has not changed Pakistani or Indian policies one iota, nor has the host of academic exchanges and track-two conferences in the last few decades, regardless of how worthwhile.

Increasing trade and transit would be more meaningful; it would build constituencies in both countries that would support an end to conflict and favor peace. Unleashing the economic potential of a unified South Asian market could do for Pakistan and its neighbors what the European Union did for Europe, creating a common sense of identity and a common interest in peace. Tourism between the two would build a healthy mutual understanding and familiarity that could reunite what partition broke apart, creating a subcontinent at peace, not war.

Today the amount of direct trade between the two is relatively small. The total trade between Pakistan and India in 2011 was $2.6 billion. In 2010 India exported about $2 billion to Pakistan and imported about $300 million. That is twice the amount in 2006 and almost ten times the amount in 2001, but it is still fairly small. *The Economist* estimates that bilateral trade would grow tenfold, to $25 billion a year, if all trade barriers were removed.[11] Indirect trade (usually via Dubai or Singapore) is much greater, but it is very hard to quantify. Direct flights between the cities of India and Pakistan are rare; it is usually easier to travel via a third nation like the United Arab Emirates. Both governments' intelligence and security services scrutinize visitors from the other side on the assumption that they are up to no good and should be watched carefully—or better yet, kept out. Nonetheless, modest but important progress has been made in the last decade. Most recently, on September 8, 2012, the two countries signed an agreement to ease visa requirements; children under twelve years of age and adults over sixty-five will no longer need a visa. But Prime Minister Singh made clear that the Mumbai masterminds must be brought to justice for a greater loosening of travel requirements to occur.[12]

There is certainly much interest in India in more trade and transit. Successive Indian governments, both of the Congress Party and the Bharatiya Janata Party, have talked about more economic interaction and freer trade. Once, in a public speech, Prime Minister Singh famously dreamed about a day when he could breakfast in New Delhi, lunch in Lahore, and dine in Kabul. In August 2012, India unilaterally decided to allow direct foreign investment in India from Pakistan, which one expert has called a "huge psychological blow to elements hostile to improved ties."[13] There is much less interest in Pakistan, but it is growing. Pakistan's finance minister, Abdul Hafeez Shaikh, told a Brookings Institution audience in June 2012 that in the past when he was asked how to improve Pakistan's economic prospects, he facetiously advocated moving the whole country to the Alps and becoming part of the European Union. Now, he said, he realizes that the Himalayas are really the better venue since Pakistan is superbly positioned next to the two fastest-growing economies in the world, India and China.

But Shaikh is in the minority in Pakistan; the majority still fears India as a partner. Some fear that the larger Indian economy will swamp Pakistan with cheap products; others fear that it will make Pakistan dependent on India. Those who are the most hawkish on India, of course, oppose more trade as dealing with the enemy. The army has traditionally been very skeptical of improved trade, transit, and communications. In 2012 Lashkar-e-Tayyiba founder Hafiz Muhammad Saeed, the mastermind of the Mumbai massacre, organized massive demonstrations in Lahore, Karachi, and Islamabad against trade with India and relations with the United States. Efforts to encourage free trade usually get bogged down in bureaucratic red tape. While talk about a South Asia free trade zone is a perennial staple of regional summits, in reality there is little trade between the subcontinent's two biggest countries.

South Asia does have a regional organization, the South Asia Association for Regional Cooperation (SAARC), which has its headquarters in Kathmandu, Nepal. But unlike the European Union or the Association for Southeast Asian Nations, the SAARC is largely a hollow shell; although it aspires to be more, its member states are unwilling to give it much authority. Pakistan and the smaller states like Nepal and Bangladesh fear that it will be dominated by India and become an instrument for Indian hegemony. A visit to SAARC headquarters quickly leaves one with the sense that it is a Potemkin village, not a South Asian version of EU headquarters in Brussels. Nonetheless, the bureaucrats who work at SAARC can quickly come up with mountains of data on why increased trade and transit would benefit all South Asians.

However, as mentioned, increased trade and transit can also be seen as part of hegemonic ambitions and so fuel mistrust and conspiracy theories. Indian-Afghan cooperation since 9/11 is a case in point. Since 2002, India has helped to reduce Afghanistan's historical dependency on Pakistan as an outlet for trade by building a highway, Route 606, connecting the Afghan ring highway to an Iranian highway that goes on to the Arabian Sea at Chabahar, Iran. The road was constructed by India as an economic assistance project for Afghanistan; costing $136 million, it runs just over 200 kilometers across the Baluchistan desert. India turned the finished project over to Afghanistan in January 2009. Now India is considering adding a railroad line that would link the Afghan mineral mines around Hajigak to Chabahar to provide a transit route for exports. These projects are good for Afghanistan; they help to improve its economy and reduce its overdependence on Pakistan, especially on Karachi's harbor. But they also fuel Pakistani paranoia and fear of encirclement by India. If you are an officer in the Inter-Services Intelligence Directorate of the Pakistani army, it is not hard to see the India-Afghan-Iran economic pact as part of a plot to weaken Pakistan. As the United States and NATO draw down their forces in Afghanistan in 2014, turning the war over to the Afghans, the competition between India and Pakistan for influence there is all but certain to grow. A new "great game" will be fought in Afghanistan between New Delhi and Islamabad.[14] So any economic approach to resolving South Asia's problems also requires a political approach to resolving the disputes that keep Pakistan's borders unresolved.

Global and U.S. diplomacy should therefore focus on these two critical issues: Pakistan's relations with Afghanistan and its relations with India. The Afghan-Pakistan border, 1,610 miles long, runs through the heart of al Qaeda's sanctuary in South Asia. This border, the so-called Durand Line, divides the Pashtun and Baluchi peoples, and it has never been accepted by any Afghan government because it was unilaterally imposed by the British colonial government in 1893. Kabul governments have always been reluctant to formally give up their claim to a larger "Pashtunistan"; even the pro-Pakistan Islamic Emirate of Afghanistan under the Taliban did not accept the Durand Line. It is unlikely that the government of President Hamid Karzai could accept the line formally and finally any more than its predecessors could. But the United States and NATO should work with Kabul and Islamabad to accept publicly that the line cannot be modified or altered without the consent of both governments. Such acceptance of the de facto permanence of the border should also set the stage for greater willingness on both sides to police the line and to regard it as a real international frontier. It clearly would not stop smuggling and infiltration overnight—or even over several years—but it would provide a basis for long-term cooperation between Kabul and Islamabad, something lacking in the past.

Since the United States has so much at stake in the stabilization of this border area and in preventing it from remaining an al Qaeda safe haven, the United States, the United Nations, and the International Security Assistance Force should be prepared to endorse an agreement between Pakistan and Afghanistan. Pakistan, in turn, would need to address the insecurity of its badlands in the north and responsibly administer them like any other part of the country. Ronald Neuman, a former U.S. ambassador to Afghanistan, has rightly characterized the current situation as "borderline insanity" and suggested that resolving its ambiguity is part of the "big think" solution to the threat posed by the badlands.[15] India also could endorse the border to remove any suspicions that it wants to help Afghanistan take over Pakistani territory in Baluchistan or the Federally Administered Tribal Areas. That alone would not eliminate Pakistani fears of an Afghan-Indian plot to carve up their country, but it would be a good start. A broad regional agreement on the permanence of the Durand Line and Afghan neutrality in the Indo-Pakistani rivalry would help undermine conspiracy theorists in Pakistan who feed on the border dispute.

To effectively promote and encourage border stabilization, the United States and NATO have to stay in Afghanistan and continue to lead the International Security Assistance Force there. Americans are rightly frustrated that this has become the longest war in U.S. history, with no end in sight. Obama inherited a disaster there from Bush, and he has spent four years trying to build an Afghan army that can cope with the Taliban without foreign combat troops. Obama has developed a strategy to dramatically draw down the NATO force in Afghanistan by 2014; however, he has also signed a long-term strategic agreement with Kabul to maintain an American military presence in Afghanistan to back up the Afghan army for at least another ten years, until 2025, and to use Afghan bases for counterterrorism missions in Afghanistan and Pakistan. So the United States is planning to be in Afghanistan for the long haul. What actually transpires in Afghanistan over the next few years could, of course, be very different from what the United States has planned. It needs Afghanistan to be able continue the drone war against al Qaeda for the indefinite future; it also needs access to Afghan bases for SEAL raids like the one in which bin Laden was killed. If that operation had been launched from an aircraft carrier in the Arabian Sea, it would have failed as disastrously as the 1980 mission to rescue the Iran hostages. Geography matters.

But it is unclear whether the Afghan government and army will be able to withstand the pressure of the Taliban and the ISI when American and other NATO forces leave. It is a gamble. If the government succeeds, it will have a stabilizing impact. If it fails, the region will be further destabilized and the most extreme Islamists will have achieved a great victory. Yet America and NATO cannot and should not stay indefinitely. It is time to see whether the Afghans can manage—with extensive help, but without thousands of foreign boots on the ground. The best solution would be a political process that brings at least some of the Taliban into an accommodation with the legitimate government in Kabul. The Pashtun community needs to be better represented in the Kabul process, and perhaps some Taliban are ready for a cease-fire and talks. Greater devolution of political power to the provinces would be a mechanism for a political endgame to what is now a thirty-five-year-old civil war. Holbrooke's successor, Ambassador Mark Grossman, tried during 2010–12 to engage the Taliban. At first there was some hope for guarded optimism when the Taliban met with various foreign powers, including Germany, and signaled interest in some dialogue with NATO, although not with Karzai. The Taliban agreed to open an office in Qatar to serve as a venue for discussions, starting with a possible prisoner swap. Hamid Gul, a former head of ISI and a well-known supporter of the Taliban and al Qaeda, expressed interest through intermediaries in starting a dialogue with America, allegedly on behalf of Mullah Omar. Then, in September 2011, an assassin killed the Afghan lead negotiator in Kabul, Burhanuddin Rabbani, a former president of Afghanistan. In March 2012 the Taliban suspended all talks of a political deal and halted work on their Doha office. They claimed that the American side had failed to live up to its promise to release prisoners held in Guantánamo Bay, Cuba. The political process has since lain dormant.

It could revive if the Taliban decided that it would be better to talk than to continue to hope for a military victory. Pakistan, with its huge influence on the Taliban and its control of much of the leadership, including Mullah Omar and the Haqqani family (all of whom live in Pakistan), could help considerably. A political process in Afghanistan would be good for Afghans, and it could open the door to improved relations between Washington and

Islamabad. So far that has not tempted Pakistan. The generals who run Pakistan are convinced that military victory is still possible in Afghanistan and that the NATO alliance will not have the stomach to fight on. They read the polls in America and Europe that show growing dissatisfaction with the war, and they conclude time is on the Taliban's side. They may be right.

But power abhors a vacuum, and if America and NATO abandon Kabul and the anti-Taliban Northern Alliance of Tajiks, Uzbeks, and Shia (a majority of Afghans), others will step in to support them. That is what happened in the 1990s. When the first CIA team went into Afghanistan in 2001 after 9/11, the Iranian intelligence service was already there, helping the Tajiks and Shia.[16] The Russians, Indians, and Central Asians were also still backing Ahmad Shah Massoud. In the future, their capacity to help an anti-Taliban coalition will be greater than ever. Pakistan will create its own worst nightmare, an Afghan state allied with India on its western border. The generals in Rawalpindi seem oblivious to the self-fulfilling nature of their paranoia.

THE HEART OF THE MATTER

The other and far more critical issue for American diplomacy to address is the underlying problem that drives Pakistan's relationship with terrorism: India and Kashmir. This is the real potential game changer. The Pakistani state and its army have been obsessed with India since its creation in 1947. The ISI created much of the modern jihadist infrastructure in South Asia to fight India asymmetrically, either directly in Kashmir or indirectly in Afghanistan, in order to defend Pakistan's strategic depth.

What was the princely state of Kashmir and Jammu before 1947 was roughly the size of Minnesota. Today the area includes several regions, the most famous being the Valley of Kashmir, in the Indian province of Jammu and Kashmir, whose capital is Srinagar. Although the valley is part of India, its 4.7 million inhabitants are almost entirely Muslim; most Hindus have fled the violence that has existed there since 1990. South of the valley is Jammu, whose 4.5 million inhabitants are primarily Hindu. To the east, on the border with China, is Ladakh, also a part of Jammu and Kashmir, which has only 200,000 people, largely Buddhists; a Shia Muslim minority resides around Kargil. Pakistan-controlled Kashmir is divided between the Northern Areas, above Kargil, and Azad Kashmir, west of the Valley of Kashmir and almost adjacent to Islamabad; Azad Kashmir includes just over 3 million Muslims. The Northern Areas is a large but sparsely populated region that is physically cut off from Azad Kashmir by mountains and linked directly to Pakistan. Its roughly 1 million inhabitants are also almost entirely Muslim. To its east is the territory ceded to China by Ayub Khan in 1963. China also occupies an area called Aksai Chin, part of Indian-claimed territory east of Ladakh.[17] Both are largely uninhabited.

From the Pakistani perspective, an optimal resolution of Kashmir would lead to the unification of the province, or at least the Muslim-dominated Valley of Kashmir and Srinagar, with Pakistan. With Kashmir "reunited" with Pakistan, the requirement for nuclear weapons would be reduced, if not eliminated, and the need for a jihadist option to compel Indian withdrawal from the valley would be gone. That is precisely the outcome that Pakistani leaders have in mind when they urge American and other world leaders to devote diplomatic and political energy to the Kashmir issue. It is, of course, a completely unrealistic scenario. India has made it clear that it will not withdraw from Kashmir. On the contrary, India argues it has already made a major concession by its de facto acceptance of the partition of the state among itself, Pakistan, and China. India is probably prepared to accept the line of control, in effect the cease-fire line of 1948, as the ultimate border with Pakistan, but it is not willing to accept a fundamental redrawing of borders to put the valley under Pakistan's sovereignty.

India is right to argue that it should not be asked to give up Kashmir. But India needs also to recognize that its hopes and

aspirations for a bright shining future are unlikely to material-
ize if its neighbor to the west is a failing state or worse, a jihadist
state with a new Zia ul-Haq in charge, armed with more than
200 nuclear weapons and taking advice from Hafiz Saeed. As the
stronger power in the equation, with a far more stable and predictable political system, India is also much better equipped to make
the kind of diplomatic moves needed to break the logjam in South
Asia that has prevented a breakthrough to real regional peace since
1947. Because it is strong, it can take action. It can reduce the size
of its military footprint in Kashmir and encourage more dialogue
about the future; it also can and must take greater action to prevent human rights abuses. As Spiderman says, "With great power
comes great responsibility." That applies to great countries as well
as comic book superheroes.

There is a way to resolve the Kashmir problem along the lines
of Indian thinking. It is similar if not identical to the proposal
that John Kenneth Galbraith made back in 1962, not for a territorial compromise but for a broader deal that makes Kashmir
a zone of peace and prosperity between India and Pakistan, like
the Saar region between France and Germany. The basis for such
an approach would be the Indo-Pakistani bilateral dialogue. That
dialogue has already produced a series of confidence-building measures between the two countries by reopening a few transportation
links, setting up hotlines between military commands, and engaging in periodic discussions at the foreign secretary–level on all the
issues that divide the two. Unfortunately, the dialogue has not
seriously addressed the Kashmir issue because of the significant
gulf between the two parties and India's understandable refusal to
negotiate while it is still a target of terrorist attacks planned and
organized in Pakistan. And since Musharraf exited the scene, the
two countries have not gone very far in their back-channel talks on
how to resolve Kashmir.

The United States has long been reluctant to engage more actively
in the Kashmir dispute in light of the Indian posture that outside

intervention is unwarranted and that Kashmir is a purely bilateral issue. Faced with the likelihood of Indian rejection of outside intervention, American diplomacy has put the Kashmir problem in the "too-hard" category and left it to simmer. The results have been all too predictable. The Kashmir issue periodically boils over and the United States and the international community have to step in to try to prevent a full-scale war. That was the case during the Kargil crisis in 1999, after the terrorist attack on the Indian parliament in December 2001, and again in 2002, when India mobilized its army for war along the Pakistani border. The specter of war was again in the air in 2008.

American reluctance is understandable. The major thesis of this book and its review of American diplomacy in South Asia for the last seven decades is that the United States has been unable to achieve most of its goals in the region; every president from Roosevelt to Obama has found the subcontinent to be a tough place to get ahead. Dealing with India and Pakistan has been a zero-sum game, and often American presidents have struck out with both sides. In 1965, 1971, and 1998, the United States sanctioned both countries and achieved virtually none of its goals. The puzzle has been too hard to put together.

Howard Schaffer, a former American ambassador, has argued persuasively that the Kashmir issue in particular has been very resistant to U.S. intervention. The title of his masterly study on American diplomacy, *The Limits of Influence,* underscores that point. He rightly notes that no president since Kennedy even seriously attempted to intervene in Kashmir—and Kennedy struck out. But Schaffer also rightly argues that the issue is too important to be neglected and that the timing for an American initiative is more propitious now because of the rapprochement between India and America.[18]

Indians and Pakistanis will have to be the primary actors in efforts to shape their future. That is how it should be. American diplomacy in South Asia will always be secondary to their diplomacy. History has shown that American actions can make a bad situation worse, and it has shown only limited evidence that they can make things fundamentally better. The United States is best at conflict management, not conflict resolution. So humility is in order in thinking about grand projects in South Asia.

But that should not be an excuse for defeatism. A unique opportunity now exists for quiet American diplomacy to help advance the Kashmir issue to a better, more stable solution. The U.S.-India civil nuclear deal has created a steadier and more enduring basis for U.S.-Indian relations than at any time in history. The deal removes the central obstacle to closer strategic ties between Washington and New Delhi, the nuclear proliferation problem, which held up the development of their relationship for two decades. Obama's support for a permanent Indian seat at the UN Security Council, the so-called high table of world leadership, has added more weight to the new policy of strategic partnership, and the U.S. rapprochement with India, begun by President Clinton and advanced by presidents Bush and Obama, is now supported by an almost unique bipartisan consensus in Congress and in the U.S. foreign policy establishment.

The next president in this new era of U.S.-Indian strategic partnership will have an opportunity. Washington should quietly but forcefully encourage New Delhi to be more flexible on Kashmir. It is clearly in the American interest to try to defuse a lingering conflict that has generated global terrorism and repeatedly threatened to create a full-scale military confrontation on the subcontinent. It is also in India's interest to find a solution to the conflict, which has gone on far too long. Since the Kargil war in 1999, the Indians have been more open to an American role in Kashmir because they sense that Washington is fundamentally in favor of a resolution to maintain the status quo, which India can accept.

The key to Indian cooperation will be whether the United States can make clear to Pakistan that some red lines regarding terrorism are real, especially a red line on Lashkar-e-Tayyiba. If Sonia Gandhi and Prime Minister Singh can point to real evidence that

LeT is being broken up and dismantled in Pakistan, then they will have the political clout to advance the back-channel talks to secure a peace breakthrough.

What would a peace deal look like? Would it be a Galbraith solution, like the one on the Saar? A Kashmir solution would have to be based on a formula for making the line of control both a permanent, conventional international border (perhaps with some minor modifications) and a permeable frontier between the two parts of Kashmir so that the Kashmiri people could live more normal lives. A special condominium might be created to allow the two constituencies to work together on issues specific to the region, such as transportation, the environment, sports, and tourism. For example, both the Indian and Pakistani currencies could become legal tender on both sides of the border, an idea recently floated in India. That would be a win-win-win approach. The Kashmiris would be the biggest winners since they would finally have peace and would be reunited. Pakistan would be a winner since it would no longer have to spend so much of its limited resources on trying to keep up with much larger India; it also could finally attack the jihadist monster that it has created, which threatens its democracy and future. India would be a winner as well, since it would no longer face an insurgency in Kashmir and terrorism in its cities.

The Kashmir solution would be embedded in a larger regional framework that strengthens the South Asia Association for Regional Cooperation and removes both formal and informal trade barriers. Visa requirements for travel between the South Asian countries would be removed or at least required for only a small number of military and diplomatic personnel. Average citizens should be able to travel and trade without complex border controls, much as Americans travel to Canada or Europeans travel within the European Union. As transit and trade grow, so would cooperation on the environment, water resources, and other issues.

In short, Galbraith's concept of Kashmir as a place of reconciliation, like the Saar region between France and Germany, would be implemented. Given the history of pervasive mistrust on both sides, it is unlikely that the two states will be able to reach such an agreement on their own. A quiet American effort led by the president to promote a solution is probably necessary to any effort to move the parties toward an agreement. It should not be a formal, public initiative—discretion and privacy are essential.

While U.S.-India relations are well poised to make such an effort, U.S.-Pakistani relations have deteriorated sharply in the last several years and are unlikely to rebound anytime soon. The decades of mistrust and betrayal between the two countries have left an enormous trust deficit. Americans are deeply troubled that Pakistan backs the Taliban, which is killing American troops in Afghanistan, and that Osama bin Laden was able to hide in the heart of the Pakistani national security establishment in Abbottabad for more than five years. Pakistanis believe that America has let them down repeatedly over the years, that it wages an illegal drone war on their territory, and that it is more interested in building ties to India than to Pakistan (they are probably right about India). Pakistan's former ambassador to Washington, Husain Haqqani, has suggested that it is time for Pakistan and America to get a divorce.

This is where other states, such as China, Saudi Arabia, the United Arab Emirates, and other Arab Gulf states can play a central role. China is Pakistan's all-weather friend: 90 percent of Pakistanis trust China. Riyadh, Abu Dhabi, and Dubai are second homes for many Pakistani leaders. Saudi Arabia and the United Arab Emirates are trusted partners. Quiet, behind-the-scenes Chinese and Arab diplomacy with Islamabad and quiet work between Washington and New Delhi could become a mechanism to push India and Pakistan toward engaging in bilateral interaction.

Other partners could help, too. The United Kingdom has a unique place in the history of South Asia. It both unified the subcontinent and divided it. It gave South Asians their common language. Today there is a large, vibrant South Asian diaspora in the United Kingdom—2 million British residents are either Pakistanis or descendants of Pakistani immigrants, and 700,000 are Kashmiris—and England is a favored destination for South Asian students and holiday makers. London can play a big role in helping to bring peace to the region. It can also take the lead in getting the European Union to be more active in diplomacy relating to South Asia. The special Anglo-American relationship has long worked as a force multiplier in South Asia.

In his second term, President Obama should quietly but persistently work to create a coalition of friends of Pakistan that will come together to back a peace offensive to resolve South Asia's unfinished business in Kashmir. It will not be easy, but it is critical. The choice is really between risking Armageddon and creating Nirvana. Resolution of the Kashmir issue would go a long way toward making Pakistan a more normal state and reducing its preoccupation with India. It would also remove a major rationale for the army's disproportionate role in Pakistani national security affairs; that in turn would help to ensure the survival of genuine civilian democratic rule in the country. A resolution of the major outstanding issue between Islamabad and New Delhi would reduce the arms race between them and the risk of nuclear conflict. By eliminating Pakistan's desire to wage asymmetric warfare against India, it would also discourage Pakistan from making alliances with the Taliban, Lashkar-e-Tayyiba, and al Qaeda. Former ambassador William Milam, a seasoned South Asia hand, has rightly stressed that the "India-Centricity of the Pakistani mindset is the most important factor and variable" in the future of the country.[19]

Such an agreement would not resolve all the tensions between the two neighbors; however, their disputes on issues other than Kashmir are comparatively trivial. More than anything else, a Kashmir deal would set the stage for a different era in the subcontinent and for more productive interaction between the international community and Pakistan. It could set the stage for a genuine rapprochement between India and Pakistan and nurture trade and economic interaction, which could transform the subcontinent for the better. A virtuous cycle could develop, making the subcontinent a zone of peace and prosperity, not war and terrorism.

South Asia will always be on the opposite side of the globe from North America. The citizens of the two regions do not share a border, but they do share much history. Americans are notoriously averse to studying their history to understand why others like or dislike them. South Asians, in contrast, tend to wallow in their history and nurse their traditional animosities. Both need to revisit how they have interacted for the five centuries since Europe "discovered" them both in the 1490s. Only by learning from their past can they escape its deadly embrace. Today Americans, Indians, and Pakistanis share the dubious distinction of being nuclear weapons states. All have an awesome power to destroy. They urgently need to ensure that their actions never lead to Armageddon. They urgently need to seek a better future. Finding a way to put the pieces of the puzzle together to achieve that future is their common challenge.

NOTES

CHAPTER 1

1. See the *Hindustan Times* collection of articles about the attack, *26/11: The Attack on Mumbai* (New Delhi: Hindustan Times and Penguin, 2009), pp. 38–39, for my commentary during the attack on al Qaeda's likely role.

2. Laurence Chandy and Geoffrey Gertz, *Poverty in Numbers: The Changing State of Global Poverty* (Brookings, 2011), p. 12.

3. Niall Ferguson, "Lights Out in India," *Daily Beast*, August 6, 2012.

4. Saleem Shaikh, "Need to Contain Surging Population," *Daily Times* [Karachi], August 7, 2012. Michael Lugelman, "Don't Drop That Bomb on Me," paper presented at the Woodrow Wilson International Center for Scholars, Washington, June 9, 2010.

5. The details of the attack have been widely reported. A good summary is found in Angel Rabasa and others, "The Lessons of Mumbai," Occasional Paper (Santa Monica, Calif.: RAND, 2009) (www.rand.org/pubs/occasional_papers/2009/RAND_OP249.pdf), which also includes a useful chronology of the incident. Qasab's confession was reported by the BBC, among others. See BBC News, "Excerpts from Mumbai Suspect's Confession," July 20, 2009 (http://news.bbc.co.uk/2/hi/south_asia/8160243.stm).

6. Rommel Rodrigues, *Kasab: The Face of 26/11* (New Delhi: Penguin, 2010), pp. 76, 108–09.

7. Ibid., p. 103.

8 See the guilty plea agreement, *United States of America* v. *David Coleman Headley*, No. 09 CR 830-3, U.S. District Court, Northern District of Illinois, March 2010. The prosecutor was Patrick Fitzgerald. It is also useful to see the indictment released by the U.S. Department of Justice on October 27, 2009.

9. National Investigation Agency, "The Interrogation of David Coleman Headley," June 3–9, 2010 (www.investigateproject.org).

10. Ibid., p. 92.

11. "Mumbai Attacks: ISI Leaders Had No Involvement, Says Headley," *Express Tribune*, June 1, 2011 (http://tribune.com.pk/story/179550/isi-leadership-not-involved-in-mumbai-attack-planning/).

12. "Saudi Arabia, U.S., and India Cooperate to Capture Mumbai '26/11' Attacker Abu Jindal," *Jamestown Militant Leadership Monitor*, vol. 3, no. 6 (July 1, 2012).

13. Animesh Roul, "Dawood Ibrahim: India's Elusive Most-Wanted Man," *Jamestown Militant Leadership Monitor*, vol. 1, no. 6 (June 30, 2010).

14. *United States of America* v. *David Coleman Headley.*

15. See Nawaz Sharif interview, "Vajpayee May Have Dealt Differently with Jaswant Singh," *Hindustan Times*, August 23, 2009. Sharif says, "Look at the colossal damage that we have done to our own economies by the arms race."

16. Steve Coll, "The Back Channel: India and Pakistan Negotiate on Kashmir," *New Yorker*, March 2, 2009.

17. See his interview with *Der Spiegel*, "Obama Is Aiming at the Right Things," *Der Spiegel*, July 6, 2009.

18. Pratik Parija, "President Zardari Says Pakistan Won't Use Nuclear Weapons First," Bloomberg News, November 22, 2008, and "Fury over Zardari Kashmir Comments," BBC News, October 6, 2008.

19. Vined Sharma and Zia Huq, "There Is a Bit of India in Every Pakistani: Zardari," *Hindustan Times*, November 22, 2008.

20. Syed Saleem Shahzad, *Inside al Qaeda and the Taliban: Beyond bin Laden and 9/11* (London: Palgrave, 2011), pp. 67–71.

21. David Ignatius, "The Bin Laden Plot to Kill President Obama," *Washington Post*, March 16, 2012.

22. For the creation of Lashkar-e-Tayyiba, see Wilson John, "Lashkar-e-Tayyeba," Pakistan Security Research Unit Brief 12, University of Bradford [U.K.], May 21, 2007. For more on Azzam, see Thomas Hegghammer, "Abdullah Azzam, the Imam of Jihad," in *Al Qaeda in Its Own Words,* edited by Giles Keppel and Jean-Pierre Milelli (London: Belknap, 2008).

23. Hassan Abbas, *Pakistan's Drift into Extremism: Allah, the Army, and America's War on Terror* (London, East Gate, 2005), p. 211.

24. See Arif Jamal, *Shadow War: The Untold Story of Jihad in Kashmir* (Brooklyn, N.Y.: Melville House, 2009).

25. Quoted in Yoginder Sikand, "Islamist Militancy in Kashmir: The Case of Lashkar-i Tayyeba," *South Asian Citizens Web*, November 20, 2003 (www.sacw.net/DC/CommunalismCollection/ArticlesArchive/sikand20Nov2003.html).

26. See Praveen Swami, "The Well-Tempered Jihad: The Politics and Practice of Post-2002 Islamist Terrorism in India," *Contemporary South Asia*, vol. 16, no. 3 (September 2008), p. 317.

27. Ibid., p. 316.

28. Jamal, *Shadow War*, p. 13.

29. Jane Perlez and Salman Masood, "Terror Ties Run Deep in Pakistan, Mumbai Case Shows," *New York Times*, July 27, 2009.

30. Abbas, *Pakistan's Drift into Extremism*, p. 212.

31. Bernard-Henri Levy, *Who Killed Daniel Pearl?* (Hoboken, N.J.: Melville, 2003), p. 437. See also Bernard-Henri Levy, "Let's Give Pakistan the Attention It Deserves," *Wall Street Journal*, December 9, 2008.

32. See Mukhtar A. Khan, "Hafiz Mohammad Saeed: India's Most-Wanted Man Free Again in Pakistan," *Jamestown Terrorism Monitor*, July 27, 2009.

33. Michael Jacobson, "Saudi Efforts to Combat Terrorist Financing," *Policy Watch 1555* (Washington Institute for Near East Policy, July 21, 2009).

34. John Kiriakou, *The Reluctant Spy: My Secret Life in the CIA's War on Terror* (New York: Random House, 2010).

35. See Stephen Tankel, *Lashkar-e-Taiba: From 9/11 to Mumbai* (London: International Centre for the Study of Radicalisation and Political Violence, 2009), pp. 9–10. Tankel has also written a superb study of LeT, *Storming the World Stage: The Story of Lashkar-e-Taiba* (Columbia University Press, 2011).

36. Tankel, *Lashkar-e-Taiba: From 9/11 to Mumbai*, pp. 12–18.

37. One al Qaeda spokesman in 2009, Abu Yahya al Libi, did laud "the lions of Mumbai" in a statement but said nothing more. Another, Mustafa abu al Yazid, heralded the "heroes of Mumbai" in a statement threatening more attacks on economic targets around the globe.

38. Zaid Hamid, *Mumbai: Dance of the Devil, Hindu Zionists, Mumbai Attacks, and the Indian Dossier against Pakistan* (Rawalpindi: Brass Tacks Security Think Tank and Defence Analysis Consulting, 2009).

39. Rahul Singh, "India, Pak Were on Brink of War after 26/11," *Hindustan Times*, June 1, 2009.

40. See Walter C. Ladwig III, "A Cold Start for Hot Wars? The Indian Army's New Limited War Doctrine," *International Security*, vol. 32, no. 3 (Winter 2007–08), pp. 158–90.

CHAPTER 2

1. Patrick Wintour, "No Decision on Speeding Up Afghan Troop Withdrawal in 2013," *The Guardian*, December 13, 2011.

2. There is a huge literature on the British Empire in India. Among the best works are Lawrence James, *Raj: The Making and Unmaking of British India* (New York: St. Martins, 1997); Jac Weller, *Wellington in India* (London: Greenhill, 1953); William Dalrymple, *The Last Moghul: The Fall of a Dynasty: Delhi, 1857* (New Delhi: Penguin, 2006), and Denise Dersin, *What Life was Like in the Jewel in the Crown: British India AD 1600–1905* (Alexandria, Va.: Time Life Books, 1999). Even larger is the literature on partition. Among the best works are Larry Collins and Dominique Lapierre, *Freedom at Midnight* (London: Harper Collins, 1975); Stanley Wolpert, *Shameful Flight: The Last Years of the British Empire in India* (Oxford University Press, 2006); Alex von Tunzelmann, *Indian Summer: The Secret History of the End of an Empire* (New York: Picador, 2007); Yasmin Khan, *The Great Partition: The Making of India and Pakistan* (Yale University Press, 2007); and Narendra Singh Sarila, *The Shadow of the Great Game: The Untold Story of India's Partition* (New Delhi: Harper Collins, 2005).

3. "The Company That Ruled the Waves," *The Economist*, December 17, 2011, pp. 109–11.

4. Saul David, *Victoria's Wars: The Rise of Empire* (London: Penguin, 2007), p. 283.

5. "A Mohammedan Conspiracy for the Sovereignty of India," *New York Times*, September 13, 1857.

6. Guy Gugliotta, New Estimate Raises Civil War Death Toll," *New York Times*, April 2, 2012 (www.nytimes.com/2012/04/03/science/civil-war-toll-up-by-20-percent-in-new-estimate.html?pagewanted=all).

7. William S. McFeeley, *Grant* (New York: Norton, 1974), pp. 472–73. John Russell Young, *Around the World with General Grant* (Johns Hopkins University Press, 2002) is an edited reissue of an account of the trip originally published in 1879 by a journalist who accompanied the Grants.

8. See, for example, Prasannan Parthasarathi, *Why Europe Grew Rich and Asia Did Not: Global Economic Divergence, 1600–1850* (Cambridge University Press, 2011).

9. Ironically, the two fought on the same battlefield in South Africa, Churchill as a soldier and journalist, Gandhi as an ambulance driver, in the Boer War.

10. Romain Hayes, *Subhas Chandra Bose in Nazi Germany* (Columbia University Press, 2011), pp. 89, 102, 111, 141.

11. Dennis Kux, *India and the United States: Estranged Democracies, 1941–1991* (Washington: National Defense University Press, 1992), p. 24.

12. Bob Spitz, *Dearie: The Remarkable Life of Julia Child* (New York: Knopf, 2012).

13. Kux, *India and the United States*.

14. Madhusree Mukerjee, *Churchill's Secret War: The British Empire and the Ravaging of India during World War II* (New York: Basic Books, 2010), and Arthur Herman, *Gandhi and Churchill: The Epic Rivalry That Destroyed an Empire and Forged Our Age* (New York: Bantam, 2008), are two excellent new studies of the partition issue. Both conclude that Churchill was a critical player in the creation of Pakistan. The definitive biography of Jinnah is Stanley Wolpert, *Jinnah of Pakistan* (Oxford University Press, 1985). Jaswant Singh's *Jinnah: India, Partition, Independence* (New Delhi: Rupa, 2009) is a must-read for an Indian perspective.

15. Arthur Bryant, *Triumph in the West, 1939–1945: Based on the Diaries and Autobiographical Notes of Field Marshall the Viscount Alan Brooke* (London: Collins, 1959), p. 158.

16. Hayes, *Subhas Chandra Bose in Nazi Germany*, p. 133.

17. Kux, *India and the United States*, p. 32.

18. "Tata for Now," *The Economist*, September 10, 2011, pp. 61–62.

CHAPTER 3

1. Farooq Naseem Bajwa, *Pakistan and the West: The First Decade, 1947–1957* (Karachi: Oxford University Press, 1996), p. 2.

2. Stanley Wolpert, *Shameful Flight: The Last Years of the British Empire in India* (Oxford University Press, 2006).

3. Although Nimitz never wrote his memoirs, a historian at the U.S. Naval Academy was given access to his papers, so the inside story on the first American who tried to make peace in Kashmir is available.

4. E. B. Potter, *Nimitz* (Annapolis, Md.: U.S. Naval Institute Press, 1976), p. 439.

5. Ibid., p. 451.

6. Howard Schaffer, *The Limits of Influence: America's Role in Kashmir* (Brookings, 2009), p. 26.

7. Bajwa, *Pakistan and the West*, p. 38.

8. Ibid., p. 10.

9. Shashi Tharoor, *Nehru: The Invention of India* (New York: Arcade, 2003), p. 205.

10. Bajwa, *Pakistan and the West*, p. 56.

11. Dennis Kux, *Disenchanted Allies: The United States and Pakistan, 1947–2000* (Johns Hopkins University Press, 2001), p. 61.

12. Ibid., p. 131.

13. Steve Inskeep, *Instant City: Life and Death in Karachi* (New York: Penguin Press, 2011), p. 86.

14. Kux, *Disenchanted Allies*, pp. 99–101.

15. Clint Hill, *Mrs. Kennedy and Me* (New York: Gallery, 2012), p. 138. Hill describes how he had to fight Galbraith's desire to get Mrs. Kennedy to more and more of India by expanding her schedule to twenty hours every day of the visit, ignoring her need to get a good night's sleep.

16. John Kenneth Galbraith, *Ambassador's Journal* (Boston: Houghton Mifflin Company, 1969), p. 307.

17. Odd Arne Westad, *Restless Empire: China and the World since 1750* (New York: Basic Books, 2012), p. 342.

18. Yaacov Vertzberger, "India's Strategic Posture and the Border War Defeat of 1962: A Case Study in Miscalculation," *Journal of Strategic Studies*, vol. 5, no. 3 (September 1982).

19. Galbraith, *Ambassador's Journal*, p. 378.

20. It has been the home of the American ambassador to India ever since.

21. Galbraith, *Ambassador's Journal*, p. 446.

22. Ibid., p. 372.

23. Ibid., p. 446.

24. Timothy Crawford, *Pivotal Deterrence: Third Party Statecraft and the Pursuit of Peace* (Cornell University Press, 2003), p. 153.

25. Quoted in Kux, *Disenchanted Allies*, p. 136.

26. Ibid., p. 146.

27. Anand Giridharadas, "JFK Faced India-China Dilemma," *New York Times*, August 26, 2005.

28. Crawford, *Pivotal Deterrence*, p. 157.

29. Ibid., pp. 138–61.

30. Stanley Wolpert, *Zulfi Bhutto of Pakistan: His Life and Times* (Karachi: Oxford University Press, 1993), p. 98.

31. Ibid., p. 155.

32. David Ludden, "The Politics of Independence in Bangladesh," *South Asia Journal*, no. 3 (January 2012), p. 77.

33. Richard Sisson and Leo E. Rose, *War and Secession: Pakistan, India, and the Creation of Bangladesh* (University of California Press, 1990), pp. 135–37.

34. Christopher Van Hollen, "The Tilt Policy Revisited: Nixon-Kissinger Geopolitics and South Asia," *Asian Survey*, vol. 20, no. 4 (April 1980), p. 347. Hollen

was the deputy assistant secretary of state for South Asia and was present in the room when Kissinger spoke.

35. "Dissent from U.S. Policy toward Pakistan," American Consul, Dacca, April 6, 1971. The full cable has been declassified and can be accessed in "The Tilt: The U.S. and the South Asian Crisis of 1971," National Security Archive Electronic Briefing Book 79, edited by Sajit Gandhi, December 16, 2002.

36. See National Security Archive Electronic Briefing Book 79, document 20.

37. National Security Archive Electronic Briefing Book 79, document 32.

38. Dennis Kux, *India and the United States: Estranged Democracies* (Washington: National Defense University Press, 1992), p. 304.

39. Van Hollen, "The Tilt Policy Revisited," p. 351.

40. Wolpert, *Zulfi Bhutto of Pakistan*, p. 165.

41. Kux, *Disenchanted Allies*, p. 339.

42. "Post Mortem Report: An Examination of the Intelligence Community's Performance before the Indian Nuclear Test of May 1974," Director of Central Intelligence, Top Secret Talent Keyhole, July 1974 (declassified and available at the National Security Archives).

43. "Indian Nuclear Developments and Their Likely Implications," Special National Intelligence Estimate 31–72 (declassified and available at the National Security Archives).

CHAPTER 4

1. Stanley Wolpert, *Zulfi Bhutto of Pakistan: His Life and Times* (Oxford University Press, 1993), p. 262.

2. Dennis Kux, *India and the United States: Estranged Democracies* (Washington: National Defense University Press, 1992), p. 367.

3. Author's interview with His Royal Highness Prince Hassan bin Talal, April 11, 2010.

4. Shuja Nawaz, *Crossed Swords: Pakistan, Its Army, and the Wars Within* (Karachi: Oxford University Press, 2008). p.361.

5. Seyyed Vali Reza Nasr, *The Vanguard of the Islamic Revolution* (University of California Press, 1994), p. 189.

6. Nawaz, *Crossed Swords*, p. 361.

7. C. Uday Bhaskar, "Hamid Karzai Clarification and Grey Sheen over Af-Pak," *Economic Times*, October 26, 2011.

8. Steve Coll, *Ghost Wars* (New York: Penguin, 2004), p. 180.

9. Ayesha Siddiqa, *Military Inc.: Inside Pakistan's Military Economy* (London: Pluto Press, 2007). p. 186

10. Mohammad Yousaf and Mark Adkin, *The Bear Trap: Afghanistan's Untold Story* (London: Leo Cooper, 1992), p. 22. Yousaf was the ISI Afghan bureau chief from 1983 to 1987, and the book is dedicated to General Akhtar Rahman. This is the definitive account of the ISI's war from a Pakistani perspective.

11. Mohammad Yousaf, *Silent Soldier: The Man behind the Afghan Jehad* (Lahore: Jang Publishers, 1991), p. 27.

12. Daveed Gartenstein-Ross, "Religious Militancy in Pakistan's Military and Inter-Services Intelligence Agency," *Afghanistan-Pakistan Theater: Militant Islam, Security, and Stability* (Washington: FDD Press, 2010), p. 33.

13. Yousaf, *Silent Soldier*, pp. 16 and 70.

14. Fouad Ajami, "With Us or against Us," *New York Times*, January 7, 2007, p. 14

15. Vali R. Nasr, "International Politics, Domestic Imperatives, and Identity Mobilization: Sectarianism in Pakistan, 1979–1998, *Comparative Politics*, vol. 32, no. 2 (January 2000), pp. 171-90.

16. Nawaz, *Crossed Swords*, pp. 372–73. Prince Turki confirmed this account in an interview with me.

17. Ibid., p. 386.

18. S. Frederick Starr, *Xinjiang: China's Muslim Borderland* (New York: M.E. Sharpe, 2004).

19. Ibid., p. 375.

20. Carlotta Gall of the *New York Times* interviewed the ISI trainer, Colonel Imam, in 2010. I am indebted to her for this information on Mullah Omar's ISI background. Colonel Imam also mentioned training Omar to Christina Lamb in "The Taliban Will Never Be Defeated," *London Sunday Times*, June 7, 2009. Imam claims the ISI trained more than 95,000 Afghans.

21. S. M. A. Hussaini, *Air Warriors of Pakistan* (Lahore: Ferozsons, 1980).

22. Yousaf, *Bear Trap*, pp. 191–95.

23. Yousaf, *Silent Soldier*, p. 42.

24. Gregory Feifer, *The Great Gamble: The Soviet War in Afghanistan* (New York: Harper, 2009), p.130. Feifer's book is the best account available on the Soviet side of the war. The Soviets probably invaded Afghanistan more to defend the communist regime there than to advance to the Arabian Sea, but that is clearer now than it was at the time.

25. Yousaf, *Bear Trap*, p. 97.

26. Shahriar Khan, *Genocide and War Crimes in Bangladesh* (Dhaka: Forum for Secular Bangladesh, 2012).

27. Arif Jamal, *Shadow War: The Untold Story of the Jihad in Kashmir* (Brooklyn: Melville House, 2009), pp. 107–11.

28. Ibid., p. 115.

29. The authoritative account of the CIA relationship with the mujahedin and the decisions made within the agency and the White House is by Robert Gates, *From the Shadows: The Ultimate Insider's Story of Five Presidents and How They Won the Cold War* (New York: Simon and Schuster, 1996), p. 147. George Crile's masterpiece, *Charlie Wilson's War* (New York: Grove Press, 2001), adds insight and color to the story.

30. Janet Blight and others, *Becoming Enemies: U.S.-Iran Relations and the Iran-Iraq War, 1979–1988* (Plymouth, U.K.: Rowman and Littlefield, 2012), p. 66.

31. Gates, *From the Shadows*, p. 321.

32. Charles Cogan, "Partners in Time: The CIA and Afghanistan since 1979," *World Policy Journal*, vol. 10, no. 2 (Summer 1993), p. 76.

33. Ibid., p. 79.

34. George Crile, *Charlie Wilson's War*, pp. 502–03.

35. Interview with Zvi Rafiah, May 10, 2010. Zvi was Charlie's Israeli contact.

36. Casey's trip is recounted by Charles Cogan in "Partners in Time," pp. 73–82. Cogan was the CIA's Near East and South Asia division chief in the Directorate of Operations at the time; he went with Casey on all his visits to the region. Bob Gates also recounts the first Zia-Casey meeting in his book; see Gates, *From the Shadows*.

37. Dennis Kux, *The United States and Pakistan, 1947–2000: Disenchanted Allies* (Johns Hopkins University, 2001), p. 279.

38. Ibid., p. 281.

39. Ibid., p. 289.

40. Author's interview with Robin Raphel, May 12, 2012.

41. Yousaf, *Bear Trap*, p. 234.

42. Barbara Crossette, "Who Killed Zia?" *World Policy Journal*, vol. 22, no. 3 (Fall 2005), pp. 94-102.

43. Nawaz, *Crossed Swords*, pp. 393–405.

44. Tariq Ali, *The Assassination: Who Killed Indira?* (Calcutta: Seagull, 2008). See also Katherine Frank, *Indira: The Life of Indira Nehru Gandhi* (London: Harper Collins, 2001).

45. Krishnaswamy Sundarji, *Blind Men of Hindoostan: Indo-Pak Nuclear War* (New Delhi: UBS Publishers, 1993).

46. The best chronicle of the Brass Tacks crisis is by Stephen Cohen, P. R. Chari, and Pervaiz Iqbal Cheema, *Four Crises and a Peace Process: American Engagement in South Asia* (Brookings, 2007).

CHAPTER 5

1. Fatima Bhutto, *Songs of Blood and Sword: A Daughter's Memoir* (London: Jonathan Cape, 2010).

2. "Visit of Pakistan's Prime Minister (Mohtarma Benazir Bhutto and George Bush Addresses)," transcript, *Department of State Bulletin*, October 1, 1989.

3. Mohammad Yousaf and Mark Adkin, *The Bear Trap: Afghanistan's Untold Story* (London: Leo Cooper, 1992), p. 220.

4. Separate author's interviews with two former Indian intelligence officers in 2012.

5. Arif Jamal, *Shadow War: The Untold Story of Jihad in Kashmir* (Brooklyn, N.Y.: Melville House, 2009), p. 128.

6. Benazir Bhutto, *Reconciliation, Islam, Democracy, and the West* (New York: Harper Collins, 2008), pp. 195–201.

7. Bhutto, *Songs of Blood and Sword*, p. 400.

8. Arnaud de Borchgrave, "Army Back on Top," *Washington Times*, March 30, 2010.

9. "Report of the United Nations Commission of Inquiry into the Facts and Circumstances of the Assassination of Former Pakistani Prime Minister Mohtarma Benazir Bhutto," April 2010, paragraphs 38 and 218.

10. Jamal, *Shadow War*, p. 136.

11. Zahid Hussain, *Frontline Pakistan: The Struggle with Militant Islam* (Columbia University Press, 2007), p. 54.

12. Jamal, *Shadow War*, p. 13.

13. Ibid., p. 137.

14. Ibid., pp. 147–57.

15. Arif Jamal, "South Asia's Architect of Jihad: A Profile of Commander Mohammad Ilyas Kashmiri," *Militant Leadership Monitor*, vol. 1, no. 1 (Washington: Jamestown Foundation, January 30, 2010), pp. 8–10.

16. P. R. Chari, Pervaiz Iqbal Cheema, and Stephen P. Cohen, *Four Crises and a Peace Process: American Engagement in South Asia* (Brookings, 2007), p. 86.

17. Ibid., pp. 91–98.

18. Husain Haqqani, *Pakistan: Between Mosque and Military* (Washington: Carnegie, 2005), p. 220.

19. "Dr. Abdul Qadeer Khan Discusses Nuclear Program in TV Talk Show," Karachi Aaj Television, August 31, 2009.

20. "Nawaz Sharif Met Osama Three Times, Former ISI Official," *Daily Times Monitor*, June 23, 2005.

21. Haqqani, *Pakistan: Between Mosque and Military*, p. 228.

22. The most thorough investigation has been done by Asif's brother Shuja Nawaz in *Crossed Swords: Pakistan, Its Army, and the Wars Within* (London, Oxford, 2008), Appendix 3, "Investigation into the Death of General Asif Nawaz," pp. 599–605. He states that there was no direct evidence linking Prime Minister Sharif to the death, but the mystery remains.

23. Strobe Talbott, *Engaging India: Diplomacy, Democracy, and the Bomb* (Brookings, 2006), p. 23.

24. Secretary William J. Perry, Office of the Secretary of Defense, "Establishing Strong Security Relations with India and Pakistan," Foreign Policy Association, New York, January 31, 1995.

25. Central Intelligence Agency, "India: Improved Relations with China Tempered by Conflict and Competition," September 1994; approved for unclassified release in September 2005 and available at the National Security Archives.

26. United Nations Security Council Resolution 1172, adopted by the Security Council at its 3890th meeting, on June 6, 1998.

27. Talbott, *Engaging India*, p. 61.

28. Ibid., p. 4.

29. For more information on al Qaeda, see Bruce Riedel, *The Search for al Qaeda: Its Leadership, Ideology, and Future* (Brookings, 2008).

30. Talbott, *Engaging India*, p. 119.

31. For more on this issue, see Bruce Riedel, *Deadly Embrace: Pakistan, America, and the Future of the Global Jihad* (Brookings, 2012).

32. Peter Lavoy, "Why Kargil Did Not Produce General War: The Crisis Management Strategies of Pakistan, India, and the United States," in *Asymmetric Warfare in South Asia: The Causes and Consequences of the Kargil Conflict* (Cambridge University Press, 2009), edited by Peter Lavoy, p. 180.

33. V. P. Malik, *Kargil: From Surprise to Victory* (New Delhi: Harper Collins, 2006), p. 146–47.

34. Ibid., pp. 131, 147.

35. Ibid., pp. 146–47.

36. Jaswant Singh, *A Call to Honour: In the Service of Emergent India* (New Delhi: Rupa, 2006), p. 208.

37. I have described the dialogue between the two leaders in detail in a monograph based on my notes of the meetings; see Bruce Riedel, "American Diplomacy and the 1999 Kargil Summit at Blair House" (University of Pennsylvania, Center for the Advanced Study of India, 2002).

38. Talbot, *Engaging India*, p. 161.

39. Pervez Musharraf, *In the Line of Fire: A Memoir* (New York: Free Press, 2007), pp. 58, 163.

40. Singh, *Call to Honour*, p. 230.

41. Malik, *Kargil: From Surprise to Victory*, p. 260. According to Malik's account, India also cancelled the planned testing of its long-range missile, the Agni, on July 5, 1999, to avoid inflaming the situation further.

42. Talbott, *Engaging India*, p. 167.

43. William Clinton, *My Life* (New York: Random House, 2004), p. 866.

44. Bhutto, *Reconciliation*, p. 212.

45. Malik, *Kargil: From Surprise to Victory*, p. 348.

46. Judith Miller and James Risen, "A Nuclear War Feared Possible over Kashmir," *New York Times*, August 8, 2000.

47. Clinton, *My Life*, p. 901.

CHAPTER 6

1. Rani Singh, *Sonia Gandhi: An Extraordinary Life, An Indian Destiny* (New York: Palgrave, 2011).

2. Neelesh Misra, *173 Hours in Captivity: The Hijacking of IC 814* (New Delhi: Harper Collins, 2000), p. 47.

3. Ibid., pp. 149, 170.

4. Roy Gutman, *How We Missed the Story: Osama bin Laden, the Taliban, and the Hijacking of Afghanistan* (Washington: United States Institute for Peace, 2008), p. 192.

5. Embassy of India, "Information on Hijacked Indian Airlines Flight IC 814," Washington, January 2001.

6. Jaswant Singh, *In Search of Emergent India: A Call to Honor* (Indiana University Press, 2007), p. 204.

7. Ahmed Rashid, *Descent into Chaos* (New York: Viking, 2008), p. 48.

8. George Tenet, *At the Center of the Storm: My Years at the CIA* (New York: Harper Collins, 2007), p. 147.

9. Ibid., p. 152.

10. On Bonk, see Dina Temple-Raston, "The War on Terror, Before the Shock Wore Off," *Washington Post*, September 2, 2012, p. B1-4. I was present when Berger briefed Rice. See also Richard Clarke, *Against All Enemies: Inside America's War on Terror* (New York: Free Press, 2004), p. 229.

11. Tenet, *At the Center of the Storm*, p. 141.

12. Author's interview with George Tenet, June 1, 2012.

13. Author's interview with Ambassador Chamberlin, August 24, 2010.

14. Zahid Hussain, *Frontline Pakistan: The Struggle with Militant Islam* (Columbia University Press, 2007), p.43.

15. Author's interview with Bob Grenier, May 18, 2010.

16. Pervez Musharraf, *In the Line of Fire: A Memoir* (London: Free Press, 2006), p. 202.

17. Ibid., p. 202.

18. Author's interview with Pervez Musharraf, September 30, 2009.

19. The dispersal of al Qaeda and Taliban fighters in 2002 is covered best in Anne Stenersen, "Al Qaeda's Allies: Explaining the Relationship between Al-Qaeda and Various Factions of the Taliban after 2001," New America Foundation Counterterrorism Strategy Initiative Policy Paper, April 2010 (www.newamerica.net/publications/policy/al_qaeda_s_allies).

20. "State of the Taliban," NATO TF 3-10, January 6, 2012, p. 9.

21. Author's interview with Bob Grenier.

22. Lewis G. Irwin, *Disjointed Ways, Disunified Means: Learning from America's Struggle to Build an Afghan Nation* (Carlisle, Pa.: U.S. Army War College Strategic Studies Institute, May 2012), p. 135.

23. Dov Zakheim, *A Vulcan's Tale: How the Bush Administration Mismanaged the Reconstruction of Afghanistan* (Brookings, 2010), and Ronald Neumann, *The Other War: Winning and Losing in Afghanistan* (Washington: Potomac Books, 2009). Pakistan got far more military equipment—and more sophisticated equipment— than Afghanistan did.

24. Yaniv Barzilai, *102 Days of War: How Osama bin Laden, al Qaeda, and the Taliban Survived 2001* (2013, forthcoming).

25. The most detailed account so far of bin Laden's odyssey after 2001 is Peter Bergen, *Manhunt: The Ten-Year Search for Bin Laden from 9/11 to Abbottabad* (New York: Crown, 2012).

26. Bruce Riedel, *Deadly Embrace: Pakistan, America, and the Future of the Global Jihad* (Brookings, 2012), p. x.

27. M. Ilyas Khan, "Osama bin Laden: The Night He Came for Dinner," *BBC New Magazine*, May 1, 2012. The BBC report does not identify bin Laden's host. A separate source in Pakistan confirmed that it was Khalil.

28. George Bush, *Decision Points* (New York: Crown, 2010), p. 213.

29. Stephen Cohen, P. R. Chari, and Pervaiz Iqbal Cheema, *Four Crises and a Peace Process: American Engagement in South Asia* (Brookings, 2007), p. 152.

30. Author's interview with Wendy Chamberlain.

31. Raymond E. Vickery Jr., *The Eagle and the Elephant: Strategic Aspects of U.S.-India Engagement* (Johns Hopkins Press, 2011), p. 116.

32. Cohen, Chari, and Cheema, *Four Crises and a Peace Process*, p. 166.

33. Vickery, *The Eagle and the Elephant*, p. 128.

34. Cohen, Chari, and Cheema, *Four Crises and a Peace Process*, p. 162.

35. It happened on my first day on the job at the White House as the director for South Asia affairs.

36. Tenet, *At the Center of the Storm*, p. 285.

37. International Institute for Strategic Studies, *Nuclear Black Markets: Pakistan, A. Q. Khan, and the Rise of Proliferation Networks* (London: 2007), p. 22.

38. "Dictatorship Non-existent in Pakistan: U.S.," *Pakistan Tribune*, April 1, 2006.

39. Helene Cooper and Mark Mazzetti, "Backstage, U.S. Nurtured Pakistan Rivals' Deal," *New York Times*, October 20, 2007.

40. "Report of the United Nations Commission of Inquiry into the Facts and Circumstances of the Assassination of Former Pakistani Prime Minister Mohtarma Benazir Bhutto" (United Nations), paragraph 205.

41. Ibid., paragraph 219.

42. Ibid., paragraph 208.

43. Ibid., executive summary.

44. Ibid., paragraph 218.

CHAPTER 7

1. Dov Zakheim, *A Vulcan's Tale: How the Bush Administration Mismanaged the Reconstruction of Afghanistan* (Brookings, 2010). Pakistan got much more help from Bush than did Afghanistan.

2. Bob Woodward, *Obama's Wars* (New York: Simon and Schuster, 2010). A wealth of other journalists' accounts have filled in more of the details first laid out by Woodward. See, for example, David Sanger, *Confront and Conceal: Obama's Secret Wars and Surprising Use of American Power* (New York: Crown, 2012).

3. This conversation is recounted in David Klaidman, *Kill or Capture: The War on Terror and the Soul of the Obama Presidency* (New York: Houghton Mifflin Harcourt, 2012), p. 43.

4. Mitchell D. Silber, *The Al Qaeda Factor: Plots against the West* (University of Pennsylvania Press, 2012), pp. 152–65.

5. Bin Laden's threat was included later in a long al Qaeda video on the Christmas Day attack entitled "The Final Trap."

6. Gregory D. Johnson, *The Last Refuge: Yemen, Al Qaeda, and America's War in Arabia* (New York: Norton, 2012), p. 260. Abdulmutallab told the investigators in Detroit that al-Awlaki instructed him in how to conduct the operation and provided him with the bomb. I served as an expert witness to the prosecution.

7. Sanger, *Confront and Conceal*, p. 244.

8. See New American Foundation, "The Year of the Drone: An Analysis of U.S. Drone Strikes in Pakistan, 2004–2012." The analysis is periodically updated (http://counterterrorism.newamerica.net/drones).

9. Joby Warwick, *The Triple Agent: The Al Qaeda Mole Who Infiltrated the CIA* (New York: Doubleday, 2011).

10. Alan Kronstadt, "Direct Overt U.S. Aid Appropriations and Military Reimbursements to Pakistan, FY 2002–FY 2013," Congressional Research Service, totals the aid disbursed at $25,379,000. Weapons systems provided included the 18 F-16s, 8 P-3C Orion maritime patrol aircraft, 6,000 TOW anti-tank missiles, 500 AMRAM air-to-air missiles, 6 C-130 transport aircraft, 20 Cobra attack helicopters, and a Perry-class missile frigate. About half the $25 billion was disbursed by Bush and half by Obama. The Obama total includes more economic aid due to the Kerry-Lugar bill.

11. Mark Owen and Keven Maurer, *No Easy Day: The Firsthand Account of the Mission That Killed Osama bin Laden* (New York: Dutton, 2012), 173.

12. Cyril Almeida, "The Emperors' Clothes," *Dawn*, May 6, 2011 (http://dawn.com/2011/05/06/the-emperors-clothes/).

13. Author's interview with Hina Rabbani Khar, September 15, 2012.

14. "Osama bin Laden Death: Afghanistan Had Abbottabad Lead Four Years Ago," *The Guardian*, May 5, 2011.

15. I am indebted to my Brookings colleague Vanda Felbab Brown for her research in Indonesia in October 2012 on Umar Patek, which helped clarify what remains a murky issue.

16. Husain Haqqani, *Pakistan: Between Mosque and Military* (Washington: Carnegie Endowment for International Peace, 2005).

17. David Ignatius, "Diplomacy That Needs Some Therapy," *Washington Post*, July 15, 2012, p. A21.

18. Ibid.

19. Peter Bergen, *Manhunt* (New York: Crown, 2012), p. 226.

20. "Haqqani Sought U.S. Help for COAS Gen. Kayani's Removal," *Pakistan Defence Blog*, n.d. (www.pakarmedforces.com/2012/02/haqqani-sought-us-help-for-coas.html).

21. "Pakistani Public Opinion Ever More Critical of U.S." (Washington: Pew Research Center Global Attitudes Project, June 27, 2012).

22. Pamela Constable, *Playing with Fire: Pakistan at War with Itself* (New York: Random House, 2011), p. 255.

23. Jonathan E. Hillman, "A Cold Shoulder from India," *Los Angeles Times*, June 12, 2012.

24. Amir Latif, "U.S.-India Defense Trade: Opportunities for Deepening the Partnership" (Washington: Center for Strategic and International Studies, June 2012).

25. Author's interviews with British officials, October 2012.

26. "Joint Statement on the Third U.S.-India Strategic Dialogue," U.S. Department of State, Office of the Spokesperson, June 13, 21012.

CHAPTER 8

1. See, for example, Ahmed Rashid, *Pakistan on the Brink: The Future of America, Pakistan, and Afghanistan* (New York: Viking, 2012); Stephen Cohen, *The Future of Pakistan* (Brookings, 2011); Maleeha Lodhi, *Pakistan: Beyond the Crisis State* (Oxford University Press, 2011); and Pamela Constable, *Playing with Fire: Pakistan at War with Itself* (New York: Random House, 2011).

2. Nadeem Hotiana, "Sunday Dialogue: Pakistan-Afghan Options," *New York Times*, November 4, 2012.

3. Steve Coll, "Sporting Chance: Can a Sex Symbol and Cricket Legend Run Pakistan?" *New Yorker*, August 13 and 20, 2012.

4. All the military figures are from International Institute of Strategic Studies, *The Military Balance* (2012).

5. Iskandar Rehman, "Drowning Stability: The Perils of Naval Nuclearization and Brinkmanship in the Indian Ocean," *Naval War College Review*, vol. 65, no. 4 (Autumn 2012).

6. Paul Kerr and Mary Beth Nikitin, "Pakistan's Nuclear Weapons: Proliferation and Security Issues" (Congressional Research Service, June 26, 2012).

7. See, for example, James Blight and Janet Lang, *The Armageddon Letters: Kennedy/Khruschev/Castro in the Cuban Missile Crisis* (New York: Rowman and Littlefield, 2012).

8. George Tenet, *At the Center of the Storm: My Years at the CIA* (New York: Harper Collins, 2007).

9. Banyan, "Nuclear Profusion," *The Economist*, August 25, 2012, p. 33.

10. See Polly Nayak and Michael Krepon, "U.S. Crisis Management and South Asia's Twin Peaks Crisis" (Washington: Stimson Center, 2006), and Nayak and Krepon, "The Unfinished Crisis: U.S. Crisis Management after the 2008 Mumbai Attack" (Washington: Stimson Center, 2012).

11. "India and Its Near Abroad," *The Economist*, February 18, 2012.

12. Salman Masood, "India and Pakistan Sign Visa Agreement, Easing Travel," *New York Times*, September 9, 2012.

13. Rohit Viswanath, "Investing in Peace," Issue Brief, Wadhwani Chair in India-U.S. Policy Studies (Washington: Center for Strategic and International Studies, August 8, 2012).

14. Larry Hanauer and Peter Chalk, "India's and Pakistan's Strategies in Afghanistan: Implications for the United States and the Region (Santa Monica, Calif.: RAND, 2012).

15. Ronald E. Neuman, *The Other War: Winning and Losing in Afghanistan* (Washington: Potomac Books, 2009).

16. Gary Schroen, *First In: An Insider's Account of How the CIA Spearheaded the War on Terror in Afghanistan* (New York: Ballantine, 2005), pp. 1, 120.

17. Howard B. Schaffer, *The Limits of Influence: America's Role in Kashmir* (Washington: Brookings. 2009), p. 2.

18. Ibid., pp. ix–x.

19. William Milam, "Factors Shaping the Future," in *The Future of Pakistan*, edited by Stephen Cohen (Brookings, 2011).

INDEX

Personal names starting with al are alphabetized by the following part of the name.

219